THE CHILDREN OF
Fatima

BLESSED
FRANCISCO
&
BLESSED
JACINTA MARTO

THE CHILDREN OF

BLESSED FRANCISCO

BLESSED JACINTA MARTO

LEO MADIGAN

OUR SUNDAY VISITOR PUBLISHING DIVISION
OUR SUNDAY VISITOR, INC.
HUNTINGTON, INDIANA 46750

To Father Edwin Gordon
who, though blind, sees clearly the significance of Fatima,
knows the way there and leads many.

Our Sunday Visitor Publishing Division
Our Sunday Visitor, Inc.
200 Noll Plaza
Huntington, IN 46750

ISBN: 1-931709-57-2 (Inventory No. T34)
LCCN: 2002115699

Cover design by Rebecca Heaston
Cover photo: Immaculate Heart of Mary statue in the Holy House, USA. Courtesy of World Apostolate of Fatima USA, Inc.
Interior design by Robert L. Hoffman
Interior photos courtesy Dr. Luciano Cristino of the Fatima Sanctuary Archives

PRINTED IN THE UNITED STATES OF AMERICA

TABLE OF CONTENTS

Acknowledgments

I would like to thank the following authorities for extensive help, advice, assistance, manuscript reading and guidance. Each combed the pages of this little book and corrected my errors. Those that remain are due to my own lack of judgment.

- Dominican Sisters of the Holy Rosary, Fatima, Portugal
- Lauri Duffy, Dublin, Ireland
- Donal Foley, Nottingham, England
- John Hauf, Ellicot City, Maryland, United States of America
- Paul MacLeod, Geelong, Victoria, Australia
- Marton Perim, Budapest, Hungary
- Tim Tindall-Robertson, Devon, England
- Michael Tweedale, Corpus Christi College, Oxford, England
- Bob Nesnick, who, on the streets of Fatima, told me much about Jacinta

Preface

I want to introduce two illiterate peasant children, brother and sister, Francisco and Jacinta Marto, both beatified by the Catholic Church. Their very brief lives were as ordinary and as predictable as those of the sheep they tended. The only exceptional thing that happened to them is the reason for their fame, though not for their beatification. A year or two before their deaths, at nine and ten years old, they were visited by a young woman who herself had died more than eighteen hundred years earlier.

She didn't appear as a ghost, haunting the dark caverns of the night to inspire fear and foreboding. She came to them at midday when the sun was at its highest. But she was more radiant than that sun; her presence was more compelling. She said she came from heaven, and she told the shepherds how we, too, the banished children of Eve, can get there.

This woman, who later told them she was the Lady of the Rosary, visited the children on six occasions and confided many other things as well. Some they didn't understand at the time, but in those cases their understanding wasn't required. What they did comprehend was that they had been created for heaven, where creatures love their God and give Him the glory that is His due — and where He loves them and allows them to share in that glory. This knowledge took possession of their hearts, and they longed to go there.

Within eighteen months the boy was dead, and a year later his sister passed away. Only their cousin and fellow seer, Lucia dos Santos, remained on this earth to be a living witness to the message of the Lady of the Rosary.

But apart from these visits from heaven (which, although they have the strongest possible papal approval, are not required matters of Faith), their lives were circumscribed, and their activities commonplace. They were born, lived, and died as peasants. Yet they are known and revered throughout the world, and shall continue to be known and revered when the great and the glamorous of the twentieth century no longer merit a footnote in the history books. The reason why is one of those glorious and simple paradoxes by which heaven confounds our logic and unseats our arrogance.

When the Kingdom comes, it will be the Francisco and Jacinta Martos who will take the places of the monarchs and generals in the halls of glory.

CHAPTER ONE

It is all too easy to imagine Portugal at the time of the Fatima apparitions as holy-picture perfect. The reality was quite the opposite. A powerful atheistic element had infiltrated Portuguese politics and aligned itself to the forces of Republicanism, whose promoters used blood and Masonic influence to further their cause. After grasping the reins of power, it showed that its true goal was the persecution of the Church.

Unlike any other European nation, Portugal had never experienced a regicide. Among the three successive ruling houses, no monarch had been assassinated until the twentieth century, when radical forces gained the upper hand.

In 1908, as King Dom Carlos I was traveling along Lisbon's riverfront in an open carriage, he was attacked by group belonging to a secret political society (the *cabonari*). A young man shot the king in the head, but the carriage managed to break away. At the corner of the square, a bearded man shot and killed the heir to the throne, Prince Luis Filipe. Though the regicides were not the work of a Republican group, the Republican leadership made no protest about the murders. In fact, they added to a fund set up to aid families of the killers.

The prince's younger brother, Dom Manuel, was also in the carriage but was only wounded in the arm. He was destined to be the last of the Portuguese royals, and his reign was brief. In October 1910, he was forced from his throne by the anti-monarchists. He sailed on the yacht *Dona Amélia* to settle in Twickenham, England, and a Republican government was formed in Lisbon.

This administration was headed by Teófilo Braga, the high priest of positivism, the theory that contends that sense perceptions are the only admissible basis for human knowledge and precise thought. His cabinet members were all positivistic acolytes, but one in particular, the minister of justice, Afonso Costa, took the theory to extremes. He was a fanatic, a rabid anticlerical in the mold of a Diocletian.

On introducing his laws of separation of Church and State, Costa declared that "in two generations Catholicism will be completely eliminated from Portugal." With a ferocity that bordered on mania, and that even caused his fellow Republicans to blanch, he divested the state of every manifestation of faith: Religious oaths ceased to have legal force. Religious instruction in schools and the teaching of theology in the universities were abolished. Jesuits were declared, by virtue of their allegiance to the Society of Jesus, to have forfeited their Portuguese nationality.

Everything was secularized, including marriages, burials and cemeteries. The army was forbidden to participate in religious observances, and saints' feast days were no longer kept as holidays. The wearing of cassocks was prohibited. In April 1911, a law placed the administration of parish churches in lay committees called "Cultural Associations." Bequests to the Church were prohibited; the state provided pensions for priests, however.

Most of the Portuguese hierarchy and clergy protested against the Costa measures with singular courage, which resulted in their banishment. The cardinal patriarch of Lisbon, along with the archbishops of Braga and Evora and the bishops of Porto and Viseu, were exiled.

The overthrow of the monarchy was followed by years of mercurial governments. The Republicans split into various groups. Members of Costa's faction called themselves Democrats, a mutation that contemporary Americans might find difficult to conceive.

In 1915 the Democrats seized power under João Pinheiro Chegas, but he was shot by a political opponent and lost sight in one eye. Costa, while traveling on a Lisbon tram, suddenly interpreted the vehicle's jolting as a machine bound for hell and jumped through the window. He fractured his skull on the cobbled street, but healed quickly. By the end of the year, he was prime minister.

Local government, too, was parceled into the hands of anti-religious, largely Masonic, sympathizers. In Vila Nova de Ourém, the administrative center encompassed a large area including Fatima. It was run by Arturo Oliveira Santos, a scrap-metal merchant in his early thirties. Around this time his wife, Adalina, gave birth to their sixth child, to whom he gave the name Afonso Costa after the fanatical prime minister. Appointed on May 14, 1915, Arturo Santos held the post until December 8, 1917. During his tenure, he took it upon himself to intervene in the course of the Fatima apparitions.

Under Prime Minister Costa, anti-religious policies reached a fever pitch. Had it not been for World War I, Portugal, not Albania, might have been the first country to declare that it had eliminated all religion within its borders and proclaim itself the first atheist state in the world. Costa's government, collaborating with the Allies on the war, took instructions from London to commandeer thirty-six German ships harboring in Portuguese ports. This, not surprisingly, provoked Germany to declare war on Portugal. After a brief attempt at coalition with the Evolutionist Party, Costa became prime minister again and remained so all through 1917; that is, through all the months of the Fatima apparitions.

But Costa's star was dimming. Indeed, it was soon to be extinguished altogether. The day after the Miracle of the Sun — which happened on October 13, 1917 — was a Sunday, and the day of the Portuguese municipal elections. At the time, the Lisbon press reported the three main parties — the Democrats, Republicans and Evolutionists — had lost ninety-five thousand votes to Catholic sympathizers in the capital alone.

Costa's government, which the strictures of war had made intensely unpopular, was overthrown on December 5, 1917, by a military coup.

Although the end to this unhappy abuse of power would seem to be one of the immediate fruits of the Fatima apparitions, revolutions continued to erupt in Portugal with monotonous regularity. There were no less than sixteen between 1910 and 1926. Credible democracy didn't reach Portugal till 1974.

Chapter Two

Aljustrel is one of a number of villages making up the parish of Fatima in the district of Vila Nova de Ourém and the Diocese of Leiria. It is situated some eighty miles north of Lisbon on a plateau behind two ranges of hills, the Serra de Aire and the Serra de Candeeiros, which lie across the land like rounded loaves of bread.

In the teens of the twentieth century, Aljustrel was a small cluster of thirty-three houses, too unimportant ever to have had a written history. Seer Lucia dos Santos would later note:

> In the early days of the Republic, during which the Church suffered a good deal of persecution, the practice of religion had to be restricted and hidden. The churches were kept shut. It was forbidden to hold processions or to ring bells. Priests were arrested and male and female religious were expelled from the country and so on. In Fatima, however, persecution was not quite so severe, possibly because it was off the beaten track and almost unknown; but even so the parish priest had to tread very carefully. My mother never appeared to be afraid. We lived our lives tranquilly and little was said in our house about the situation. I do, however, remember hearing my mother speak regretfully of the death of the king and the young prince; and at night when my father was leading the grace, she would suggest to him that we should say an Our Father for the eternal repose of the king and the prince. If people

who came to the house did happen to speak about these things, my mother used to say that the rich are like cocks. They all want to perch on the roof and give orders, and so they went about killing one another, closing the churches and forbidding the people to go there to pray.

In this territory, everyone was related, if only by a distant marriage. It was where no one locked a door if the house was left untended — or if they did, neighbors knew in which wall niche the key was left in case of an emergency.

There were no indigenous beggars, no burglars.

Crops and animals provided all that was needed to sustain the inhabitants between birth and death. Each household had plots of land in the area. These were handed down from previous generations, yielded as wedding portions, purchased, swapped, or borrowed. In this one they might grow their rows of corn or potatoes; in that one cabbage, turnips, beans, onions, and tomatoes, according to the suitability of the soil and the proximity to water. The rocky slopes would yield enough grazing for sheep and goats, and even the most barren plot would provide a few olives and a supply of firewood. Time was mostly measured by the seasons for planting and harvesting, for lambing and shearing.

Lucia told a story that illustrates how closely residents linked early summer crops to the feast of Pentecost. During a catechism class, the parish priest asked who knew the fruits of the Holy Spirit. She promptly answered, "Broad beans, peas, and cherries."

It's not difficult to imagine the men and the youths of the families spending their days working their own fields as well as the fields of widows and older relatives. It's easy to picture villagers using and storing the produce, exchanging and bartering some items, taking any surplus to market.

Elsewhere in the pasture grounds, the younger children would be occupied with tending the sheep. They would alternate the areas daily (ensuring flocks had access to water as well as pasture), keep the animals out of vegetable patches and, most importantly, make sure they stayed together.

At home, mothers planned the meals for the coming days. Older unmarried girls would be released from the looms or the care of the infants to collect wood and pinecones that they would carry in bundles on their heads. On their arms would be baskets of greens and fruits and perhaps chestnuts, walnuts, and wild herbs.

Breakfast would often be a bowl of curds with bread broken up in it. In the middle of the morning, there was usually a cup of goat's milk served with bread, cheese and olives. The midday meal was always a hot one, perhaps potatoes boiled with pork, sausage or spare ribs. There might be pigs' ears or feet, or even rabbit or hare, partridge or thrush or suckling pig. There was no lack of variety. Bread was generally baked on a particular day of the week. A great favorite was a mixture of bread, sugar and wine. With that touch of the quirky that can raise a menu to an art form, this dish was known as "weary-horse soup."

At sunset, when the church bells tolled the Angelus, all would stand and take off their hats and, holding the typical local headgear in their hands, would pray. This was also the signal for the people to go to their own houses and take their supper together.

At the end of the evening meal, the head of the household would lead the thanksgiving with a litany of Our Fathers, Hail Marys, and Glory Bes for all the intentions that occurred to him. After that, the mother would take over the saying of the Rosary or a "crown" of seven mysteries in honor of Our Lady of Sorrows. Then there would be a few minutes of conversation, combined with the allotment of work for the following day, and they were off to bed, for the night would be short.

Lent was strictly, yet doubtless joyously, observed. No meat was eaten, but plenty of root crops and fish from the nets of the Atlantic port of Nazaré appeared on the tables: cod, mackerel, sardines and clams. Potatoes, sliced onions, hard-boiled eggs, salt, olive oil, and dressings meant that the fast was observed, but no one went hungry. Sometimes even the young who were not re-quired to observe the regulations were given the Lenten fare on the principle, as Lucia's mother said, "You can only bend a cucumber when it's young."

The sheep that the younger members of the families took to pasture were merino, the large white breed with plenty of wool and milk. Almost all the ewes would bear twin lambs each season. A flock of thirty would be the norm for most families, but in the lambing season this would jump to nearer a hundred. The male offspring would mostly be killed for family consumption, while the females would be spared for wool and breeding. The old ewes would be sold, along with the surplus female lambs.

As the weather grew warm, the sheep would be shorn of their winter coats. The women of the house would wash the wool and prepare it for the carders, who would wirecomb it to untangle the fibers. Then it would be sent to the local factory to be spun and dyed in whatever color the lady of the house stipulated.

The villagers rarely traveled except to market, but after the apparitions Lucia was taken to Santarem. When she returned to Aljustrel, she described to the children who used to come and play in her front yard the great novelty that she had seen:

> A whole lot of little houses, trotting along one behind the other, with neither horses nor donkeys to pull them, with lots of people inside looking out the windows, and a great chimney in the front belching out smoke and hooting like a whole lot of horns sounding at once.

It was a life of quiet peace and joy in an area of such insignificance that even the turbulent politics of Lisbon, which seemed intent on destroying the very soul of its own nation, could do little to disturb.

Faith was the fire that powered such villages, and the sacraments provided the fuel. The Eucharist was paramount, of course, but here the sacrament of matrimony came into its own. Conjugal happiness and family harmony illustrated in bold relief how marriage, in essence, was a living dimension of the Eucharist. The parents accepted all the children the Lord wanted to give them, not as a burden but as a gift to enrich their homes and build up the Mystical Body of Christ. They were always careful to take their babies to the baptismal font as soon after birth as possible, to free those young souls from the bonds of original sin. A baptism was always a great festival for the family and the village. Everyone came together and celebrated with those parents who had been honored with one more gift of God.

It was at the knees of their mothers and fathers that the children learned the name of God and how to pray the Rosary. Once old enough, they were sent to catechism classes in the parish church, where they prepared for first Holy Communion. Traditionally, children had received the Eucharist for the first time around age twelve, but Pope Pius X's 1910 decree *Quam Singulari* lowered the age considerably. Even so, a thorough knowledge of the catechism was still a requisite. That was not always easy for children who couldn't read or write and had no particular motivation to learn either skill.

Seven was the age that Pius X envisaged as ideal for first receiving the Eucharist. It was at this age, too, that the children of the area began to be initiated into the life of a shepherd. Sheep were easily led, so children were able to take them to graze, and it was in this way that the youngsters grew, breathing the pure country air.

Life in Aljustrel was a circumscribed existence, with the liturgy as the calendar and the shearing, lambing, fruit picking, olive gathering and *mundança* (pig-killing) ticking off the phases of the moon. It was a life lived just outside the gates of Eden, a life almost incomprehensible to the strident egocentricity of our materialistic age, where the word "fast" is linked with food and cars, and "lent" is the past participle of a banking activity.

It was into this milieu that Francisco Marto was born in June 1908 and his sister Jacinta in March 1910, just twenty-one months later.

CHAPTER THREE

The Fatima parish record lists Francisco's baptism as June 20, 1908. It also says that he was born at three in the morning on the eleventh of that month and year. The parish priest affirms that the child is the legitimate son of Manoel Pedro Marto and Olympia de Jesus. The godparents, Francisco Lopes and Thereza de Jesus, are identified. The entry is signed by Theodoro Henriques Vieira.

A notation in the margin reads: "Died in the parish of Fatima, of this municipality, on the 4th of April 1919. Registration 173 of the same year. Villa Nova de Ourem, 10 of May 1956." The signature is illegible.

In the same book there is a similar entry for "Jacintha" (sic), who was born at four o'clock in the afternoon on the eleventh day of March. The godparents were Manoel José and Jacintha de Jesus, spinster. It finishes with the amusing: "This registration has been signed by the Reverend Administrator alone because none of them knows how to write and we don't want to waste the three-reis tax stamp. In witness whereof ..."

And in the margin of this entry: "She died in the parish of the Angels, in the city of Lisbon at three minutes past eleven, on the 20th day of February, 1920."

Jacinta's birthday was actually March 5, 1910. The law at the time required that an infant be baptized — registered — eight days after birth. In fact, the custom was to baptize when convenient to the priest and the parents and let the birthday be registered as eight days beforehand. Francisco's given date, June 20,

1908, appears to be correct, or at least none of the authorities dispute it. Lucia's birth date was registered as March 22, 1907, but she was born on the twenty-eighth and christened only a few days later.

Birthdays in terms of days and dates meant nothing in that rural society. A waspish critic might say that the first thing written about these children was a lie, but that statement itself would not be true, because to lie one must have the intention of deceiving a person who has a right to know. In this case no one intended to deceive anybody. The administration required a date of mostly illiterate people, and they were given one. It was a custom acknowledged by all. Had parents been asked to place a birth to the nearest liturgical feast or a time of planting or harvesting, then they would have exercised a far more conscientious accuracy.

Apart from adjustable birthdays and the humor of Father Vieira, these entries bring up one or two other small points. The old spelling of the name "Manuel" as "Manoel "and the children's family name "Marto" as "Martho" are interesting; also the spelling of "Jacinta" as "Jacintha."

Francisco's name needs no comment, it being the same one the Francophile father of the great saint of Assisi gave to his son. It has always been a popular Christian name in Portugal, possibly because Portugal's greatest saint, Anthony of Lisbon, was a Franciscan friar. (He was known to the world at large as "Anthony of Padua," to the chagrin of the Portuguese. St. Francis himself — they were contemporaries — referred to him as "Brother Anthony, my bishop.")

As we read in the baptismal records, the parents of Francisco and Jacinta were Manuel Pedro Marto (b. 1873) and Olympia de Jesus (b. 1869). Manuel was commonly called Ti Marto — Ti being a diminutive of *tio*, uncle. Nicknames are very common all over Portugal among the working people. Fishermen will call each other by the name of a species of fish, soldiers by some military term indicative of a quirk of feature or personality. Lucia's father, Antonio dos Santos, was so well known as *abóbora*, "pumpkin," that many acquaintances didn't know his real name. He got the somewhat clumsy sobriquet from the pumpkin-growing area he came from near São Mamede.

Francisco and Jacinta were the sixth and seventh children of their father and the eighth and ninth of their mother. When Olympia married Ti Marto she was already a widow with two sons, António and Manuel dos Santos Rosa. Her first husband, José Pereira da Rosa (1850-1895), had been the brother of Lucia's mother, Maria Rosa.

Olympia's first husband had emigrated to Brazil as a young man, but had been shipwrecked on the way. Adrift in the Atlantic, clinging to a piece of flotsam and praying energetically to Our Lady of the Rosary, he was rescued by an English steamer, which took him to Mozambique. After working in that Portuguese colony for some years, he returned to Aljustrel with enough money to repair his parents' house. This is where Lucia was born, and it is preserved as such to this day. José also built a house to accommodate his new wife, Olympia. It was here that both Fran-

Olympia Marto at the door of the Marto home.

cisco and Jacinta were to be born. This means that of the thirty-three houses in Aljustrel at that time, the same man was responsible for the two in which the seers were born.

Olympia herself was the sister of Lucia's father, hence the dos Santos name for António and Manuel. This was a rather complicated relationship. It meant that Francisco and Jacinta's maternal uncle had a wife who was also the natural aunt of their maternal half-brothers.

Of the other five children of Olympia's marriage to Ti Marto, all older than Francisco and Jacinta, first-born Teresa died in 1902 before she was two years old. Then came José, Florinda, another Teresa, and João. Both girls died young, losses that Jacinta foretold somewhat eerily shortly before her own death in 1920. João lived to be ninety-four, dying in 2000 just two weeks before the beatification of his younger siblings. He is buried in the Fatima parish cemetery in his mother's grave, at the foot of the plot where Francisco and Jacinta's remains had been before they were transferred to the transepts of the Basilica of Our Lady of the Most Holy Rosary in the Cova da Iria.

Both Ti Marto and Olympia were small and wiry, but their moral fiber was tempered steel. Never in their long lives, even when Fatima had become one of the most prominent Marian shrines in the world, did either of these two seek the slightest distinction. When cardinals and bishops from every continent came to the Cova to celebrate the Eucharist and pay homage to the Heavenly Mother who had made confidants of their children, they themselves would be lost in the common areas, sharing the prayer of the pilgrims. Even when sought out in their home in Aljustrel, they would give no leeway to the overenthusiastic devout. They would disarm these visitors but never embarrass them, silence them but never disown them.

Ti Marto, too, had spent time in Africa when he was young, a conscript in the Portuguese army. He liked to talk about his years there, not the military aspect of his sojourn but the strange animals he had seen and their vast habitat. Neither he nor Olympia touched alcohol (not even the customary table wine), but it seems that he could chat as well as any man emboldened at a bar, though always equably, always with a natural candor. Many testify that, without his being conscious of it, his faith shone.

These people lived their faith without any pretension whatsoever. Moreover, they accepted their children as precious gifts from God to nurture in that same faith by word and by example. This made for a stability and joy in the home that many pass through this life without ever having experienced. These people were living the message of Fatima, in Fatima itself, before the Blessed Virgin came to their children to ask them to deliver it to the world. It is not correct to say that she could have appeared to anybody and said the same things and made the same demands. Most children simply wouldn't have been equipped to communicate with her, because their parents had never taught them the language she spoke, the language of faith.

There is a sense in which the parents of the seers, Manuel and Olympia, are mirrors reflecting each other. Quite apart from

The Marto parents toward the end of their lives. Olympia died in 1956 and Ti Marto in 1957.

being of almost equal height and build, the harmony between them, the practical, unsentimental love, had fused them together, made them a living testimony to the divine injunction. They were indeed two in one flesh.

In Lucia's "Memoirs," Jacinta before the apparitions is hailed as the personification of enthusiasm and caprice. Initially her companionship was found to be somewhat disagreeable because of her hypersensitive temperament. She is described as "pouty" when she doesn't get her own way. In effect, she would retire to a corner and sulk — "tethering the donkey" to use the local expression. This is hardly matter for wonder in young children who have just discovered the colorful menagerie that is their own ego. What does surprise us is the speed with which Jacinta discerns and acknowledges that she must subdue those leanings in her character that were contrary to grace.

This is a tough assignment for any child. For most of us the discerning and acknowledging take a lifetime. But sometimes, when the Spirit breathes, the meek and amiable elements in the child's character come to the fore. These seek out the Hidden Jesus who, working silent marvels, subdues the snakes of pride and self-will. If the pout remains, it is now as lips shaped to kiss the Hidden Jesus. The donkey is not slaughtered; it is carrying the same Jesus across the palms of willing sacrifices and sweet aspirations, because He is the victor taking possession of the fortress of the heart.

It is not long before the "Memoirs" are speaking of Jacinta as sweet and gentle, lovable and attractive. Later she becomes "a lily of candor," "a shining pearl," "a seraph of love."

Francisco had his own menagerie, but different climates make for different fauna. His disposition didn't mark him as Jacinta's brother. He was neither capricious nor vivacious, but quiet and submissive. He allowed himself to be pushed around. The story of the Nazeré handkerchief illustrates this.

Someone had brought him a little souvenir back from the coastal resort of Nazeré. Printed on the handkerchief was an image of Our Lady of Nazeré. We can picture this handkerchief and its new owner being the focus of attention for the children of the inland village. It passed from hand to admiring hand until it vanished altogether. Presently it was found secreted in the pocket of another boy. Of course this new possessor of the cloth argued that his was a different handkerchief; that he, too, had a friend just back from Nazeré and so on. But the point is that Francisco's reaction was "Let him have it. What does a handkerchief matter to me?" Lucia's comment on this was: "It's my opinion that if he had lived to manhood his greatest defect would have been 'never mind.' "

In the terms of our metaphor, as he was neither indulging his beasts nor nourishing them, they would either starve to death or feed on him. Nonchalance, coolness in contemporary parlance, is all very well, but it must have a strength directing it or it becomes a negative, emptiness hooked on nothing, a commercial for a product that was never in business.

We know of two little crimes Francisco committed: stealing a coin from his father to buy a music box and throwing stones at boys from Boleiros. The first, while a version of the sort of thing we all do as children, is nonetheless different because we go on to steal bigger and brighter coins to buy stereos and such, some of us eventually graduating to symphony orchestras. Francisco must have been found out and put to shame or confessed the deed because the girls knew of it when he came to make his dying confession.

As to throwing stones at the boys from Boleiros, well, we simply don't know the circumstances. Vandalism in peacetime becomes valor in war. Perhaps the Boleiros boys were attacking the Aljustrel boys, innocents all, who were constrained to retaliate in self-defense. Perhaps somebody had been reading Joshua or Judges or Chronicles aloud in his hearing, and he was moved to imitation. We know Francisco wasn't belligerent by nature so, dropping all the piety for a moment, don't we secretly want to stand up and clap to see a bit of the Tom Sawyer emerging from among the candles and incense?

If Jacinta could wander dreamily in the midst of her flock holding a lamb in her arms and say that she wanted to do the same as Our Lord in the holy picture, maybe Francisco was motivated by a like sentiment but chose, rather, to identify with Jesus as he lashed out at the merchants in the Temple.

Even so, whatever the sins, it was Jacinta who spoke for them both when, at their favorite hideout by the well (hidden behind chestnut trees and piles of stones and brambles), she said, "Our poor, dear Lord! I'll never sin again! I don't want Our Lord to suffer anymore!"

Children's games are invariably fascinating. They are the foundation bricks of the individual, and ultimately of society. In Aljustrel during the years of World War I, the children played games called pebbles, buttons, pass the ring, hit the mark, quoits and cards (especially a game called *Bisca,* which was Francisco's favorite, though, as he always lost, this predilection doesn't suggest any notable skill).

Jacinta's favorite game was "forfeits" in which the loser must do whatever the winner commands. The religious significance of the rules must have become apparent to the children as they developed. If you played the game with God, you had already lost through original sin, but by accepting the forfeits, you become amalgamated with the winner. It was the lesson of the Cross played out in the marketplace. In the beginning, Jacinta's companions might have chided her with something equivalent to:

"We piped for you and you would not dance; We mourned for you and you would not weep."

But, as we see from an incident later reported by Lucia, Jacinta quickly learned about losing and winning and the value of forfeits, even if it meant bending the rules, as when she was told to hug and kiss Lucia's brother Manuel. She answered:

> "No! Tell me to do something else." She pointed to the crucifix on the wall. "Tell me to go and kiss that crucifix over there."
>
> "All right! Get up on a chair, bring the crucifix over here, kneel down and give him three hugs and three kisses, one for Francisco, one for me and one for yourself."
>
> She ran to get the crucifix and kissed and hugged it with such devotion that I have never forgotten it. Then, looking attentively at the figure of Our Lord, she asked,
>
> "Why is Our Lord nailed to a cross like that?"
>
> "Because He died for us."
>
> "Tell me how it happened."

When Lucia was older, she described Jacinta to an interviewer:

> "She was the normal height for a well-developed child of six, robust by nature, more slim than fat, skin tanned by the mountain air as well as by the sun, large brown eyes, sparkling, enhanced by long lashes and dark eyebrows. She had a sweet, and at the same time tender look. Photos of her show her with a sullen look but they were taken in the sun. That was not her natural look."

In the same interview, Francisco merits a brief reference:

> "The same description could serve for Francisco because physically they were very alike. His face was more inclined to be round than oblong, though his features were anything but coarse."

Elsewhere the "Memoirs" say that he was always friendly and smiling, though if other children swore or did something untoward he would simply walk away. This wasn't, we may assume, as a show of rudeness or malice, but with the same automatic disinterest that one might display in avoiding territory when a sign says "Keep off the grass." If asked why he was leaving, Francisco would say that he didn't want to play anymore or "Because you're not good." Given what we know of him, the latter sounds more like a blunt statement of fact than a confrontational red flag.

Jacinta's response to errant playmates was the same, but in reverse. She would tell them "Don't do that, for you are offending the Lord our God, and he is already so much offended." If the recipient of this advice scoffed at her, or said she was being prissily pious, Jacinta would look at that child very seriously and walk away without a word.

So, Francisco would walk away first, then if pressed, censure. Jacinta would censure, then if pressed, walk away. But at the end of the day Jacinta would, as Lucia charmingly observes, "take her brother by the hand, and go home."

For country folk, the beacons that lit up the Portuguese calendar were the liturgical feasts — Christmas, St. Joseph, St. Anthony, the Sacred Heart, Our Lady of the Rosary — along with Carnival, weddings and the like. These gave color and joy to the arduous regularity of rural lives. For children, feasts meant Mass (with singing, incense and processions), followed by games, dressing up, stalls, raffles, cakes and dancing.

During one Corpus Christi procession, a very young Jacinta was among the girls casting petals before the Child Jesus, whom, she had been told, the priest would be carrying. Excitement at the prospect of seeing the Child Jesus filled the days leading up to the feast but, during the procession itself, Jacinta simply stared expectantly at the priest carrying the monstrance with the Sacred Host. Afterwards, she was asked why she hadn't strewn her petals. She answered, quite reasonably, that she hadn't seen the Child Jesus. "Did you see him?" she asked Lucia.

> "Of course not. The Child Jesus in the Host can't be seen. He's hidden."
> "And when you go to Communion do you talk to him?"
> "Yes."
> "Well, why can't you see him?"
> "Because he's hidden."

The faith that had been kindled from the cradle took flame with the concept of the Hidden Jesus. The expression stayed among the children and became their verbal rubric to identify the Eucharist. Hidden Jesus gives the word "seer" a new dimension; it raises sight to the elevation of faith.

Festivals also meant music, singing and dancing, and the children carried the artistry learned at the festivals to their games and into the pastures with their sheep. Jacinta excelled at dancing. To express herself by launching into dance seems to have been as natural to Jacinta as talking, an aptitude she was to employ most movingly in the prison cell in Ourem when she danced as a prelude to what she understood was to be her own death.

Francisco had no taste for dancing; his talent was with the flute. He would provide the music while others danced and sang, yet he wasn't restricted to performers or an audience. He was happy perched on a rock alone, coaxing melodies out of his hollowed cane with nothing but the bleating of the sheep, the chorus of the cicadas and the varied input of birds as accompaniment.

Given the uncomplicated tenor of his temperament, it's not surprising to learn of Francisco's special feeling for birds. (Once, at the Carreira pond, he ran all the way up the hill to Aljustrel to fetch a couple of pennies to ransom a bird from a boy who had caught it.) Their simplicity, alluded to by Christ himself as models of trust in Providence, was the perfect mirror of his thinking.

There is a refreshing wisdom to be found in focusing on Francisco sharing the bread in his lunch bag with the thrushes and the finches and the wrens.

But note that it is the birds and not Francisco that are the center of this exercise. They are not there waiting on the whims of his largesse, ready to fluff his self-esteem by approaching and eating out of his hand. Francisco would simply crumb the bread, spread it on a rock and move away. The object was to feed the birds, not his ego. And when they had dined and were flying off chirping and twittering, Francisco — from his hideout — would join in the medley.

The image of Francisco chirruping with the birds can be linked with Jacinta who, when in the hills with her sheep, would stand on high ground and shout. The young girl delighted in the echo that would bounce through the gullies and over the rocks. Soon she was calling "Maria!" to hear the mountains repeat it, and then the whole Hail Mary, word for word. She waited until the echo of one had disappeared down the concentric tunnels of sound before calling out the next.

CHAPTER FOUR

Apart from what they learned at their parent's knees and from catechism classes in the parish church, the Marto children had no formal education before the apparitions. It wasn't a matter of being deprived of education; book learning simply didn't feature as a priority in remote rural life in the Portugal of the time. Some, like Lucia's mother, could read after a fashion, but it doesn't appear to have been a skill that was greatly envied.

The children of that community took it for granted that their lives would follow the same pattern as their parents and neighbors. It was a life concerned with family, with agriculture, with domestic livestock, with barter, birth, marriage, children, honorable death. Money played no great part in the established scheme of things, and learning even less.

From their earliest years, the three children were drawn together, not as into a secretive clique that excluded others, but in the natural arrangements involving interests, compatibility, affection and family familiarity. It started with Jacinta. She idolized Lucia and consciously set her up as the principle icon among her peers.

Today observers might explain this attachment by pairing them under the same star sign, Aries. But we don't need astrologers to tell us that there is nothing more natural than a younger child finding an older one worthy of intense affection and consequent imitation. This is healthy; and grace, when hearts are open to it, delights in using the affiliation to further its purposes.

When Lucia's elder sister ceased looking after the family flock and went out to work, it was time for Lucia to take over the role of shepherdess. Jacinta was still four and Francisco six. Before this separation, a monumental happening in a child's life, they had spent their days playing together with no responsibilities apart from doing what they were told. Both Francisco and Jacinta took the news as an intrusion, as tragic in its own way as a death. Each felt that way for quite different reasons.

Jacinta was to lose the constant presence of her heroine, mentor, cousin and friend. Francisco, however, while also experiencing Lucia's proposed absence, felt his own role as big brother more keenly. He seems to have had an independence in his character that wasn't based on ego. It was one that expressed itself in submitting to others — not, as the psychologists might deduce, as an expression of weak will or even indifference. It was, rather, as a man who was so conscious of the nobility of his manhood, so confident of its unassailability, that he could afford to allow others to help themselves to his treasury. This was possible because he had grasped the essential paradox that the more exploited he was, the richer he became. It had every appearance of weakness, yet it was an enviable strength. There was no explaining it. It wasn't based on economics or physics. Its dynamic came from love. Christ had the same peculiar characteristic. It led Him to the bloody cross, the greatest triumph in the history of mankind.

Jacinta implored her mother to let her and Francisco take out their sheep and look after them along with Lucia and her flock. Francisco joined in the plea, rather as a way of showing solidarity with Jacinta than in furthering his own interests. Olympia, however, refused to allow her youngest to take the Marto sheep out to pasture, not even with Lucia who, after all, was only in her eighth year herself.

The two younger children could do nothing more about it. They could only play during the day — alone, with each other or with other village youngsters. At dusk they could wander beyond Aljustrel and linger on the sheep tracks, keeping a lookout for Lucia bringing her flock home. Then, together again, the trio could pen the animals.

It was on nights such as those, Lucia's father told her, that the moon was Our Lady's lamp, and the stars the lamps of the angels. These heavenly beings, he taught her, brighten each night by placing their lights in the windows of heaven so that we might see our way at night. The sun, he added, was Our Lord's lamp, which He would light up every day to keep people warm and make it possible for them to see to work.

This simple and delightful explanation of the universe must have made a great impression on the children because Lucia refers to the image several times in her "Memoirs." She wrote that during this time, when she alone was permitted to mind the sheep, every day her cousins would come to meet her at dusk. Then they would make for the threshing floor and run and play for a while, waiting for Our Lady and the angels to light their lamps and put them at the window to give them light. On moonless nights, they would say that there was no oil for Our Lady's lamp.

Referring to Francisco's cool, unhurried manner at this time, she said that in the evenings he would wait for Lucia's homecoming. She noted that it wasn't out of affection for her, but rather to please Jacinta. As soon as Jacinta heard the tinkling of sheep bells, she would run out to meet her cousin, but Francisco would sit on the stone steps of the front door and wait.

Yes, Lucia is contradicting herself here. At one point Francisco and Jacinta go to meet her, and in the next Jacinta alone runs to join her while Francisco remains seated on the steps. Of course, both statements are true. The "Memoirs" were written years apart, and anyway, if we knew all the facts as the angels know them, the contradictions, like the contradictions in the Gospels, bolster the truth, in some inapprehensible way, by their very contrariety.

If they were written to deceive, she would have taken pains to eliminate them, or at least to whitewash the sepulcher. Lucia has probably never read her own words since she wrote them.

Perhaps it was during this time, 1915 — two years before the apparitions of the Blessed Virgin — that a series of incidents occurred that, though they were out of the ordinary, were nevertheless relegated to the cellars of Lucia's mind. They remained there until Father Manuel Nunes Formigão, an eminent cleric from Santarem who had faith in the children's story from the beginning, conducted a series of interviews with them beginning in September 1917 and took extensive notes on what they said. On November 2, having heard references to possible angelic visitations from Lucia's mother, Father Formigão had a conversation with Lucia that went, in part, like this:

Q: You haven't told me what you saw some time ago. I would like to know what you saw and the circumstances under which you saw it. Are you sure that you saw a white face?

A: Yes. I saw the face at Cabeço.

Q: Was it on the ground or up in a tree?

A: I saw it above a holm oak.

Q: And what did this face seem like to you?

A: It seemed to me like a person wrapped up in a sheet.

Q: Did it speak to you?

A: No, it said nothing.

Q: Were you alone at the time or were you with other people?

A: The first time I was with Thereza Mathais from Casa Velha, and Maria Pereira.

Q: Did they also see this white figure?

A: They said that they did.

Q: And the second time, who was present?

A: There was Manuel das Neves, and Manuel de
    Jesus. The third time there was only me and João
    Marto who said he saw nothing.

Q: How was the figure dressed?

A: All in white. I didn't see any arms or feet.

Q: Who saw the face first?

A: The others saw it first and told me.

Q: Who do you think the face could have belonged
    to? Was it Our Lady?

A: I am certain that it wasn't Our Lady.

While this encounter didn't directly concern Francisco and
Jacinta, these events can be seen as the first stirrings of the supernatural activity around Fatima. They are a prelude to the gates of
heaven bursting open. Soon the Queen of Heaven herself would
visit, bringing a suprabundance of graces to the people of this
rocky, lackluster landscape.

In that early stage, Lucia had told no one what she had seen,
but her companions had had no such inhibitions. By that evening,
it was the talk of the village. Soon Lucia's mother was asking her,
"They are saying that you saw something up on Cabeço. What
was it? What did you see up there?" Because the young girl didn't
know what she had seen, she found it difficult to answer truthfully. In her confusion she said, "It looked like a person wrapped
up in a sheet."

Her mother considered this, then dismissed the statement as
childish nonsense. In doing so, she began a pattern of doubt that
would cause Lucia years of suffering.

Up to that time, Lucia had been the coddled baby of the family, the object of caresses and kisses, of constant and spontaneous
affection. Suddenly, her sisters mocked her. Her brothers taunted
her with questions like "How is your friend who is wrapped up in
a sheet?" and "Have you seen any statues made of snow recently?"
It wasn't just her own family, but the whole village, who laughed

at her. The residents — and family members — had no way of knowing that she was being groomed in humility because she was to be the key confidant in heaven's most public manifestation of Mercy since Christ lived among us. Little Lucia had no way of knowing that either.

Lucia has said specifically that she never mentioned the apparitions to her cousins, though it seems extraordinary that she wouldn't have confided in them when they played together. There was no one else she could spill her troubles to, especially since her immediate family was among the chief scoffers. Furthermore, it is unlikely that Francisco and Jacinta wouldn't have heard talk of "something strange" that local children claimed to have seen in the groves. Particularly so, since their cousin and intimate was said to be one of those seers.

It is not difficult to gauge the reaction of the Marto cousins. First, they would believe in Lucia implicitly. Then they would puzzle over why everybody else didn't as well. Vaguely human figures transparent with light that made them look as if they were wrapped in sheets — particularly when floating among tree branches — weren't matter for dispute. Either they had been there or they hadn't. And if Lucia said that she saw them, then she saw them.

Francisco and Jacinta probably couldn't understand what the fuss was about. On the second and following occasions when the nebulous figure was seen — and other children spoke of it — Lucia was blamed and reprimanded for inciting trouble. She probably turned immediately to her little cousins for solace even if she didn't specifically mention what she was seeking solace for.

This harsh treatment of Lucia served to draw the three even closer together and made the Marto children even more eager to take over the pasturing of the family sheep. They longed to spend their days in the grazing fields with Lucia, to talk and play there with no one else to disturb them.

At that time, it was customary for two flocks to be grazing together. Lucia had already been combining her sheep with those being tended by other neighborhood children. Among them, as she mentioned to Father Formigão, were Tereza's, Maria's and Manuel's. If Francisco and Jacinta could take the Marto flock with Lucia's, the three could be together and the other children could take their flocks to other pastures.

It was Jacinta — not both Martos — who wanted to be with Lucia, and taking care of the family flock was the means to this end. She was not discouraged, even though by this time Lucia had teamed up with Francisco and Jacinta's slightly older brother, João (the Portuguese for John, it's pronounced joe-ówng). While Lucia didn't find his company as compatible as that of her younger cousins, she later admitted that at this stage, she had no outstanding affection for Francisco or Jacinta.

Although attracted by a certain sweetness and gentleness in Jacinta's disposition, Lucia was not blind to the disagreeable characteristics her little cousin betrayed when they played together. The younger girl was possessive and manipulative. She wanted her own way. When she couldn't get it, the storm clouds would gather over that tiny brow and the stubborn mule in her would take to kicking and pouting. Sweet talk wouldn't bring her round. Nothing but everybody else submitting to her will would suffice.

Francisco, while lobbying for the shepherding job as insistently as his sister, was doing it for her sake. If she was to be allowed to go shepherding at all, she was far too young to do so alone; Francisco had to be part of the deal. When Olympia got annoyed at their insistence, Francisco would say, "Mother, it doesn't matter to me. It is Jacinta who wants to go." Whatever the motive, it all seemed so simple to their young minds. They pestered their mother with their scheme until, like the harassed judge in the Gospels, she gave in and allowed the two, young as they were, to pasture the family sheep with Lucia.

Overjoyed with this longed-for concession, the three made plans. It was decided that whoever was first to take a flock from the pens would lead it down the road to the pool at Barreiro to await the arrival of the other. Once the cousins had met up, they would decide where to take their charges.

Families had pockets of land scattered all over the area. Choices of sites for a day's grazing doubled when two flocks were combined. However, the pastures on this rocky and often dry terrain were hardly lush. Even the most undiscerning of sheep would have its work cut out for it getting in a good day's feeding.

This consortium of Lucia and the Marto children was probably initiated in the early spring of 1916, well more than a year before the apparitions of the Blessed Virgin in the Cova da Iria. But this year was not a blank space in the short life of the Marto seers, not a year that we can pass over simply as a period of waiting. Quite unbeknown to them, this year was, as it were, a novitiate, and their novice master was an angelic being sent from heaven to prepare them for their very singular vocation.

Indeed, reading between the lines of Lucia's fourth "Memoir," it would seem that much of the period was spent in a state of deep prayer. It was a devotion that took possession of their souls but that, on an exterior level, and perhaps even to their own immediate consciousness, did not betray its presence.

CHAPTER FIVE

Sometime in 1916, probably in early summer, Lucia, Francisco and Jacinta took the sheep to a place called Cabeço (the top of the hill), a steep, rocky, wooded area to the north of Aljustrel. Toward midday a light drizzle started. The children took shelter in a small cave nearby where, seated beneath an overhanging lip of the rock, they opened the lunches that Francisco carried in his shoulder bag: bread, cheese, olives, fruit and water in a skin bottle.

When they had finished this simple meal, they knelt to say their Rosary, possibly reminded by the Angelus bell ringing from the parish church a little more than a mile to the south. (Because Portugal observed "government time," nature said it was only eleven when the bell rang at "noon.") The little shepherds took their beads from their pockets and started the prayer. The vocal prayer had lost much of its savor by becoming routine, and the children were just saying the two words "Our Father" on the larger beads without the praise, the petition or the penance. On the series of ten smaller beads, they were simply repeating "Hail Mary! Holy Mary!" A charming greeting if heartfelt, to be sure, but it was hardly praying the Rosary. It wasn't a burgeoning contempt for religion but, more prosaically, an eagerness to get to a game they called "pebbles."

After the slight shower had passed and the sun was shining in the grove, the children remained in the cave, which gave a good view of the placidly grazing sheep. Then, with no warning, a strong wind, seemingly from nowhere, began to toss the branches of the trees. At once the youngsters grew apprehensive and lost interest in their game.

There was an ominous force in the stiff breeze. Frightened, they drew closer to each other. There was a moment of tightrope tension and then they saw, quite plainly, a young man — a youth, very beautiful, suffused with light — standing in the rays of the sun. He began walking toward them over the tops of the olive trees. It was as if there were an invisible path leading directly to the mouth of the cave, and the splendid being walked down it till he stood before them.

In the New Testament, when an angel appeared to Zechariah (the father of John the Baptist), to Mary and then to the Bethlehem shepherds, he — it always seems to be a male body that angels assume — invariably began with an exhortation not to be afraid. This suggests that in each case the human being involved was clutched by a mighty fear. Matthew describes the angelic presence graphi-

The cave of the first angelic appearance, with local children, circa 1946.

cally when writing about the aftermath of the Resurrection: "His appearance was like lightning, and his clothing white as snow. For fear of him the guards shook and became like dead men. But the angel said to the women, 'Do not be afraid. . . .' "

At Fatima, the shining youth spoke first. "Do not be afraid!" he said. "I am the Angel of Peace. Pray with me." Why, we might wonder, did this visitor say "I am the angel of peace"? Was it a qualifier for "Do not be afraid"? In other words, "Do not be afraid *because* I am an Angel of Peace." Where there is peace, there can be no fear. Fear is canceled out by peace. Peace is the air of heaven; fear is the air of hell. Of course the angel could have omitted identifying himself, but would doing so have altered the flavor of the injunction "Pray with me"? Were the children being asked to pray with him in his capacity as "an" or "the" Angel of Peace, or were they being asked to pray with him anyway?

After his introduction, the angel knelt and, leaning forward, touched his forehead on the ground. He prayed, "My God, I believe, I adore, I hope and I love You! I ask pardon of You for all those who do not believe, do not adore, do not hope and do not love You."

Standing, he said to the children, "Pray thus; the Hearts of Jesus and Mary are attentive to the voice of your supplication."

This is the first mention in the Fatima story of the Heart of Mary. The heart, of course, refers to the love of the person concerned because the heart is the seat of the affections. In this case, it is love beyond anything we can imagine. It is love of the intensity of divine love, not because Mary is divine, but because the object of her love is Divinity itself, and her whole being is so immersed in that Divinity that she has become one with It.

From the first mention of the Heart of Mary — by the priest Simeon in the Temple of Jerusalem — through Sts. John Eudes and Louis Grignion de Montfort, awareness of devotion to the Heart of Mary in the divine scheme had been growing till in the early twentieth century, it pleased heaven to announce this refuge for recidivistic man. In the history books of the Kingdom, this announcement will be the foreword to one of the major chapters of God's mercy in dealing with us — perhaps even the last and greatest of those chapters.

And that announcement was made here, in the olive groves of Cabeço, to three illiterate children who had just eaten their lunch and then skimmed over their Rosary in order to play a game.

We are not told whether the angel retreated as he had come, or simply vanished. As he seems simply to have appeared and disappeared on subsequent visits, we might suppose that the initial approach was a courtesy to dilute the children's alarm.

During this supernatural encounter and all that followed, both with the angel and with Our Lady, Francisco could not hear what the apparition was saying. He could hear Lucia's response, and see as well as the girls, but to the actual sounds of heaven he was deaf. Some writers on the Fatima phenomenon have tried to explain this by claiming that Francisco was of a lesser spiritual and moral caliber than Lucia and Jacinta. They give the impression that there was something wanting in his character. This is a hasty and unworthy judgement by the writers who employed their talents to announce an important truth and as offensive to the memory of Francisco as an accusation of godlessness.

After the angel had left the three children that first day, the intense supernatural atmosphere continued for a long time. They remained prostrate, offering the same prayer over and over. The presence of God was so intense and intimate that they did not even speak to each other. On the following day, they felt their spirits still immersed in that atmosphere but were conscious that it was slowly disappearing. None of them felt the need to bind each other to secrecy. This was something so intensely intimate that silence on the matter was instinctive.

Although few, if any, of us have had a comparable experience, we can nonetheless relate to it. The true supernatural —

"true" to distinguish it from the bogus of spooks and spells and petulant devilry — dwells at no distance from us. Indeed, it is closer to each individual than thought can fathom. It is not a foreign country, but the true territory of our soul. So our notion of it, even if dislocated by original sin, shouldn't be a surprise. As with prayer, it is a recognition unimpeded by the senses, and for that reason both more difficult to express and more difficult to evade.

But the children were pragmatic enough not to cling to the delight of the experience. They learned quickly that, while the memory of the event remains fresh for longer, the spiritually sumptuous aspect fades like a plucked flower. Lucia later commented that "if it were not for the events that followed, sooner or later I would have forgotten it." This would be equally true of Francisco and Jacinta.

—∞—

While the experience of the angel bonded them, we can't help asking if they regarded his visit as universal experience. Did this sort of thing happen to everybody in some form or another but, as with a number of areas of life, was it socially politic for it to remain a subject taboo for general discussion?

It is said that St. Padre Pio's diabolical visions were counter-balanced by apparitions of the Blessed Virgin Mary and his guardian angel. But he never thought that these were anything out of the ordinary. It was not until he was almost thirty years old that he asked his spiritual director, "Don't you see Our Lady?" When the answer was no, Padre Pio is said to have commented, "You are saying that out of humility."

Then, too, Catherine Emmerich (1769–1802), whose entire life seemed to alternate between vivid ecstatic experiences and acute physical suffering, wrote that she thought "everyone had visions, as well as myself, consequently I used to speak of them quite freely, but when my playmates contradicted or ridiculed me on the subject I became pensive and silent." Very quickly she learned to keep her own counsel, and it is not unreasonable to wonder whether our Aljustrel shepherds thought along the same lines.

But they had no way of knowing whether contact with the spiritual world was common or not; and probably no curiosity either. The experience itself was enough to cope with. Their role was that of passive seers. Perhaps that is one reason why heaven usually confides its plans to unlettered children, because their capacity to love and wonder and listen is not yet engrossed by a need to question and analyze.

It is also worth noting here that *none of the children felt the need to recommend secrecy* to each other. Lucia had had the unpleasant experience of being laughed at over the incident of the "figure in the sheet." While neither Francisco nor Jacinta had shared the sight of that figure, or the ridicule that followed, they are included in this unspoken conspiracy of silence. After the first apparition of Our Lady, however, the situation was quite the reverse, and Lucia felt compelled to caution her cousins to keep silent.

Clearly, the psychological effect produced in the children by the angel was quite different from that engendered by Our Lady. The angelic presence produced a sense of annihilation that even caused physical exhaustion, whereas the presence of Our Lady left the children filled with peace and an expansive joy that did not prevent them from speaking of it afterward.

This difference between annihilation and peace with effusive gladness seems to satisfy our grasp of the right order of things while still remaining inexplicable. St. Paul tells the Hebrews that "it is a fearful thing to fall into the hands of the living God," and we can apprehend the truth of the statement. But if anybody, even a comparable authority, were to say "It is a fearful thing to fall into the hands of the Mother of God," is there a soul on earth who would fail to question it?

As Lucia suggests, it is a matter worth pondering that the children confided in no one after this and two subsequent angelic visitations in the spring and summer 1916. Of themselves, normal children are not capable of such secrecy. Only a malign force, such as suggested in the Henry James novel *The Turn of the Screw*, or a morbid, excessively introspective disposition could maintain continued silence on phenomenal events; or, as in this case, a discretion imposed by heaven, such as Christ charges Peter, James and John with after the Transfiguration on Mount Tabor. Children who are deluded or intent on a hoax, even if they managed to refrain from talking of the matter outside their own circle, would certainly develop personality changes, arrogance and a disdain for authority.

Chapter Six

The human psyche is so constructed that the impact of even such a naked confrontation with the angelic world as befell the Aljustrel children diminished with time. Gradually, it gave ground to the daily routine of family life, weather and husbandry. This is a natural progression, and presumably the wills of the seers were no less attuned to the will of God simply because the red-hot enthusiasm fired by the presence of the angel had cooled.

But these are children of predilection. They are being formed for a mission. So, as a teacher will jolt the class to renewed attention and the drill sergeant lambaste his recruits, so heaven again sent an angel some weeks later. He appeared beside them suddenly and, without any preliminary small talk, asked:

> "What are you doing? Pray! Pray a great deal! The most Holy Hearts of Jesus and of Mary have merciful designs for you. Offer prayers and sacrifices constantly to the Most High."

Here we have a rhetorical question, a command, a reinforcement of the command, a justification for the command, and a further, more comprehensive, repetition of the command. Clearly the injunction to pray is the paramount message the angel has to communicate, but the children are not simply told to pray. They are given a reason.

It's not uncommon for adults to talk down to children, to expect blind obedience from them, and for those same adults to consider themselves masters of child psychology, too. But heaven talks down to nobody. The three are not simply told to pray; they are told *why* they must pray. And the reason is a startling one. What makes it so is contained in the word "merciful." Into the concept of mercy can be read the immeasurable distance between divine bounty and human nothingness. The essence of the Divine is alive in the Heart of Jesus by incarnation, and in the Heart of Mary by grace. Here at Fatima, heaven is once again going to communicate physically — though not sacramentally — with humanity. From our vantage point, we miss the scale of this undertaking. If God wishes to appear among us, or delegate Our Lady to do so, we argue, all He has to do is to will it.

Heaven was about to speak directly to us once more. Our representatives, the negotiators, had been selected by heaven and were undergoing a training as intense as any astronaut preparing to plunge into space. These representatives were, in the light of eternity, three of the most important human beings in the world at the time: Lucia dos Santos, nine; Francisco Marto, eight; and Jacinta Marto, six. They had never been to school and had never traveled more than a few miles from their village of thirty-three houses. The motor car was still a novelty. Electricity, the telephone, the movies, hadn't yet reached their backwater. Nevertheless, they were heaven's choice for the merciful designs of the Hearts of Jesus and Mary.

The children were playing near a well at the bottom of the garden behind Lucia's home. Some years before, a small child of the family had fallen down another well closer to the house. In her grief, Lucia's mother had it sealed up. It is because of that tragedy, and to prevent its repetition, that this well — called Arneiro, the dry, barren place — had a slab covering most of its opening.

Some yards away, Lucia's father kept beehives. Wild bees were drawn to the area and their small combs between twigs provide instant honey for children brave enough to pluck them. Perhaps they were harvesting this wild honey when the angel appeared to them and demanded the prayers and the sacrifices.

Lucia, the spokesperson for the trio, had the presence of mind to ask a most sensible question. "How are we to make sacrifices?" There was no lack of good will on the children's part, simply inexperience. Perhaps this is true of most people, and Lucia is spokesperson for all of us. But, alas, it would seem that most aren't aware that they have been spoken for and consequently have never heard the answer.

> "In everything you can, offer a sacrifice as an act of reparation for sins by which He (The Most High) is of-fended, and of supplication for the conversion of sinners."

Reparation and supplication — this is exactly what Our Lady would ask for when she herself came. Clearly, heaven felt that the lesson could not be repeated often enough.

> "This will draw peace upon your country. I am its guard-ian angel, the Angel of Portugal. Above all accept and endure with submission the suffering which the Lord will send you."

These words of the angel illumined the children's spirits so that they understood, in a measure, who God is, how much He loves mankind and wishes to be loved, the value of sacrifice, how sacrifice pleases God and how He accepts sacrifice to convert sinners. Because of this knowledge, they offered Our Lord every-thing that mortified them, but without looking around for other mortifications or penances. The immediate effect of this appari-tion, however, was that they remained for hours with their fore-heads touching the ground, repeating the prayer the angel had taught them.

Francisco, who, as with the first apparition, couldn't hear what the angel had said, asked the girls to repeat it. They were still so stunned by the supernatural experience that they said they would tell him the next day. He inquired no further then, but the next day he asked, "Did you sleep last night? I was thinking all the time about the angel and what it might be that he said." When they repeated the angel's words he asked, "Who is the Most High? What does it mean, 'The Hearts of Jesus and Mary are attentive to the voice of your supplications'?"

He asked so many questions that Jacinta said, "Look, don't talk so much about these things! I don't know what I feel, I can't speak or sing, nor play, and I haven't enough strength for anything."

"Neither have I," said Francisco. "But what of it? The angel is more beautiful than all this. Let me think about him!"

The children's exhaustion is interesting, even if inexplicable. Few of the biblical reports of encounters with the angelic world make specific mention of such an aftereffect, though it is not unknown. The Old Testament prophet Daniel is graphic about it: "My strength left me, and my complexion grew deathly pale, and I retained no strength."

We aren't given a word about any specific event that occurred between the angelic apparitions. In its way, this tells us all we need to know; that is, that Francisco and Jacinta led perfectly normal lives, that nothing in their talk or conduct betrayed that they had been in the confidence of angels. If they were a little more reserved or tractable around the house than before, it would not have been a sullen reservation or a morbid tractability. That would have been noted and brought to light later. There is no recorded criticism of the children's personal behavior from family, neighbors or acquaintances during or after the apparitions. No tantrums, no attention seeking, no excessive highs or lows, even though there was no shortage of devil's advocates ready to pounce on any such manifestation.

The children's great champion from the earliest days, Father Formigão — whose own cause for beatification is currently being considered in Rome — wrote in the months immediately after the apparitions:

They are free of any symptoms whatsoever of sickness. Moreover they have never been sick. There is no indication whatever that permits us to believe that nerves played any predominant part in their temperament. That is how it was before the events at the Cova da Iria, and that is how it was after. They have, on the contrary, calm and well-balanced personalities. They are neither intent nor pensive. Carefree and outgoing, they like to play with children of their own age. Happy by nature, their happiness is simple, frank, childlike....Their piety was no greater than that of children of their age. Francisco and Jacinta haven't even made their first Communion.... Lucia, cross-examined after the apparitions about the power of Our Lady, declared with the greatest of ingenuity, that in her opinion she was superior to God. This was the state, in the question of religion, in which the spirit of the seers of Aljustrel was found when the Most Holy Virgin Mary appeared to them.

This error in doctrine provides a remarkable insight into the children's guileless thinking. Had the superiority of the Blessed Virgin been a tenet of Lucia's own devising, and had she espoused and continued to defend it, the whole Fatima phenomenon today would be no more than a curiosity for students of religious fads. The physical presence of Our Lady herself, the urgency and truth of her message, would not have survived in the consciousness of humanity had one of the seers deliberately rejected a truth and upheld an untruth. That is the extent to which heaven puts itself at our mercy in this world; that's how seriously heaven respects the free will it has given each individual. It can either be the glory or the curse of all.

Life went on in Aljustrel. Heaven was forming its novices, but this formation went unobserved in the homes and lanes of the village. It was an interior working of grace, like a conversion; a spiritual pregnancy, like the establishment of Eucharistic life in the soul. The children had no inkling that they were especially chosen. True, they had been told that the Hearts of Jesus and Mary had designs on them, but that didn't mean that the Hearts of Jesus and Mary didn't have designs on everybody else as well.

Lucia didn't record their understanding of their privilege, probably because they didn't have any, nor did she indicate any curiosity on their part concerning their role in the supernatural manifestations. Yet the concepts of prayer and of sacrifices, and the religious rationale that gave them substance, seeped into their thinking, became customary and desirable, transforming them radically without touching a hair of their heads or altering so much as a mannerism. They were being coaxed from even the legitimate delights that nature had to offer, and weaned slowly toward the things of heaven.

However, even if they had had full knowledge of what was happening to them, no human agent could have prepared them for what was to be bestowed on them during their third and final encounter with the angel.

CHAPTER SEVEN

One day, while pasturing their sheep in the hills behind Aljustrel, the shepherds decided to pray in the hollow among the rocks. Once there, they knelt down with their foreheads touching the ground, and began to repeat the prayer of the angel: "My God, I believe, I adore, I hope and I love You…" After a time, they became aware of an extraordinary light shining on them. They looked up to find the angel standing over them. In his left hand, he held a chalice with a Host suspended above it. Drops of blood fell from the Host into the chalice. Leaving the chalice suspended in the air, the angel knelt down and made the seers repeat three times: "Most Holy Trinity, Father, Son and Holy Spirit, I offer you the most precious Body and Blood, Soul and Divinity of Jesus Christ, present in all the tabernacles of the world, in reparation for all the outrages, sacrileges and indifference with which He Himself is offended. And through the infinite merits of His most Sacred Heart and of the Immaculate Heart of Mary, I beg of You the conversion of poor sinners." Then, rising, he took the chalice and the Host in his hands. He gave the Sacred Host to Lucia and shared the Blood from the chalice between Jacinta and Francisco, saying as he did so: "Take and drink the Body and Blood of Jesus Christ, horribly outraged by ungrateful men. Make reparation for their crimes and console your God." Once again, he prostrated on the ground and repeated with them, three times more, the same prayer: "Most Holy Trinity . . ." Then he disappeared. They remained prostrated for a long time, repeating the same words over and over again. When at last they stood up, they noticed that it was already dark, and time to return home.

This account is adapted from Lucia's "Second Memoir." She repeats the story in much the same words in her "Fourth Memoir," except for the addition of the words "I adore You profoundly" after "Father, Son and Holy Spirit." Either way, it is a prayer of great beauty and theological depth. It assimilates the person praying it into the priesthood of the Mystical Body. In that sense it is, in its own way, a little Mass.

Then, too, given the deep distress Our Lady was later to declare concerning the evils that Russia's atheistic communism was to let loose in the world, it might have been more than mere coincidence that the Eucharist as administered here at Cabeço used both kinds of the Sacred Species. This is how Holy Communion has always been distributed in the Eastern Rites and the Russian Orthodox Church, though not, at the time, in the Roman Rite.

Some days later, as the intense supernatural effects were wearing off, Francisco asked Lucia:

> "The angel gave you Holy Communion, but what was it that he gave to Jacinta and me?"
> "It was Holy Communion, too; it was the Blood that fell from the Host."
> "I felt that God was within me, but I didn't know how!"

One of the most impressive aspects of the story so far is the unquestioning compliance of the children. We are used to being told to take matters into our own hands, to make decisions, to establish ourselves in command of a situation, but here we are confronted with the significance of a contrasting virtue. It is humility in the face of a superior force for good. Our protagonists had no trouble recognizing and responding to the angel, because they had no experience in relying on their own wills. For this reason they were still sensitive to the subtle breezes of heaven. They had an instinct still soft from the Creator's touch, still undiscovered by the corroding exigencies of the world. Such trust only flowers in the climate of childhood, though it has a counterpart that is nurtured in grace. It is this that Christ Himself spoke of when He said, "Unless you change and become like children, you will never enter the kingdom of heaven" and "Blessed are the poor in spirit...."

The children's compliance was consistent from the first appearance of the angel. It became more pronounced during and after the apparitions of the Blessed Virgin. In some inexplicable way, it contained within itself a proof of the authenticity of the Fatima phenomenon; not as a proof that would be acceptable in a court of law, or that would convince a scientist in a laboratory, but credible evidence to minds familiar with the quiet understatement of the Gospels and open to the place of the Virgin Mary in God's redemptive plan for mankind. Again, the messengers emerged as the embodiment of the message.

The Reading for the Mass of Blesseds Francisco and Jacinta is the passage from the First Book of Samuel. Samuel, as a boy, was lying in the sanctuary in the presence of the ark when Yahweh called him three times by name. Each time the boy thought it was the old priest Eli calling. On the first two occasions Eli tells him to go back and lie down for he has not called. The third time Eli realizes that it is Yahweh calling and tells Samuel that if the call comes again he is to answer, "Speak, Lord, for your servant is listening."

The significance of the story in relation to the Marto children is open to a variety of interpretations, but the most obvious must be the three appearances of the angels representing the call of heaven, calls that, though not ignored or rejected through pride, are misunderstood. We can sympathize with the bafflement of Samuel, just as we can sympathize with the incomprehension of the Aljustrel children. And we can sympathize with the questioning compliance of Samuel, the Martos children and their cousin. They were all frightened and quite out of their depth while, at the same time, securely anchored in, and protected by, Truth.

When Yahweh speaks to Samuel, He says, "I am about to do something in Israel that will make both ears of anyone who hears of it tingle." At that time and place, the statement referred to the punishment being prepared for the sons of Eli who "were scoundrels and cared nothing for Yahweh and whose sin was very great...because they treated the offering made to Yahweh with contempt." To our shepherds, the Samuels of the new dispensation, the Eucharistic Christ may well have been whispering the same sentence as He entered their beings. Judgment and threat are implied here too, but hope and joy are paramount. Something truly stupendous was about to take place, heavenly lightning was about to strike, and Francisco, Jacinta and Lucia would be the conductors.

The angel taught them another prayer. It is one so simple, so majestic, so perfect for a communicant carrying the Eucharist in his being that it would not be irreverent to speculate that the Blessed Virgin herself had composed it in heaven and entrusted it to her angelic emissary to teach to the children to prepare their souls for her coming.

"Most Holy Trinity, Father, Son and Holy Spirit, I adore you profoundly...."

The children didn't question this prayer. They didn't instigate inquiries into the nature of the Trinity or the depth of profundity of adoration required. They understood a little, but by accepting the words and praying them an apprehension of the unfathomable mystery grew. Imagine if the voice of Yahweh had taught the same prayer to Samuel, the Temple boy in the loincloth and the little tunic brought to him each year by his mother.

"And I offer you the most precious Body, Blood, Soul and Divinity of Jesus Christ, present in all the tabernacles of the world...."

Samuel would have had no notion of the meaning of the words. They might just as well have been spoken in an alien language. The same would be true for Abraham, Moses, David and even John the Baptist. However, both he and they, I suspect, would have repeated them as taught and believed them ardently, because their faith didn't demand understanding. Their faith was rooted in their God, Yahweh, the speaker of the words, not in their own interpretations.

It is enlightening, though, to reflect that the words of the prayer were not the total mystery to the illiterate peasant children of Aljustrel that they would have been to Abraham, Moses, David and John the Baptist. Yet we who have the inestimable treasures of the Christian dispensation all around us place little or no value on them. Indeed, taken as a body, we seem to live lives more wanton and contemptuous of God's law than Eli's sons could have imagined.

"...present in all the tabernacles of the world, in reparation for all the outrages, sacrileges and indifference with which He Himself is offended."

This prayer enables us —fantastic though it seems — to offer something to God: something that He wants and that He will accept.

"...and through the infinite merits of His most Sacred Heart, and the Immaculate Heart of Mary, I beg of You the conversion of poor sinners."

At this point, theologians hasten to prevent unlearned folk from falling into doctrinal error by pointing out that the word "infinite" refers to the merits of Christ, but not of Mary. Yet, if we look closely, the word does invite this interpretation. The origi-

nal Portuguese doesn't even carry a comma after "Sacred Heart":
"...*pelos méritos infinitos do Seu Santíssimo Coração e do Coraçao Imaculado de Maria...*"

The theologians are right, of course, but there is really no need to castigate the comma for failing to appear, because the union of these two beings, one of whom is both fully divine and fully human, is such a complete fusion of love that the will of one is wholly the will of the other, and what is attributed to one can be safely attributed to the other.

Mary's merits may be said to be infinite because they are subsumed in the merits of Christ just as rain falling on the ocean becomes a part of that ocean, shares in its grandeur and in its powers. The merits of the Immaculate Heart may be said to be infinite, not because of any power of Mary herself, but because love is infinite. On one hand we must beware of heresy, but on the other we can leave the finer points to the academics. No soul was ever damned for not being able to spell theology.

The infant Jesus being suckled at His mother's breast didn't pause to expand on the theology of their relationship. Their very presence there in the Bethlehem cave was for your sake and mine, and the closer we get to them in unquestioning prayer, the more we are admitted into the understanding of these mysteries. It is here, in this simplicity, that children become the role models. This is what Francisco and Jacinta Marto did, and why the Church honors them today.

For Francisco and Jacinta, this encounter with the angel at Cabeço was their first Communion. They are surely unique in being introduced to the Eucharist at the hands of an angelic being and with the Blood of Christ rather than the Body.

Approximately eighteen miles from Fatima is a town about which the locals tell an interesting story. The parish traditionally held the feast of St. Michael, September 29, as a holy day. The chief religious event was the Mass in honor of the archangel, followed by a Eucharistic procession.

After the procession in 1916, the pastor took the lunette holding the Host from the monstrance and deposited it in the tabernacle. He also, somewhat unconventionally, kept his chalice in the tabernacle, to which he alone had a key.

When he unlocked the tabernacle the following day to prepare for Mass, the large Host was missing and the chalice had been moved. The cleric was greatly perturbed, but there was little he could do other than tell his bishop and a few close friends, and offer reparation for what he looked upon as a breach of priestly trust: not being able to account for a consecrated Host in his care.

The matter was a burden to him all his life, although several months before his death he told friends, without explanation, that he was no longer troubled over the matter of the Host that went missing in 1916.

It was only in the "Second Memoir," written November 7-21, 1937 — which happened to be two months after the death of this parish priest — that Lucia revealed that the angel had appeared to them before the apparitions of the Blessed Virgin. This was the first time anyone heard of the angelic visitations and of the extraordinary administration of the Eucharist. This means the parish priest could not have learned from human sources of the Cabeço incident, which happened about the same time the Host disappeared from his tabernacle.

So, whether the Host and chalice used at Cabeço were, in fact, from this nearby church is a matter of private speculation. It hardly adds anything to the message of Fatima or furthers our insight into the disposition of the seers. What we can be sure of, in faith, is that the children received and bore within themselves the Body, Blood, Soul and Divinity of Jesus Christ just as truly as Our Lord is present in all the tabernacles of the world, and just as truly as He was present in the womb of the Blessed Virgin after the angel Gabriel appeared to her and she consented to be the Mother of God.

We don't know the exact dates of the angelic visitations around Aljustrel in 1916, though Lucia does say that it was probably in "October or towards the end of September, as we were no longer returning home for the siesta." This would certainly fit in with the story from the nearby parish. It would also make the time between the sublime Eucharistic event at Cabeço and the May 1917 apparition almost the length of a pregnancy.

During the weeks that followed, the children imitated the angel by prostrating themselves on the ground and repeating the Holy Trinity prayer. At times the force of the presence of God seemed to deprive them even of the use of their bodily senses. During those days, Lucia attests, the peace and happiness they felt were great, but wholly interior, for their souls were completely immersed in God. The physical exhaustion they underwent was also great.

Heaven was teaching them, with lessons at the same time sweet and compelling, the dynamics of the angel's injunction "Console your God."

Chapter Eight

So the stage was set. The religious sensitivity of the children had been introduced to a state of elevated prayer in preparation for their audiences with the Queen of Heaven. They themselves didn't know it, and there is no reason why they should. In their innocence, they attached no importance to themselves. Students of Marian apparitions may speculate whether Juan Diego, or Melanie and Maximin, or Bernadette were subjected to a comparable grooming in the supernatural before the Blessed Virgin made herself known to them at Guadalupe, La Salette and Lourdes. There is no way of knowing. However, in the case of Fatima, the very thoroughness of the preparation of the seers indicates something of the importance heaven attached to the royal visits of 1917.

These preparations emphasize, too, that the apparitions of the Blessed Virgin were not simply an accident, not a sudden whim of heaven to look in on the disruptive nursery in an effort to quell the mayhem. They seem to be part of an infinitely wider plan, a divine strategy encompassing all of time from the expulsion from Eden to that day when "as lightning comes from the east and flashes as far as the west, so will be the coming of the Son of Man."

For a reader eager to pursue the suggestion, a hint of the pattern emerges in a recent book called, *Marian Apparitions, the Bible, and the Modern World* by Donal Anthony Foley (Gracewing, 2002). For all of us, what is important to appreciate — not necessarily to understand — is that there *is* a pattern in the seamless garment. Nothing, not the falling of a leaf, nor a confused plea to the Deity, nor a stellar implosion, is arbitrary. And, if the Church acknowledges and endorses a direct communication from heaven — within the confines of her authority to do so — that communication is as much for each one of us to mull over, to ponder on and delight in with holy fear, as it was for the chosen seers.

In the bliss of heaven, when we can view the divine agenda as a whole, a biography of the seers of Fatima, as indeed all Holy Scripture, could be the story of any one of us — in substance, if not in detail.

However, back in Aljustrel around the hearths of the Marto family, there was no indication of anything extraordinary taking place in the lives of their youngest children. Those children might have appeared a little subdued and thoughtful at times. Later the parents recalled that the pair were often huddled together in secret converse with Lucia, but these variations and intensities are normal features of the climate of childhood, part of the cracking of the shell and the emergence of individuality. Nothing betrayed their experiences with the angel, and they confided in no one. Indeed, as we have seen, it was more than twenty years before Lucia, under obedience, told of the angelic visits; and by that time, her cousins had long since been taken to heaven.

It was Sunday, May 13, 1917, one p.m. by government time; noon by the sun.

On that day, on which the curtain was to rise on a new act in the great drama of God's dealings with mankind, Lucia, Francisco and Jacinta had climbed the rise at the eastern end of the Cova da Iria. This is the place where the basilica now stands.

Around them their flocks grazed on the sparse grasses that managed to sprout between the stones. The children's chief responsibility was to keep the sheep from wandering down to the floor of the Cova to feast on the vegetable garden where Lucia's father had planted cabbage, corn, carrots, beans and tomatoes.

The youngsters were playing a game. The idea seems to have been to use stones to make a plan of a house on the ground. The amusement offers unlimited stimulus for the imagination, and they might have spent all that warm Sunday afternoon at it. But eternity had other plans.

They had built a stone circle around a small shrub (a *moita*, which thrives in arid soil), when a flash of light cut across the clear sky. It was a blink of a burning paradise. The shepherds — with experience of the supernatural, it is true, but with no further expectation — interpreted this momentary illumination as lightning before a summer storm. Sudden summer storms were dangerous, and lightning had been known to strike and kill sheep, so they abandoned their game and began to corral their flocks for an urgent scamper home.

Turning from their architectural enterprise, they hastened down the hill, intending to spread out to encircle the sheep and move them on together. But straightaway the heavens blinked again. Had the children thought about it they might have suspected that this lightning wasn't like any other lightning they had witnessed. It wasn't a sudden gash of molten gold, or a jagged prong of light that illuminated the world for an instant, sparks from a stratospheric anvil. This light was more dazzling but more suffused, light generated by a benign intensity rather than thrown off from a flame.

But it didn't occur to the little shepherds to speculate on the source of the light. No matter what generated these explosions they must remove their sheep, and themselves, from the apparent threat.

Where the land started to level out, and the sheep began to jostle along the rough path between the vegetable garden and the manure mounds, the children stopped, stunned with wonder. In the trees the birds sang their customary medley of chirps and

warbles, and summer insects droned lazily among the thin flowers of dry-ground herbs, but Francisco and Jacinta and their elder
cousin saw or heard none of these things. They had halted because, immediately in front of them, on a holm oak sapling no
taller than Jacinta herself, stood a young woman.

She made nonsense of gravity by standing on top of a tender
shrub. In spite of glowing with an effulgence of which the "lightning" a few moments before had been less than a bland overture,
despite being more spectacularly beautiful than any description
could have prepared them for, she caused the children to be frozen with amazement and fear.

"I was so frightened," Lucia was to tell Father Formigão later,
"that I wanted to run away with Jacinta and Francisco; but she
told us not to be afraid for she would do us no harm."

We get the impression that, great as this initial fear was, it
was not that awful dread, that clawing apprehension that is said
to be a feature of mysterious encounters. Agog and mesmerized
they remained, but the fear quickly evaporated, because the beautiful young woman had an aura that did not inhibit them, a gentleness, a compassion, a motherly magnetism.

Some commentators, relying more on imagination and gossip
than on authenticated reports, claim that Francisco couldn't see
the Lady at first. They say his reaction was to throw a stone at
this tree that seemed to engross Jacinta and Lucia. I can find no
evidence for or against his inability to see the Lady in the initial
stages of the apparition, but the stone throwing is not true. At
the time of the apparitions, Lucia herself told Father José Ferreira
de Lacerda, who had heard the same rumor, "Francisco threw no
stone."

Anyway, it seems out of character. The boyish and tribal exu-
berance that induced him to throw stones at the boys from Boleiros
would not present itself when faced with someone who was clearly
a Lady, in the social sense of the word, and so dazzling and beautiful, pure and holy. Francisco might well have been a very young

and illiterate peasant, but there was nobility in his nine-year-old psyche, one born of sound family values, the stuff that forms gentlemen. And, further, his experience with the angels would have suggested from the outset that this majestic being, whose very gaze invited confidence, was from the same plane as the angel.

The Lady emitted a supernal light that enfolded them like heat. They were only a yard or so away from her. Shortly she spoke to them. Some years later, when she was seventeen, Lucia described the voice of Our Lady as "soft but clearly audible." Lucia was the only one of the children who answered. Francisco couldn't hear what the Lady said, though he could see the visitor and hear Lucia's replies. Jacinta did not speak to the Lady during the Cova da Iria apparitions, possibly through shyness. She probably did speak during several private apparitions she was given subsequently, both in the parish church and during her illness.

On that first visit to all three children, this is the conversation that passed between the Lady and Lucia:

Lady:	**Do not be afraid, I will do you no harm.**
Lucia:	Where are you from?
Lady:	**I am from heaven.**
Lucia:	What do you want of me?
Lady:	**I have come to ask you to come here for six months in succession, on the thirteenth, at this same hour. Later on I will tell you who I am and what I want. Afterwards I will return here yet a seventh time.**
Lucia:	Shall I go to heaven, too?
Lady:	**Yes, you will.**
Lucia:	And Jacinta?
Lady:	**She will go also.**
Lucia:	And Francisco?
Lady:	**He will go there to, but he must say many Rosaries.**

Lucia: Is Maria das Neves in heaven?
Lady: **Yes, she is.**
Lucia: And Amélia?
Lady: **She will be in purgatory until the end of the world.**
Are you willing to offer yourselves to God and bear all the sufferings He wills to send you, as an act of reparation for the sins by which He is offended, and of supplication for the conversion of sinners?
Lucia: Yes, we are willing!
Lady: **Then you are going to have much to suffer, but the grace of God will be your comfort.**

These are the bare words of the conversations recalled by Lucia more than twenty years after that day. Needless to say, this is an English translation, in essence faithful to the Portuguese, but even the Portuguese doesn't claim to be unequivocally verbatim. Other things are said, or alluded to, in the contemporary transcripts of the interrogations of the seers.

Words are not necessarily the sum of a conversation, or even its essential ingredient. Even so, it's worthwhile to look at this exchange a little more closely before moving on to other aspects of the meeting.

"Do not be afraid, I will do you no harm."

There is a similarity to St. Luke's account of the Annunciation. The Lady tells the children not to be frightened, just as the angel had told her not to be afraid at Nazareth. We don't have to be mystics to appreciate that a direct encounter with the supernatural would induce fear. Again, this is not necessarily a gut-wrenching dread, but the fear of the creature out of its element: Cinderella at the ball, or Mowgli in the officer's mess. Reverent fear.

Gabriel said that Mary had found favor with God, which implies that Gabriel had come from heaven, where he had been entrusted with this confidence. The Lady tells the children that she has come from heaven. Both heavenly visitors ask if those on earth will participate in a divine arrangement: Mary to conceive the Christ by the direct power of the Holy Spirit and the children to accept sacrificial suffering. Both Mary and the children agree to the proposition. Mary's child will develop in her womb over a nine-month period. The children are told to meet with the Lady regularly in the same place at the same time for six months before she will fully reveal who she is.

I'm not proposing that there is any profound significance in these parallels, but if nothing else they do indicate the immense and continuing courtesy of heaven. God Himself respects the free will of every individual, even when putting the life of His Son into the hands of a teenage girl, even when trusting illiterate peasant children with a serious warning for the world and the burden of reparation for offended Majesty.

Notice that it is not a matter of a promise of rewards. Mary never for a moment doubted her own salvation, for that would have been tantamount to distrusting God, and the children had already been told that they would be going to heaven. Their participation in sacrificial suffering was not a condition of admission into paradise.

"Where are you from?"

The Portuguese here has *"Donde é vossemecê?"* English translations tend to substitute a pallid "you" for *vossemecê*, which is an expression of respect from a person of a lower social order to one of a higher. "Where does your Ladyship come from?" might be a more faithful rendering.

If this were a work of fiction, just about every writer in the universe would put the words "Who are you?" in Lucia's mouth. Why is it that the young girl automatically asks where the Lady comes from before asking who she is? Is this question meant in the sense that she wasn't there a moment ago, so where had she been hiding? Or had she been spirited there by the lightning? Or is she so utterly unlike any being the children have seen or heard of before, that her place of origin stimulates their curiosity more than her identity?

But, if we consider it, the Lady is not utterly unlike anyone they have seen before. Only last summer they had seen — and been addressed by and spent time with — a being who had said he was the Angel of Portugal, the Angel of Peace. His presence, too, had drawn them into the shoreless and compelling vortex of the supernatural. Even if that memory had become dormant, suddenly, near this Lady, it was alive again.

But the Lady was greater, much greater than the angel. She didn't just glow, she was made of light — pure crystalline light, brighter than any fire, brighter than any sun, light of a different nature, of a different essence, uncreated light. Her face, her hands, her feet, her simple white gown and long white veil were composed of and reflected light of unfathomable beauty. And, although her manner showed that she was approachable, affable even, the children understood, by intuition — or inspiration, who knows? — that she was the queen of the angel's country. That may have been why Lucia didn't ask for details of who she was. Queenship, after all, is an absolute. Of more immediate interest was what country her Ladyship, Her Majesty, was queen of. Wherever it was, it must be the most perfect kingdom possible.

The first written record of the apparitions is from the pen of the parish priest of Fatima, Father Manuel Marques Ferreira (1880–1945), who interviewed the children on May 27, just two weeks after the first apparition. According to his notes, the conversation was reported as follows, though it must be remembered that he probably didn't attach much importance to the matter. It seems likely he suspected that it was probably childish imaginings and therefore transcribed what was said in the manner of a busy parish priest rather than as scholars of the future might have wished. The exchange is essentially the same as that reported by Sister Lucia in her "Fourth Memoir," except for the added question and answer:

> "Can Your Ladyship tell me if the war is going to last a long time or if it is going to finish shortly?"
>
> "I cannot tell you that until I have also told you what I am here for."

In the opening paragraphs of the "Fourth Memoir," Lucia writes that she "shall not knowingly omit anything, though I suppose I may forget just a few details of minor importance." Lucia's question about the war hardly seems minor, particularly as it appears to have been asked even before the matter of the children's going to heaven was posed. And the Lady's answer to the question of where she is from is particularly telling.

"I am from heaven."

There is no beating about the bush here, no buildup to a dramatic revelation. A candid question receives a candid answer. It is even more succinct in the original: *"Sou do Céu."* "I am from heaven." The children had no trouble in believing the claim. It wasn't the sort of thing a human being could say unless it were true and, anyway, everything about this visitor spoke of heaven, the great city of God. The light from which she was made was God's light because no light could be brighter. The little shepherds couldn't look at her face very long. After a minute or two the light burned their eyes, not with pain but with beauty. No eye could gaze continually on such beauty without fusing. Human eyes simply aren't made to carry the weight of beauty like that.

It is interesting that in her testimony, Lucia's mother said that when she first questioned her daughter about the child's claim, the girl reported that the Lady pointed up to the sky to indicate the position of heaven.

"What do you want of me?"
"E que é que Vossemecê me quer?"

This seems a strange question, given the situation and the conversants. In the normal course of introductory small talk, regardless of age and social differences, one party doesn't automatically ask "What do you want of me?" The meeting had been only a few moments so far. What made Lucia suppose that the Lady, no matter how extraordinary she appeared, wanted anything from her? Or was it she supposed that if the Lady had gone to the trouble of coming from heaven it wouldn't be simply to pass the time of day?

It could be that the encounters with the angel leapt vividly back into her consciousness, especially that one at the well of Arneiro when the angel chided them with the words :"Pray! Pray very much!" Perhaps they hadn't offered enough prayers, perhaps they had grown too lax about sacrifices and here was a queenly figure from heaven come to reprimand them.

Even if these words are reported exactly as spoken, we have no way of knowing the manner in which they were said. Different stresses on different words would indicate different interpretations.

- "*What* do you want of me?" might suggest the interpretation just given.

- "What do *you* want of me?" Though spoken with great respect, stressing the "you," the *Vossemecé*, is a contrast to the angel. Does your Ladyship want more prayers and sacrifices? Next to the well, the angel had said, "*The Hearts of Jesus and Mary have designs on you.*" Was this a new phase of the designs? Was something over and above prayer and sacrifice wanted now? Indeed, was this Mary herself, come to tell more about the designs?

- "What do you want of *me*?" It's a little curious that Lucia uses the personal "me" instead of "us." She was the oldest of the three, and so both the representative and the protector of her cousins. In her 1941 "Memoir," Lucia used the first-person plural: "in the presence of Our Lady we felt a certain communicative enthusiasm" (*"produziam em nós"*). Why "me" in 1917, unless it was in a profound sense of humility in the presence of the heavenly Queen. Was the child implying "What can a Lady as splendid as Your Excellency possibly want with an unlettered peasant girl like me?"

"I have come to ask you to come here for six months in succession, on the thirteenth day, at this same hour. Later on I will tell you who I am and what I want. Afterwards I will return here yet a seventh time."

Again a straightforward answer to a question. A request, followed by two promises; all admirably precise and simple, no maybes, no conditions, no small print. She immediately tells what she wants: The children are to return at set times. She adds that she will reveal her identity and the chief import of her mission, but not yet.

This statement of the Lady, "Later on I will tell you who I am," is open to various interpretations, but I would suggest that the children had no doubt that their visitor was the Blessed Virgin herself. That evening Jacinta was to tell her mother that she had seen Our Lady. Then, too, Francisco's exclamation after the apparition ("Oh my dear Our Lady . . .") strongly suggests this. When Our Lady says that later on she will tell them who she is, she probably means under which of her votive personas she is appearing, under which aspect God wants her to be honored here.

In fact it was as "Our Lady of the Rosary" that she eventually made herself known in October. The time had also come to launch the cult of her Immaculate Heart; but to confide all this to the children on their first encounter was more than they could absorb. A mother adapts herself to the limits of her little ones.

Note, too, that Lucia asked, "What do you want of me?" The reply, while answering the question perfectly, also answers the unasked question, "Why have you come here?" That would have been a more obvious query under the circumstances.

The difficulty in this communication of the Lady is the statement that she will return to this place a seventh time. According to Father Formigão in *The Wonderful Events of Fatima* (1921), Jacinta had said that Our Lady was going to appear one more time at the Cova da Iria, but not to her, for she would be dead.

The notes to the "Fourth Memoir" of Sister Lucia, first published in 1976, say:

> This "seventh time" refers to the 16th June 1921, the eve of Lucia's departure to Vilar de Oporto. The apparition in question had a personal message for Lucia, which she did not consider necessary to relate here.

Although the notes weren't written by Lucia, we must, I suppose, take this explanation as approved by Lucia herself. Still, why she should write the Lady's words in 1941 and not allude to the promised apparition as already having taken place seems uncharacteristic and odd. That's especially so as she must have known that the world is full of people ready to take up, and make capital out of, such open statements. Perhaps this unsupported footnote can be questioned, but one shies away from enrolling oneself among the ranks of the alarmists.

"Shall I go to heaven too?"
"Yes, you will."

This exchange is so simple and direct that we are inclined to skip over it. In fact it is rich matter for meditation. The child's question would disarm a diplomat but charm a queen. The Lady doesn't say " Wait and see" or "If you're good." She answers in three words (her reply takes only two in Portuguese). She tells this ten-year-old what almost no human being has been told by comparable authority since Christ promised the thief crucified with Him that on that same day they would be together in Paradise.

No novelist creating this situation from a pious imagination would dare to attribute such an unambiguous affirmative to Our Lady. The fiction writer would resort to charismatic platitudes; smiles — knowing, heavenly and mysterious; advice to pray; anything but a plain "yes" or "no."

Indeed, meditation on this absurdly simple dialogue between peasant and Lady, subject and queen, daughter and mother, will reveal subtleties of poetry and depths of spirituality that a reader in haste can't guess at.

"And Jacinta?"

This really is a child talking. Her companions are an extension of herself. A script writer might use exactly the same words but not achieve the effect. No matter how talented the artist is, he can't create reality. Creative art is still necessarily interpretive. Only saints and children are sufficiently uninhibited to create without recourse to art.

"She will go also."

Only saints and children — and the Queen of Heaven, because she is the most blessed of both.

"And Francisco?"
"He will go there to, but he must say many Rosaries."

When relating this exchange, most of the books recounting the story say that the Lady looked at Francisco in a manner that seems to cast doubt on his moral health. For instance, among the best texts, Father John De Marchi in *Fatima From the Beginning* (1950) writes: "At this point the eyes of Our Lady rested on the little boy with something of censure and disapproval, the reason for which is not given us to know." And Dominican Archbishop Finbar Ryan in *Our Lady of Fatima*

(1939) notes: "The Lady turns to the little boy with a look of maternal tenderness mingled with reproof .... "

I am not disputing these opinions, but I can't find any mention of a part-compassionate, part-censorious look afforded to Francisco by the Blessed Virgin in any of the statements, depositions or interviews of the seers.

There are vast treasure houses of insight into many aspects of the Mother of Jesus in the authenticated reports of the Fatima apparitions. The more we read, pray and think about her along the lines of the material given, the more we see a mother, a queen, a young woman not only full of grace but overflowing with that fullness that is, after all, the very life of God. We can't help feeling, as we gaze at her with the eyes of faith, that looks of censure or reproof, if they were to be given at all, would be reserved for far more obstinate and unrepentant sinners than the mild-mannered, nine-year-old Francisco.

In that very early account, Father Ferreira's report says: "He still has to say his beads." Then, too, a committee cross-examination of Lucia when she was seventeen records her words as: "She said that he was (going to go to heaven), but that he should say the Rosary."

Wherever the accentuation fell in the "soft but clearly audible voice," it is an arresting statement. At first glance one is inclined to put Francisco in the dock. Was something wrong with him? Was he fostering secret vices? Why was he singled out as needing to pray many Rosaries?

This statements has always attracted controversy and numerous interpretations are offered. Here are a few of them:

1. The most obvious, on the principle that "there are no tricks in plain and simple faith," is that Francisco would go to heaven, but there was time for many Rosaries before that happened. Here is the true mother of a soul speaking. No

threats spiced with conditions. A positive answer and an admonition presented as a suggestion.

2. That Francisco wasn't as attentive to his religious life as the girls; that he was in danger of his religious observance becoming a formality and that only by means of the Rosary could his heart be rechanneled toward the "one thing necessary." This is true as far as it goes, but the trouble with the statement is that the Rosary could be interpreted as a punishment, and that the girls, presumably being more virtuous, need not say as many as Francisco. That interpretation is nonsense and must be discredited.

3. That because Francisco cannot hear what the Lady is saying, and the girls will have to repeat this sentence to him later, he must be made aware that his foreknowledge of an assured place in heaven is not being offered as a free ride. Prayer is as necessary for those who have been granted that information as for anyone else. But, at the same time, his not being able to hear what is said does not mean that he is just a hanger-on in this company. This is a special message for him, a guarantee of his equal importance with his fellow seers. Indeed, when the girls later repeat the message he crossed his hands on his chest and exclaimed, "Oh, my dear Our Lady! I'll say as many Rosaries as you want!"

4. That it was simply a gentle ploy on the part of Our Lady to stay Lucia's innocent eagerness to know who was going to heaven. Supernaturally aroused, like St. Peter on Mount Tabor, the girl might have gone on all afternoon with a litany of names against which she could chalk off their destination in the next world. As it was, the fascination of the ultimate fate of her acquaintances was too strong and she still persisted, albeit with names of acquaintances already dead.

"Is Maria das Neves in heaven?"
"Yes, she is."
"And Amélia?"
"She will be in purgatory until the end of the world."

Even if the Lady's message for Francisco was a gentle hint to Lucia to stop the list, the visitor continues to answer the questions with consummate courtesy. In the case of Amélia, whom Lucia says was between eighteen and twenty, the information the Lady gave was so startling that the questions quite dried up.

This is not the place to discuss the theology of purgatory. Nevertheless, because Lucia is relating Our Lady's words, we must take them seriously. Many commentators on this statement launch into theories about "time off" for Masses, prayers and indulgences. This is, roughly, the teaching of the Church — so it would not contradict the spirit of Our Lady's words if we found that Amélia is even now in heaven with Francisco and Jacinta — but two other points are worth considering here.

First, Our Lady was talking from the perspective of eternity, and that is foreign territory to our finite minds. Second, when Lucia was questioned about the apparent severity of the statement, she is reported to have said that she didn't consider it surprising, as a soul can go to hell for eternity for deliberately missing Mass on a Sunday.

As to Francisco's not being able to hear the Lady, just as he was not able to hear the angel the previous year, there is an argument, or theory if you like, that could explain the anomaly without pointing at any unspecified flaws in Francisco's character. The opinions of a devout woman I know illustrate this mildly slanderous sort of thinking. She argues that the boy was spiritually deaf. There is no telling her that sound is not a spiritual faculty. Of course she could claim to be speaking metaphorically, but the angel at Cabeço and the Lady at the Cova da Iria were speaking recognizable words, in the seventh-most-spoken language in the world, and using human voices.

We don't know for certain why Francisco couldn't hear what was said, and neither did he. Because it didn't appear to bother him, there is no reason why it should bother us. Even so, there is another explanation worth considering. Perhaps Francisco's inability to hear was a gentle guarantee from heaven of the validity of the events at the Cova da Iria for those with the wit to recognize it.

Let's look at it this way. In the parish of Fatima, about a mile from St. Anthony's parish church, at the end of a promontory of hills to the southeast, is a church named for Our Lady of Ortiga. (*Ortiga* is the Portuguese word for the English "brambles.") It is a fine church, much loved by the locals.

The story of its beginnings goes back many centuries to some undated time. The land thereabouts was owned by a farmer, one of whose children, a daughter, was unable to hear or speak. With this disability, she wasn't considered much use for anything on the farm except minding the sheep, so she spent her days with the animals in pasture.

One day, in the field, she looked up to find a most beautiful Lady standing directly in front of her. She hadn't seen the Lady approach, and there was no horse or carriage, but there this woman was, standing and smiling at her. In a gentle voice the Lady greeted her and asked what she was doing. The girl said she was looking after the family sheep. The Lady asked if she would be so kind as to give her one of the sheep. The girl was flustered. She wanted to give the Lady a sheep but they weren't hers to give. "Oh yes," she said, "but I'll have to run to the house and ask my father first."

"Would you do that for me? I should be most grateful."

So the girl ran down to her home in the valley. "There is a beautiful lady," she blurted out to her father, "who wants one of our sheep. Please, can I give her one? She is so kind and . . ."

The father was astonished to hear his daughter speaking. "A lady!" he said. "And you could hear her! And you are talking to me! Give her a sheep by all means. Give her anything she wants. Give her the whole bleating flock. This is unbelievable"

The girl ran back up to the pasture. The Lady was still there. The girl reported what her father had said and they spoke together a little more. Then the Lady said, very graciously, "I would be most obliged if you would tell your father that I would like a chapel to be built here in my honor."

Then, as suddenly as she had come, she disappeared. At that very moment the girl's father, who had followed his daughter, came running onto the scene. The girl told him all that the Lady had said. As they were pondering these wonderful events, the father noticed something unusual lying beside them entangled in the brambles.

Together they unraveled it and found that it was a statue of the Virgin and Child carved in wood. Wonder was following fast upon wonder that day. They took the statue back to the farmhouse and called all the family and neighbors together to discuss the astonishing events and to decide exactly what these things could mean.

It was decided that a chapel would be built there, in the village, and everyone fetched tools to start work the next morning. When everybody went to bed, the statue was left in a place of honor on the family altar. But when they got up in the morning, it was not there. Neither were the tools. They turned the house upside down, but these things could not be found. Again the neighbors were summoned, and after a briefing, sent out in all directions to scour the countryside. The search took all morning but eventually the statue was found.

It was lying exactly where it had been discovered the day before, among the brambles where the Lady had appeared. And alongside it lay the tools. By this it was evident that here was the site where the Lady wanted the chapel built in her honor. And so it was done, just as she had asked. And it is still there to this day: Our Lady of Ortiga, Our Lady of the Brambles.

The point being made here is that if the girl had not been unable to hear or speak, it is unlikely that anyone would have believed her. Of itself, a statue among brambles is not enough to convince people of heavenly apparitions. It could be asked why the Lady didn't show herself to the girl's father, and to the neighbors, too. And the same question could be extended to Fatima in 1917 — to La Salette, Lourdes, Guadalupe and the other Marian apparitions. The only answer forthcoming is that we are not fully aware of our own perversity. God Himself did just that, and we tried him as a criminal and executed Him. Even on our own terms, we have no right to question heaven's discretion after that.

Simply put: Francisco's inability to hear the Lady may have been for our benefit rather than for his humiliation.

> **"Are you willing to offer yourselves to God and bear all the sufferings He wills to send you, as an act of reparation for the sins by which He is offended, and of supplication for the conversion of sinners?"**
> **"Yes, we are willing!"**

The small talk is over. Now comes the request, the real answer to Lucia's question, "What do you want of me?" It is a terrible request, terrible in itself, and terrible in that it should have to be made at all. But it is the only request for a voluntary action that God can ask of a child of Adam. Anything else is His for the taking anyway, and the creature has nothing else of his or her own to give. On the face of it, this is a lot to ask of a seven-, a nine- and a ten-year-old, just as Divine Motherhood was a lot to ask of the young Virgin of Nazareth. But as it is the same young Virgin who is making the request, any criticism is shamed to silence.

Again, note the simplicity of the presentation, a simplicity and directness that could be cold and formal if the words alone were the criteria. But, given what we have already seen of the Lady, they must have been spoken with love and tenderness and solicitude; irresistible qualities that draw an immediate "let it be done" from the children.

Some theologians might balk at the wording of the request. They might want to insert ancillary clauses into the sentence to reassure the children that although suffering of itself was negative, its acceptance was being sought as a continuing sacrifice in union with the sufferings of Christ that, Christ being God, could alone bridge the abyss between the Creator and the errant creature. But the Lady wasn't there to give a theology lesson. She asked the children to sacrifice themselves, and they said "yes."

"Then you are going to have much to suffer, but the grace of God will be your comfort."

The request is uncompromising. It offers no more than a severe raft on which to ride the tides of suffering until we reflect that "comfort" means "strength," in this case the might of God. And "grace" in this context means the very life of God.

Sin, Julian of Norwich teaches, has no substance and can only be recognized by the pain it causes. It is only by bearing pain that the power of sin can be broken. Left to ourselves, the pain is unbearable and the sin unavoidable. But with every nerve and muscle of the soul taut with the strength of God, and the heart and mind pulsing with the life of God, sin is vanquished and suffering is burned as fuel to carry the soul up to the very lap of the Trinity. Grace and comfort are understatements on the Lady's lips. She only reveals them by degrees in the tutorial of prayer.

On a more pragmatic note, it's odd that none of the interrogators of the seers are recorded as inquiring if the children understand what the Lady is asking of them, the purpose and nature of sacrificial suffering. A reader of faith will claim that heaven would not impose on these youths something they didn't understand, something they acquiesced to under the spell of the moment. And that reader of faith would be right, but that same person cannot help wondering about the degree of each seer's comprehension. Can seven-, nine- and ten-year-olds intelligently accept or refuse a sacrificial role, or is an overview of the function in some manner infused? Perhaps the most intriguing, and for that matter endearing, child who accepted suffering as a gift from "Holy God" was the Irish girl, Nellie Organ (1903–1908), known as Little Nellie of Holy God. The study of her short life will well-reward a reader interested in the phenomenon.

So much for conversation. But words between people are only signals sent out in passing. We long for closer intimacy, a merging of hearts and minds and wills, a fusing with the solder of trust, respect and love. Left to ourselves, we search for this intimacy in carnal couplings, possessive affinities, financial puppeteering, activities programmed for failure and frustration, yet ever rosy with self-deception. But at the Cova da Iria in 1917, the Lady who visited came from heaven, where intimacy is on a level of pure spirit, the delight of God and the glory of men and angels.

After this short introductory exchange came the crucial part of the apparition. Later, when questioned, the children told of the words the Lady spoke, how she was dressed, which direction she came from and went to, and they answered all enquiries truthfully and succinctly because no one asked questions like "Did she show you any special favors?" Or "Did she open her hands and communicate a light so intense that, as it streamed from her hands, its rays penetrated your hearts and the profoundest depths of your souls, making you see yourselves in God, who was that light?" The children answered the predictable questions willingly because they were protecting the essence of the apparitions, the incommunicable experience that was for them alone.

Because our mental image of Our Lady of Fatima is formed by statues, we are inclined to approach her as if she were a wooden or plaster object. In fact she is more completely human than any other woman in creation, more completely maternal. When she does condescend to step into the valley of tears to visit individual members of her family, it would surely be unnatural for her to withhold caresses and kisses, an experience of love-in-waiting, intimacy as it exists in the kingdom of which she is queen, and of which they, as her children, are heirs.

The seers, moved by an interior impulse, fell to their knees and repeated in their hearts: "O most Holy Trinity, I adore you! My God, my God, I love You in the most Blessed Sacrament." Here is sound theology, Mary the Mediatrix giving the children a glimpse of their deepest selves in a mirror that is God, and leading them to the adoration of the Trinity, which is God, who dwells in the material Eucharist, which is God become man.

No pen can begin to write of the sublime culmination of this and subsequent apparitions; and no unaided spirit can begin to savor it any more than the children themselves could tell of it to their interrogators. The experience of "the light from her hands" (to use Lucia's phrase) can only be shared in the cloisters of private prayer. When a soul finds it, however, the whole Fatima message of intercession and sacrifice is spelled out in letters of luminosity and beauty, as if the stars of the galaxies had arranged themselves to form the words and circled the earth with them.

On that day in 1917, after a few moments — during which time, presumably, the Lady withdrew her hands and with them the light that had encompassed the children — she said:

> "Pray the Rosary every day, in order to obtain peace for the world, and the end of the war."

Anyone hearing these words at the beginning of the twenty-first century might well say that this is all very past tense, that the war the Lady spoke of finished in 1918. At the time, of course, she meant, and the children understood her to mean, the conflict we call World War I. Time, however, quickly slips into eternity and the war becomes The War: The one that has never ceased since Cain killed Abel. The War between siblings and neighbors, families and cities, tribes and nations, Christ and Satan, the ever-festering open war against sin.

Any peace for this world will be relative peace. Christ himself said, "You will hear of wars and rumors of wars," but the Rosary will obtain degrees of peace. Yet it's clear that we haven't applied heaven's simple remedy, because the monster of war has grown fatter and even more heinous during the twentieth century so that now, in the twenty-first, it can cast its shadow over the whole world and still remain faceless.

After the Lady's solemn request for the Rosary to be said daily, she began, as Lucia recalls, to rise serenely, going up toward the east, until she disappeared in the immensity of space. The light that surrounded her seemed to open up a path before her in the firmament, and for this reason they sometimes said that they saw heaven opening.

In Guadalupe, the Rue du Bac, Lourdes, La Salette, Knock and Beauraing, Our Lady appeared in a particular place and then vanished. At Banneux she came as a small figure in the sky that approached the seers gradually. But in Fatima her approach by lightning — and, some say, by a sphere of light — was constantly spectacular. (After the October apparitions, each child testified that on that occasion she was seen bodily coming from the east, and that then she was there in the midst of brightness.) "I was blinded. I had to rub my eyes."

But they saw her depart after each apparition.

She went with her back toward the people. She went perfectly, without moving her feet. She was gone in a very short time. She came from the east and she went toward the east.

There is very likely significance in the role of the nascent east. (Spaniards visiting Fatima jocularly claim that, of course, Our Blessed Mother was coming from Spain, and returning there — a suggestion not calculated to endear them to their Lusitanian neighbors.) But however that might be, the Lady had gone off toward that compass point, and the children remained in the thrall of their experience. Apart from her compelling presence, they had actually seen their own souls, both in their individual essence and as objects of the love of God. This is the basis of mysticism. Generations of souls of all religions, and none, have longed and prayed and begged and yearned for just such an encounter. Some have been granted it in varying degrees. It is a gift of the Holy Spirit and the Spirit breathes where He will. Yet consistent personal prayer, the Rosary itself, will always be nudging the soul toward a promise of this confrontation.

And so the children stood by the little holm oak, still bathed in the aura of peace that the Lady had left behind. That was appropriate — peace in the Cove of Peace — the *Cova da Iria*. Even more appropriate, if the children thought about it at all, because that very morning at Mass in their own parish church of St. Anthony, the priest, instead of giving a sermon, had read out a letter on peace from the Pope, Benedict XV. It was a message that was read in every Catholic church throughout the world that day.

Eight days before that, on the fifth of May, the Holy Father had declared that the invocation "Queen of Peace, pray for us!" be added to the Litany of Loreto.

In his letter, the pope spoke of the horrors of war, of the frightful bloodshed that showed no sign of coming to an end. Only hands raised in prayer, he had written, could restore what hands raised in violence were destroying. All trust should be placed in *Regina Pacis*, the Queen of Peace, and every Christian in the world should implore her to intercede with God to bring an end to the horrors of war.

A local man was walking toward the children as they came out of their ecstasy. He waved his stick in the direction of the road and called something. Soon they realized he was telling them that their sheep had wandered into José Matias' bean patch. He had had to throw stones at the animals, he said, or they could have eaten all the beans. He had gone in there to check and luckily the beans had not been eaten, but what sort of shepherds were they letting the sheep out of their sight?

The children then ran after the sheep to muster them to-gether. Later that year, Francisco told Father de Lacerda that when the Lady was speaking, though the sheep walked among the corn and beans, they caused no damage. They neither toppled nor ate any.

CHAPTER NINE

As the immediate thrill of the ecstasy wore off and the children returned to the familiar sense realities of daily life, Francisco was eager for the girls to repeat the Lady's side of the conversation. He had no knowledge of their appointment to meet again on a monthly basis for the rest of the summer, nor that she had promised to eventually tell them who she was and what she wanted.

He had probably guessed that she had said she came from heaven, because Lucia had asked "Shall I go to heaven too?" He had also heard the question about his own heavenly prospects. No part of Francisco's nature was insistent or demanding; self-interest was a very low priority. But I defy any created being to have heard, as he had, Lucia's question concerning his eternal destination and not be in a state of heightened anxiety until he learned the answer.

At this point I'd like to tender a proposal, but simply as a curiosity. I have no developed views on it myself and have no wish to upset those who hold the recorded dialogue between the Blessed Virgin and the seers of Fatima as a sacred canon. Could it have been that the girls, in repeating the Lady's words, took the occasion to drum their advantage and appended the rider, "but he must say many Rosaries," when relating the Lady's statement to Francisco? No malice is being ascribed here, no blatant one-upmanship. But, after all, the final words of the Lady, "Pray the Rosary every day, in order to obtain peace for the world and the end of the war," were still echoing through their enraptured minds.

Francisco was a male. Many of the young men of the area had been conscripted and taken off to nearby Tancos, to prepare for the ghastly conflict in the trenches of northern Europe. The Rosary would be part of his war effort. The juxtaposition of the two ideas into the same sentence would be a typical "little girlish" thing to do. Given that tendency in Jacinta's character to want her own way, she was certainly capable of it. And Lucia, despite her comments on the little faults of her cousins, doesn't share any of her own with us. If she was inclined to be assertive at the expense of younger and more pliable children, particularly boys, this could explain the "but he must say many Rosaries" qualification attributed to Our Lady.

However, as already noted, Francisco's reaction on hearing that the Lady had said that he would go to heaven was an outburst of exultant happiness. He crossed his hands on his breast and said, "Oh, my dear Our Lady! I'll say as many Rosaries as you want." (Perhaps, as we're multiplying theories here, Our Lady had added the clause about Francisco having to say many Rosaries, just to elicit this delightfully spontaneous exclamation of affection from him.)

Then he had to be told about Maria das Neves being in heaven and Amelia being in purgatory. He must have been curious, too, to learn what Lucia had claimed (apparently on behalf of the three of them as she uses the plural "we") they were willing to do. When he was told that she had agreed that they would bear suffering as an act of reparation for sin and the conversion of sinners, the idea wasn't new to him. It reinforced, though as a request rather than as a demand, concepts that the angel had already introduced. The reporting of the fact they were going to have to suffer much must have occupied the minds of the children as they repeated it to Francisco, both that afternoon and during the month they spent waiting for the next promised encounter.

But such discussions wouldn't have taken the form of unanswerable questions and morbid fears of pain. They had seen themselves in "the light from her hands," themselves with and in God.

They understood the need for suffering and its transformation from sordid pain to something exquisite, to be shared in the sweet and inexplicable exchanges of love. There was no way the girls could have communicated that to Francisco, but they didn't have to, because he was as much a participant in that experience as they were. Maybe even more.

He makes one curious statement on the experience that Lucia records but provides no comment on whatsoever. Neither does she, in her writings, make any mention of seeing Christ in the light from Our Lady's hands. Francisco says: "I loved seeing the angel, but I loved still more seeing Our Lady. What I loved most of all was to see Our Lord in that light from Our Lady which penetrated our hearts."

There is no compulsion to assume that each child saw and experienced exactly the same thing when drawn into that celestial intimacy that Lucia refers to as "the light from her hands." Some things, certainly, they experienced in common, as Lucia's accounts of subsequent apparitions show. But each soul's relationship with God seems to be both communal, as a member of the Mystical Body of Christ, and exclusively personal, as the reception of the Eucharist attests. Perhaps Lucia's reluctance to do any more than briefly relate her own experience of "the light from her hands," and record first-person statements of her cousins, reflects her own unspoken intimation of the possibility that each enjoyed an individual caress from the Holy Spirit.

Throughout that afternoon of May 13, 1917, Jacinta would frequently burst out with enraptured exclamations in praise of the beauty and virtues of the Lady, even as the three children swore themselves to secrecy. Each, we can be sure, made the promise to accept suffering willingly and with every intention of honoring it. Perhaps the prospect of suffering recalled the ridicule Lucia had to endure from family and villagers when she admitted having seen the "figure in a white sheet." None of the three had spoken a word about the angelic visitations outside their own circle. But perhaps that was because there was something intense and sobering about the angel, something that sealed the lips and locked the heart, albeit a most willing heart, in an immense sanctum of adoration.

The effect of this experience was quite different. The children were expansive and reeling with joy. They were in love with an unimaginably superior person, and that person, her unimaginable superiority notwithstanding, was in love with them.

"Oh, what a lovely Lady!" Jacinta persisted in exclaiming.

"I can see what's going to happen," Lucia said to Jacinta. "You'll end up saying that to someone else."

"No, I won't. Trust me!"

The next day, Francisco told Lucia how she had reported everything at home the night before. With tears in her eyes, Jacinta said, "There was something within me that wouldn't let me keep quiet."

"Well, don't cry now, and don't tell anything about what the Lady said to us."

"But I've already told them that the Lady promised to take us to heaven."

"To think you told them that!"

"Forgive me, I won't tell anybody anything ever again!"

The manner in which Jacinta actually spoke of the events of the day was recounted by her mother in 1923. Apparently Jacinta met her parents at the street door of their house. Olympia de Jesus and Ti Marto had been to the Sunday Fair at Batalha about twelve miles away below the Serras. It was already dark. As Olympia came in through the door Jacinta, full of joy, ran up and embraced her, a thing she did not normally do, and said enthusiastically, "Oh, Mother, I saw Our Lady in the Cova da Iria today!"

Her mother was taken aback but hardly convinced. "Well then, you're quite a little saint to be seeing Our Lady, aren't you!"

Jacinta appeared unhappy at the rebuff and kept maintaining the truth of the claim. Initially Olympia was blunt in her disbelief. When she questioned Francisco on the matter, he reluctantly confirmed what his sister had said because "when my mother asked me if it were true, I had to say it was, so as not to tell a lie." Ti Marto, however, didn't accuse his daughter of lying. He believed Jacinta's story from the beginning. His attitude was that he knew her and Francisco well and they never lied, and anyway, he said, they hadn't the knowledge to invent such things.

One can't help but feel that, sincere as Jacinta's protestations of secrecy were, heaven wanted otherwise. In fact, heaven seemed determined from the outset that these supernatural happenings were not for the sole benefit of the three children. This was to be the most public and most prestigious exposure heaven had made to man since the birth of Christ, and it refused to hold the news back from the very outset. On this aspect, the seers were neither consulted nor advised. But, obliquely, they had been warned, and their sufferings to console their God had started.

Whatever Lucia or Francisco, or indeed Jacinta herself, thought at the time, it would be presumptuous of us to accuse her of breaking a trust. Francisco reproached her with "You see, it's all your fault. Why did you have to tell them?" A crying Jacinta knelt down, joined her hands and asked for forgiveness. She admitted through her tears that she had done wrong, but that she would never "tell anything to anybody again."

Superficially, she might have seemed an impulsive child, but beneath the externals her character was well-moored and anchored. She had not broken confidences before, and went on to keep her counsel over the "secrets" Our Lady confided throughout the summer. She resisted any inducement to reveal those words, even to the point of threatened death.

Fatima was a private revelation, as all such apparitions are, but a private revelation of global import. It was to be no secret. The mother had entered the nursery. Her maternal intent wasn't to be confined to the first infant she spoke to there. So perhaps the grace of silence was withheld from Jacinta on this occasion or, more positively, perhaps she was given the grace to speak in spite of her own will and the wishes of her fellow seers.

———

Once the story had been told around the hearth, it was impossible to keep it there like a family secret. Before the next midday it had spread through the village and beyond. In no time, the word — with a generous mix of skepticism and pious exclamations — was running like an electrical current through the countryside. Two recipients of the news record the fact soberly. Both were from Moita Redonda, the village nearest to the Cova da Iria. One was Maria Carreira, the invaluable custodian of the apparition site and all that concerned it. Her crippled son, João, was to be sacristan of the chapel there until his death in 1954.

The other was José Alves, who later became a generous benefactor of the shrine. Alves was to donate much of the land he owned adjacent to the Cova to be incorporated into what is now the sanctuary. The seers were often at his house with his wife and daughters. He was later to say that the seers' "story was always the same, or so my wife said. They never tried to change it. It was on account of this that I always respected them as being sincere."

Most people probably did respect the sincerity of the children, but that didn't prevent them from becoming objects of curiosity and endless interrogation. From the moment Jacinta bubbled over with the uncontainable news from heaven, none of the trio was able to lead the "normal" life of his or her peers. Fame — that omnivorous, one-dimensional weed that people will barter their integrity and self-respect for — was forced upon them that summer. All three of them handled it deftly because it failed to establish a foothold in their egos. They had no concept of fame, no knowledge of the delights it offered, and therefore no desire for it. All their longings were centered on pleasing the

Lady by working to console God and by making reparation for sinners.

This fame, this notoriety they attracted served no purpose but to supply ready fuel to burn for those ends. By means of enduring the attention, they began to suffer in a way that couldn't be detected as they played their games, mustered their sheep or sat at table. It was a suffering of alienation on an inexplicable plane: the bitterness of misunderstanding, the humiliation of being the property, as it were, of every curious passerby. And they passed by in thousands. The children were like footballs on a field: the center of attention, but to be kicked, possessed, or squabbled over.

They had agreed to accept suffering, and heaven was starting to confirm how lavish it could be with its gifts.

But we are jumping ahead. In their innocence, they were probably unaware that such suffering as their fame would attract, suffering that is spawned in the mind, is legitimate currency in the clearinghouse of love. The serious suffering was yet to come, so they devised their own deprivations. When they reached the pasture the day after the apparitions, Jacinta, sitting on a rock, declined to play. She said she was thinking and explained, "The Lady told us to say the Rosary and to make sacrifices for the conversion of sinners. So from now on, when we say the Rosary, we must say the whole Hail Mary and the whole Our Father! And the sacrifices — how are we going to make them?"

Immediately Francisco thought of one. "Let us give our lunch to the sheep."

I guess nobler sentences have been uttered, but I doubt if many have had the spontaneity, charm and ingenuity of Francisco's proposition. It is guileless enough to take heaven by surprise and melt the heart of God.

Within minutes, the contents of their lunch bags had been shared among the flock. Jacinta, still sitting meditatively on her rock, asked, "That Lady said many souls go to hell! What is hell, then?"

A conversation on the unending horrors of hell ensued, but the attentive reader of Lucia's "Memoirs" might be disconcerted because, in Lucia's own record of the May apparition, Our Lady hadn't mentioned hell at all. She didn't mention hell till she allowed them a frightening glimpse of it in July. When she appeared at Valinhos in August, she actually said that many souls go to hell.

I daresay there is an explanation for anomalies like this, but overall they hardly matter. As the Fatima scholar, Dr. Messias Coelho, wrote: "Neither the written nor the oral declarations of Sr. Lucia are inspired, nor do the necessarily present verbatim what Our Lady said."

In this period between the first and second apparition, the children began to learn something of the suffering they were to endure through the persecution of neighbors. Francisco's comment was, "Our Lady told us that we would have much to suffer, but I don't mind. I'll suffer all that she wishes! What I want is to go to heaven!" When Lucia, subjected to the disbelief of her own family, was despondent, Francisco would say, "Never mind! Didn't Our Lady say that we would have much to suffer, to make reparation to Our Lord and to her own Immaculate Heart for all the sins by which they are offended? They are so sad! If we can console them with these sufferings, how happy we shall be!"

Sometimes the boy would disappear among the rocks to be alone and pray. Once when the girls found him and asked what he was doing, he replied, "I'm thinking about God, who is so sad because of so many sins! If only I could give Him joy!"

A month to a child is a vast expanse of time, a journey with few maps or schedules. Given the little shepherds' expectations, those summer weeks from May to June must have appeared interminable. When the three were allowed, they'd take the sheep to the Cova da Iria and pray the Rosary there as the Lady had asked, but the empty Cova would only remind them of the glorious presence they yearned to behold again.

The thirteenth of June is the feast of the great St. Anthony of Lisbon, one of those sparkling few in the history of Christianity that even a convention of the canonized would elect as a saint to stand out from among them. While the Italians, who have more acknowledged saints on their books than any other nation, try to claim him by calling him Anthony of Padua, he was not Italian but Portuguese. The son of Portuguese, born, baptized and ordained in Lisbon; the glory of the Portuguese people. His feast, furthermore, is traditionally the major summer *festa*. Even now, with the clouds of secularism darkening the world, cities and villages throughout Portugal still celebrate St. Anthony's day with Masses, processions, stalls, music, fireworks and all the customary displays of communal felicity. It is a summer Christmas.

If the Marto parents had any thoughts that all talk of the Lady would evaporate in the excitement of the colorful activities planned for the parish, those ideas were soon discarded.

When Jacinta's mother asked her if she wanted to go to the St. Anthony festivities, the little one had answered, "St. Anthony's is no good; the Lady is much nicer. I'm going to the Cova and so are the others. But we would go to St. Anthony's if the Lady told us to."

With that she begged her mother and father to come with them to the Cova to see the Lady. To Jacinta it seemed the most obvious thing in the world to do, but it put the Marto parents in a dilemma. There was nothing to stop them from going with their daughter, but what fools they would look if nothing happened and they were seen by neighbors to be credulous of childish fantasies. Children were resilient. If they were proved to be acting under heated imagination or whatever, they would rally with no particular ill effects. But adults could never live down the shame of having allowed their infants to deceive them.

On the other hand, it would not be fitting for them to go to the parish *festa* while their youngest children went alone to the Cova, particularly because public curiosity, both local and beyond, was swelling hourly. So Ti Marto made a decision worthy of Solomon. They wouldn't visit either location. The usual Wednesday fair at Pedreira, some miles away, was to be incorporated into the Antonine feast, so they would go there with a view to buying oxen. Whatever events the day would furnish would be over by the time they got back to Aljustrel.

At dawn on the morning of Wednesday, June 13, Francisco and Jacinta rose to take their sheep to early pasture so they could have them back in their pen by mid-morning. One of their brothers explained that their parents had already left for the Pedreira Fair. Doubtless Jacinta was disappointed and confused, not being able to understand why they would prefer a fair to seeing the beautiful Lady. Even so, she and Francisco took their flock to up to Valinhos and brought them back at nine.

Presumably they then went to the ten o'clock Mass in the Fatima parish church. Lucia did, but separately. She tells us that she was suffering from the contemptuous attitude of her mother and sisters, which cut her to the heart and was as hurtful as open insults. People from many surrounding villages had come to Lucia's home and asked to accompany her to the Cova. They went to Mass with her and then, she said, "around eleven o'clock I left home and called at my uncle's house, where Jacinta and Francisco were waiting for me. Then we set off for the Cova da Iria, in expectation of the longed-for moment."

It was a warm day. When the children arrived with their friends, they all went to the apparition site. Some asked which tree Our Lady appeared on, and Lucia touched one. It was a sapling about a yard high. Lucia looked toward the east, then sat down near the trunk of a large holm oak. Jacinta and Francisco sat on either side of her and the other children around them.

The youngsters began to play and eat the food they brought. As time passed, Lucia became more serious and thoughtful. Jacinta, however, was playing all the time, and Lucia told her to be quiet because Our Lady would be arriving. Those who had come a long way began to eat lunch. Someone offered oranges to the children, which they accepted but didn't eat. The three of them simply sat there with the oranges in their hands. A girl from Boleiros began to read aloud from a book of prayers, and Maria Carreira asked Lucia if she thought Our Lady would be long in coming.

"She won't be long now," was her reply. All those who were there joined in the Rosary. When the girl from Boleiros was beginning the litany, Lucia interrupted, saying that there would not be time. She got up immediately and cried out "Jacinta, Our Lady must be coming. There's the lightning!"

The seers ran to the tiny holm oak with the people behind them. They all knelt on the rocks and stones. Lucia lifted her hands as if she were praying and spoke. Those present heard something like a tiny little voice answering, but they couldn't hear what it said. Maria Carreira described it as "rather like the buzzing of a bee."

CHAPTER TEN

It was Wednesday, June 13, 1917.

Lucia: What do you want of me?

Lady: I wish you to come here on the thirteenth of next month, to pray the Rosary every day, and to learn to read. Later I will tell you what I want.

[Lucia asks for a cure.]

Lady: If he is converted, he will be cured during the year.

Lucia: I would like to ask you to take us to heaven.

Lady: Yes. I will take Jacinta and Francisco soon. But you are to stay here some time longer. Jesus wishes to make use of you to make me known and loved. He wants to establish in the world devotion to my Immaculate Heart. I promise salvation to those who embrace it, and those souls will be loved by God like flowers placed by me to adorn his throne.

Lucia: Am I to stay here alone?

Lady: No, my daughter. Are you suffering a great deal? Don't lose heart. I will never forsake you. My Immaculate Heart will be your refuge and the way that will lead you to God.

The children had not doubted that the Lady would come. Doubt and disbelief were for others to cope with. The children's faith in the Lady's promise, however, didn't inhibit their relief at seeing her again or their joy in her gracious courtesy. It didn't diminish their delight in that beauty that could not be expressed or described, but which they could only gaze upon and yearn for. It was a beauty that deepened as they gazed and increased while they yearned.

"What do you want of me?"

Again there is this singular question from Lucia. It simply isn't one a child would ask a stranger, or even an acquaintance, as the Lady had now become. Or, after deliberation, is it the only question she could possibly ask? Perhaps something in the manner of the august, yet winningly natural, visitor demanded such a question?

Let's look at it this way. It might be argued that even the Queen of Heaven could make a social call without making any particular request. Yet it might equally be argued, and perhaps with more justification, that she could not return to this sinful world and refrain from asking us not to sin, refrain from trying to impress upon our sluggish and spiritually insensitive minds the terrible enormity of sin, refrain from offering her maternal aid in avoiding its horrors and securing salvation. Perhaps this urgency was part of the compelling aura that surrounded her. Perhaps the children responded to it as children will gauge the mood of a parent and adapt themselves to fit in with it. And so Lucia, though using the word "me," spoke for her cousins as well when she asked, "What do you want of me?"

Given the sublimity of the Lady, her exquisite graciousness and her aura of immediacy, perhaps Lucia's question is no longer a puzzle to us, but becomes the obvious thing to say.

It might also contain a bit of "a Lady as great as yourself can hardly have come to be entertained by the scintillating conversation of unsophisticated children from a rural village. If you want us to be your servants, just tell us what we must do."

"I wish you to come here on the thirteenth of next month, to pray the Rosary every day, and to learn to read. Later I will tell you what I want."

The Lady repeats two former requests and makes a third. Urgent as her message is, the children must pass through a period of formation before her plans for them can be implemented.

Learning to read seems a very mundane request. Those people whose faith seems to pivot on the signs and wonders attached to Fatima, Lourdes and the rest, would assume that the Lady could have waved her hand in front of Lucia and she could have been reading, writing and discoursing on the arts and sciences then and there and forevermore. But that is not heaven's way. Life and the universe are the great ongoing miracles of nature. Even when God Himself came among us, He did so through the normal channels after His conception in the womb of a virgin. So there would be no subdivision of the gift of tongues here. Reading, writing, prayer — all these skills were to be learned the hard way. It was all part of the "sweat of the brow" we inherited from Adam.

Because Lucia was speaking in the first person, it has always been assumed that the injunction to learn to read was directed solely at her, though it is hard to see why. That would also mean that only she was to return on the thirteenth of each month, pray the Rosary daily and observe the other injunctions. Clearly this is not so.

Did the prediction that Francisco and Jacinta were soon to die exempt them from education? Or is posterity inclined to consider that, in hindsight, the Lady didn't include them in the directive because Lucia was to be the one entrusted with the propagation of her message for the world? It's doubtful whether an experienced spiritual director would have agreed to their being "let off" from the study of literacy on the strength of an assurance of their early death foretold by a vision. (Even if the director was convinced of the authenticity of that vision.)

As word of the visions spread, one of the many inconveniences the children suffered was the constant succession of requests for them to ask for favors from their heavenly visitor. Already at this second apparition, the children — although generally disbelieved and ridiculed — had a list of pleas for cures. They took these seriously, being careful to remember the ones accepted and to ask for each specifically. This should be, and maybe was, an indication of the sincerity of the seers. People who are perpetrating a hoax don't normally exhibit that degree of conscientious probity.

After the Lady had repeated her requests for their monthly visits, the recitation of the Rosary, and the pursuit of literacy, Lucia considered it an appropriate place to make her first request. The Lady answered:

"If he is converted, he will be cured during the year."

The answer is kind and conditional and, in its way, could have referred to mankind as a whole had Lucia asked if she would, please, draw off the evils of the world and help us to lead substantial and fulfilling lives.

But a more pressing matter was on the child's mind. It doesn't take a graduate in psychology to deduce that the children had spoken much among themselves of the Lady and of the heaven that she came from. The fact that she had told them that they, too, would go there was too intoxicating a revelation to be left floating on the vast ocean of the future with no harbor in sight. They had turned her words over and over all month and come up with a bold solution. She was so kind and gentle, not at all the sort of person to become indignant with them. She answered questions just as she asked them, a total stranger to ambiguity or guile. She wouldn't mind. After all, she had promised, and there was nothing else at all in the world that they wanted.

Francisco and Jacinta were joint composers of the question. Lucia was the spokesperson.

"I would like to ask you to take us to heaven."

All three were riding on the answer. When it came it was as sharp and as incisive as whetted silver.

"Yes. I will take Jacinta and Francisco soon. But you are to stay here some time longer. Jesus wishes to make use of you to make me known and loved. He wants to establish in the world devotion to my Immaculate Heart. I promise salvation to those who embrace it, and those souls will be loved by God like flowers placed by me to adorn his throne."

There is a whole library in these words. The children wanted to go to heaven. During the hours of secret conferences when they were plotting and planning to ask the Lady the question, perhaps they had imagined that she would consent and take them with her when she left the Cova and glided off swiftly to the East. That was their prayer, that was the response they hoped for; and, given what they had experienced of the compliant affability of the Lady, that was what they expected. But heaven knows better.

Yes, Francisco and Jacinta would go to heaven soon. But not just "go to heaven." The Lady herself would take them.

For Francisco and Jacinta, the question, when they thought it through, must have been, "How soon is *soon?*" There were still four months at least, four more assignations on the thirteenth of each month. But they also had accepted her offer to suffer in reparation for sins and supplication for the conversion of sinners. "Suffer much," she had said. Would all that suffering be fitted into four months? Perhaps "soon" meant longer than that. They would do whatever the Lady decided, but they so wanted to go to heaven. Nothing would have any real meaning until they were in heaven.

But Lucia is to stay here some time longer. (". . . *mais algum tempo.*") Given that she is still alive eighty-plus years later (as this is being written in 2003), "some time" would seem a bit of an understatement. But the Lady is too gracious to give this information without providing an explanation: "Jesus wishes to make use of you." Jesus is at the center of the explanation, just as He is at the center of the "Hail Mary" and just as His Sacred Heart is represented on a high plinth at the center of the present-day shrine that stands on what were the rocky fields of the Cova da Iria.

To Jacinta, and to Francisco when the Lady's words were repeated to him later, it must have seemed reasonable that Lucia remain on earth for a while to do whatever Jesus wanted to be done. Lucia was the older one, the natural leader, the one who got things done. (There is no hint anywhere in this story of the children asking "Why me?" or "Why us?" There is no attempt to be humble because they have never left humility.)

If Jesus wanted to use Lucia to make the Lady better known and better loved then, Jacinta knew, Lucia must stay. How the older girl was to accomplish this was beyond speculation, but not beyond faith. Jesus wanted to establish devotion to the Lady's Immaculate Heart. Jacinta had a notion of the Sacred Heart through holy pictures and statues in homes she had visited. The Immaculate Heart was an unknown carrying a complicated label. But the Lady had said it, so it must be so. Jacinta was not confused.

Lucia's thinking ran along different tracks. "Am I to stay here alone?" It was an awful chasm that had suddenly opened out before the child. She wanted more than anything to go to heaven. She had rehearsed and rehearsed asking if the Lady would take them all to heaven — implying, if not actually saying, that they would like to go more or less immediately. And now that she had actually made the request, to be told that her companions would be going soon, but that she would have to remain on the cold earth without them was, well, daunting. No one else, no matter how sympathetic, would ever be able to understand what it was like to be with the Lady, to gaze on her beauty, to be caught up in the peace and purity that was "the light from her hands." To be alone. That was a terrible prospect.

"No, my daughter. Are you suffering a great deal?
Don't lose heart. I will never forsake you. My
Immaculate Heart will be your refuge and the
way that will lead you to God."

"No, my daughter." Every word uttered by the Lady during these apparitions has immense value. When she says "yes," the very concept of affirmation seems to set fire to heaven. And when she says "no," as here, her "no" is not a negative. She is incapable of a negative. It is a command that dispels loneliness by guaranteeing that she herself will remain, for loneliness cannot exist in her presence.

She calls Lucia "daughter." A reader's eye can easily slip over the word as being a familiar part of religious usage. But the Lady doesn't waste words. Every one she uses is chosen and sparkles with meaning. "Daughter" is not a figure of speech. In the eternal order of things, the Lady is more surely the mother of Lucia dos Santos than is Maria dos Santos in Aljustrel, who bore Lucia in her womb and fed her at the breast. By baptism — that seemingly simple ritual that is, in reality, a momentous act of purchase by God — Lucia's whole being became an integral part of the Body of Christ, and therefore as much a child of Mary as Jesus Himself. The word "daughter" here affirms this and illustrates the Church's teaching of the Mystical Body of Christ.

This young girl will not lose heart. Her heavenly mother will never forsake her. The Lady's "Immaculate Heart" — again this new and curious expression —will be her refuge and the way that will lead her to God. Had Lucia known then that she would live into her nineties, and perhaps even beyond, would she also have been able to foretell that that time would be nowhere near long enough to absorb the full riches of the Lady's sentence?

In the midst of this sentence, the Lady pauses to ask, "Are you suffering a great deal?" It was a rhetorical question, not one that required an answer. The bitterness of being mistrusted and misunderstood by her own family hung heavy on the girl's heart, and the Lady, as it were, suffered along with her.

Then, even as the visitor was speaking these words, she once again opened her hands and communicated the rays of that same immense light that had enveloped the seers the previous month. In this light they saw themselves immersed in God: Jacinta and Francisco in that part of the light that rose toward heaven, and Lucia in that poured out on the earth. In the front of the palm of Our Lady's right hand was a heart encircled by thorns that pierced it. The children understood that this was the Immaculate Heart of Mary, outraged by the sins of humanity and seeking reparation.

Again the mystical experience, "the light from the hands," the light that is the will of God. All three children had been chosen as instruments of the Divine will, the siblings in heaven and their cousin on earth. Their immediate fate was only objective. The subject was the will of God, and the will of God is the salvation of our singularly perverse species.

The Immaculate Heart, encircled by thorns that pierce it, appears not in, but in front of, the Lady's right hand. It therefore is seen in "that light from the hands," in which they experienced God. It is Our Lady's love for her children, a love that has been ridiculed and condemned. Mary's whole being is folded into God, permeated with the very essence of the Trinity, full of grace, so that a disparagement of Mary is a disparagement of God, and for that God must demand reparation. The Immaculate Heart is the last lifeline heaven can throw to shipwrecked humanity. People have only to reach for it and cling to it and it will be their refuge and lead them to God.

For those moments, the children were in a suburb of heaven. The prospect of returning to cold, humdrum earth, even for a short while, was dismal in the extreme. Yet they did not question it, for that, too, was the will of God. However, the experience could not be told on earth. They could repeat what the Lady had said, regardless of whether they were believed or not. But these things in heaven, these things they had seen in "the light from her hands," they did not tell about them. Indeed, how could they? Those things were meant to be secret and they promised they would not tell them to anybody.

CHAPTER ELEVEN

There were about fifty people present, according to what the parish priest was later told. Among them was the doughty Maria Carreira, who said Lucia stood up and called out that the Lady was going. The crowd could see only a little cloud that rose slowly and retreated toward the east. When the cloud could be seen no more, Lucia said, "She has gone back to heaven. The doors are shut." The people assembled wondered then, because the leaves and topmost branches of the holm oak sapling were all clearly bent toward the east, giving the impression that they had, indeed, been carrying a weight.

Another phenomenon visible to everybody and attested to by many was the pillar of smoke. For some inexplicable reason, it is rarely mentioned in the chronicles of Fatima. Dr. Gonçalo de Almeida Garrett was a professor at the Coimbra University and author of a 1922 pamphlet on the subject. He wrote that at each apparition, next to the holm oak tree, a cloud of smoke could be seen rising into the air. It was thin, like one produced by the burning of incense during liturgical ceremonies in churches. This phenomenon was seen by a large number of witnesses, both when Our Lady appeared to the children, and also on August 13, when the authorities had the seers in custody so that they weren't able to be at the apparition site.

The professor's son made a statement to the effect that, in the place where the children were, a column of smoke — narrow, slight and blue — ascended straight up to about six feet, where it dissipated. After a little while, it returned twice. He was convinced that the smoke was produced by a thurible.

This smoke is not mentioned in the "Memoirs." Maybe the children didn't see it. But if they did, it's questionable whether they would have been surprised. After all, they had spoken with angels and seen God — and therefore heaven — in "the light from her hands." So angelic beings bearing thuribles and offering the symbolic homage of incense smoke during an earthly visitation would arouse no wonder at all.

After this second apparition, the children walked to the Fatima parish church to join the people reciting the Rosary at the closing of the St. Anthony *festa*. They were accompanied by the fifty faithful from the Cova. It seems that all these witnesses were favorably affected by the experience. They certainly could not have spoken ill of it, or dismissed it as "little girls' games," because some three thousand people came for the July apparitions. Word of mouth is the best advertisement.

There must have been something impressive in the demeanor of the children; heaven must have veiled them with its own aura. A witness, who simply signs himself S. Bento, wrote in 1917 that in June he didn't get to the Cova in time for the happening, but spoke to the children in the churchyard in Fatima and saw in them what he referred to as "unquestionably the truth. From that moment on I believed it was the Most Holy Virgin who had come there."

The pattern of intemperate questioning, contemptuous disbelief and gratuitous insults that had been planted between May and June began to flower between June and July. And an ugly, thorny bloom it was, too. The brunt of it fell on Lucia, because her mother believed she was lying and disgracing the family. Her brothers and sisters followed their mother and missed no opportunity to ridicule and belittle their youngest sister. Her father, ill-equipped to deal with the constant disharmony in his own house, took to staying away when the daily work was over. He would be found playing cards and sharing a carafe of wine with locals in the *tasca* (a cheap bar) in Casa Velha or on the Boleiros road.

Francisco and Jacinta weren't under the same pressure of disbelief at home. Their father's facility in accepting their story and giving it credence shorn of fuss and fanfare was contagious in that small, crowded dwelling. He possessed a spiritual intuition informed by grace. But relations between siblings would never be the same again. Francisco and Jacinta could never be simply the babies of the household, the ones to pet and cuddle and play with when the mood took. They were cut off, isolated on an invisible altar from then on. No one in the family was fully conscious of the transformation yet. None of them could have spoken of it, or analyzed its causes and implications, but it was so. Francisco and Jacinta were inexplicably consecrated.

But if the Marto children weren't tormented within the family, they weren't shown any special indulgence either. And, with all the interminable questioning, they had as much to suffer outside their home as Lucia had within hers. Had they been adults, they might have built walls of silence around themselves, adjusted their body language to dissuade the curious. But with children, every adult is a self-appointed inquisitor, with a right and duty to grill mercilessly, and very confident of his or her own judgment, too.

The seers learned very quickly how to accept these cavalier invasions of their souls' territory: how to submit their wills to it in patience; how not to return rudeness for rudeness, arrogance for arrogance, contempt for stupidity. They learned how not to seek to impress, but to tell the simple truth simply, just as the Lady would have, no more, no less. They learned how to be deferential, not to joke or jest or to countenance familiarity. And they learned how to never, under any promise or threat, divulge what the Lady didn't wish divulged.

The "secrets" of Fatima seem to have occupied the attention of the public more than the theological truths that Our Lady came to emphasize. And, predictably, when those secrets were revealed, the public straightaway lost interest, because the revelation didn't conform to the world's idea of a secret. That definition has been fashioned by curiosity, set like a glittering stone in prurience and marketed by a godless media.

When Our Lady spoke with the children of Aljustrel, she made known to them some things that they were not to repeat for the time being. Some of those things (such as the vision of hell and the bishop clothed in white, which were shown to them in the July apparition), they were specifically told not to share with anyone. Others (revealed in June, such as the knowledge that the Marto children were to be taken to heaven soon and Our Lady's desire to have her Immaculate Heart honored and trusted) are recorded by Lucia as being expressly forbidden to be passed on. But the children seemed to know by intuition, or perhaps it was in the tone or the manner of the Blessed Virgin, that these things were, for the time being, matters of confidence between themselves.

Anyway, Lucia didn't reveal any of them till 1925, when Our Lady appeared to her in Tuy and asked her to promulgate the Immaculate Heart devotion. The consecration of the world to the Immaculate Heart wasn't asked for until 1928. Even then, Lucia told only her religious superiors. Most of the confidences weren't made public until the "Memoirs" were published immediately before and during the Second World War.

Had the matter been left in the hands of the children, all accounts of the apparitions and every word Our Lady spoke would have been "secret," Jacinta's initial outburst of enthusiasm notwithstanding. Lucia herself would never have spoken a word had she not been urged to do so under obedience.

So, already in June 1917, Jacinta, in her innocence, was referring to "secrets" (*segredos*), which whetted the appetite of many a sensation seeker. That also obscured the import of the initial call to prayer and penance as being the only path to the real, fulfilling, abundant love we were created to enjoy.

The one person who had a full right to question the children, indeed a duty, was the parish priest, Father Manuel Marques Ferreira. At the time, the thirty-seven-year-old had been ordained for nine years and in Fatima for three. He seems to have been a practical, conscientious man, with little sympathy for parishioners who preferred religious phenomena to a living faith. (He was of much the same admirable stamp as the Curé of Lourdes, M. Peyramale, fifty-nine years before.) To Father Ferreira, reports of the occurrences at the Cova da Iria were a nuisance that created needless work. Furthermore, given that the devil had a good fire going among the government and press of the country, any clergyman could be forgiven for being reluctant to throw fireworks into the blaze by announcing that three children were chatting on a regular basis to the Mother of Christ in a vegetable patch in a rural backwater.

Although Father Ferreira didn't believe the children's claims, he didn't want to alienate the people who were speaking of little else, and he couldn't afford to antagonize the civil powers who at that time definitely had the upper hand in the war against religion. What capital they would make out of the situation: the drowning Church trying to impose yet another vision on the people! In fact, it was the people who imposed Fatima on the Church, not the Church on the people, as Cardinal Cerejeira, the patriarch of Lisbon, was famously to say twenty-five years later.

Meanwhile, Father Ferreira followed the guidelines set by the Church for dealing with such claims. Prudently, he advised Lucia's mother not to prevent her daughter from visiting the Cova on June 13, but to bring her and her cousins to the rectory soon after so he could question them.

After Mass on the appointed day, Francisco and Jacinta walked with their father and Lucia's mother to the priest's house and started up the stairs leading to the porch. They had climbed only a few steps when Lucia's mother turned to her and exclaimed, "Don't annoy me any more! Tell the Reverend Padre now that you lied, so that on Sunday he can say in the church that it was all a lie, and that will be the end of the whole affair. A nice business, this is! All this crowd running to the Cova da Iria, just to pray in front of a holm oak bush!" The priest's sister opened the door and invited them to sit down on a bench. At last, the parish priest appeared and took them into his study.

The cleric asked Jacinta questions, but she wouldn't answer him. He said to her, "You don't seem to know anything; sit down there, or run away if you like." Jacinta took out her Rosary and started to say it, while Father Ferreira began to question Lucia, who answered well. From time to time Jacinta got up and told Lucia to be sure to explain things properly. At that Father Ferreira said rather crossly to Jacinta, "When I was asking you questions you didn't know anything, and wouldn't say a word, and now it's the other way about."

Then the priest continued to question Lucia. She was surprised that he did this so calmly, and in such a kindly manner, yet she was still fearful of what was to come.

Several different overviews are apparent in this scene.

The parish priest was efficient, matter-of-fact, professionally kind, but he had other things to do. There was no need to crush bruised reeds. This nonsense would die in a week or two, smothered by its own momentum.

Lucia's mother was harassed almost to the point of obsession. Though she was an excellent woman, it would seem that it was not to heaven's purposes to give her the grace to believe her daughter. Her standing in the community, the standing of her family, everything she lived for was being undermined by these claims of her ten-year-old, which were as persistent as they were fantastic. The parish priest was a figure of great authority whose word had the force of law. The woman's hopes were centered on him.

Francisco said nothing, or nothing worth recording. Moreover, he would have been the first to confirm that he had nothing to say. On his own testimony he couldn't hear what the Lady said. He was content to stand in the background, to merge with the furniture, to think of the God who wanted to be consoled. He was not clever in anything except in finding ways to offer his God consolations.

Jacinta was a blend of impenetrable silence followed by unabashed chattering a moment later. It might have been grounds for diagnosing insanity if it weren't such a regular feature in the behavior of little girls.

Lucia was sober with awe, respect and determination. Her mind and heart were being torn by opposing forces. She maintained an exterior balance, but her responses to the parish priest's questions were brief. They gave nothing away. Only Francisco and Jacinta had an inkling of what she was suffering, and they were powerless to help. The three children were faced with the disbelief of two adults who should be their supports and champions.

At the end of the interrogation, the priest commented, "It doesn't seem to me like a revelation from heaven. It is usual in such cases for Our Lord to tell souls to whom He makes such communications to give their confessor or parish priest an account of what has happened. But this child, on the contrary, keeps it to herself as far as she can. This may also be a deceit of the devil. We shall see. The future will show us what we are to think about it all."

Father Ferreira's report is succinct. It quotes Lucia as saying that the children saw a woman, but we wonder whether he was attending to what they told him when he writes that Francisco only saw her as she was departing.

They saw lightning, his report continues, and they started to muster their sheep. There was more lightning, after which they saw a woman on top of an oak sapling. She was dressed in white. On her feet were white socks. Her white skirt was edged with gold. She had a white cloak and a white mantle that covered her head. The mantle was not edged with gold, but the socks were shot through with gold. She had a gold cincture and some very small gold earrings. Her hands were raised, and when she spoke with fervor she opened her hands and arms.

This was written by someone in a hurry, someone who doesn't believe a word of what he is writing and is trying hard not to make a parody of it.

The parish priest's version of the dialogue between Lucia and Our Lady is similarly brief. The Lady says she comes from heaven. The children are to meet with her for six months and then she will tell them what she wants. In response to a question she can't tell them when the war will be over without also telling them what she wants.

The short exchange about going to heaven follows (about the need for Francisco to continue to say his prayers — but, here, there is no specific mention of the Rosary). The parish priest concludes: "The other two heard the questions and the answers but they didn't ask any questions."

One thing Father Ferreira didn't mention in this short report was his own suggestion to Lucia that the whole scenario might have been staged by the devil. The priest was not wrong in saying it, but because he didn't believe that Our Lady had appeared, he had no reason to believe that the devil had either. Perhaps it was his way of pointing out to the child that even if she was genuinely deluded (as opposed to telling lies), the source of the delusion posed serious questions.

It was a bitter pill for a religiously sensitive ten-year-old. Over the following days, Francisco and Jacinta could see that the thought of being deluded by the devil had unseated all Lucia's former happiness. She reasoned that, as the devil was said to bring disorder and conflict with him, and the apparitions had brought much disorder and conflict into her life and home, they must be from the devil.

"No, it's not the devil!" said Jacinta. "Not at all! The devil is very bad and ugly and he's down under the ground in hell. But that Lady is so beautiful, and we saw her go up to heaven!"

Lucia's mental and spiritual anguish during this period were clearly harrowing. She tells us of the ordeal herself with winning candor. Every soul has counterpart experiences — of different magnitudes and levels of intensity — that enable it to appreciate that sense of devastation, a black cloud that can envelope every faculty and strangle hope.

But if Lucia was suffering, so were her cousins when they saw what was happening to her. The older cousin had a dream in which the devil was trying to drag her down to hell, laughing at having deceived her. She screamed and woke her mother, then was too paralyzed with fear to tell her parent about it.

The young girl took to going off by herself to weep. Even the company of her cousins began to seem burdensome. She began to hide from them as well. They would search for her, calling out her name and receiving no answer, but she would be there all the while, hidden close to them in some corner where they never thought of looking. She lost all delight in the supernatural. Sacrifices became loathsome, mortification a dread. The Rosary itself was insipid. Eventually she told Francisco and Jacinta that she was thinking of admitting that the whole story of the Cova and the Lady was one big web of make-believe and have done with all the bother.

"Don't do that!" they beseeched her. "Don't you see that that itself would be a lie, and to tell a lie is a sin."

All through this terrible purgation, the idea planted by the parish priest — that the apparitions could be the work of the devil — grew until it was confused in her mind with reality. On the evening of July 12, Lucia told Francisco and Jacinta that they wouldn't go to the Cova the following day in case it really was the devil appearing there. They protested, but she was adamant. They were distraught. Jacinta said that she could talk to the Lady, but the prospect didn't allay her grief and she began to cry. Lucia said, with all the innocence of childhood, "Tell the Lady I'm not going because I'm afraid she may be the devil."

People were arriving in droves at the homes of the two families. They were demanding to see the children and to question them. On this evening Lucia slipped away and hid among the brambles of a neighbor's property to avoid the visitors and to be alone with her agony.

The following morning, and right up until it was time to leave for the Cova, she remained determined to stay at home. Then, suddenly, her terrible cloud lifted. In an instant she knew she had to go to the site. A strange, though welcome, force impelled her, and there was no denying it. She ran to her cousins' house. Jacinta was in her room with Francisco. They were kneeling beside the bed crying. "We aren't going without you! We don't dare. Please come, Lucia! Please!"

"Yes, I'm going."

With a surge of joy, they set out for the Cova da Iria. There were so many people all making in the same direction and all wanting to speak with them that the journey took much longer than usual.

It had been a morning of violently contrasting emotions for the three little ones. But these were only a mild preparation for the extremes of experience the Lady had planned for them that day.

CHAPTER TWELVE

The seers on July 13, 1917, in front of the Fatima parish church before the apparition on that day.

It was Friday, July 13, 1917.

> Lucia: What do you want of me?
>
> Lady: I want you to come here on the thirteenth of next month, to continue to pray the Rosary every day, in honor of Our Lady of the Ro-

sary, in order to obtain peace for the world and the end of the war, because only she can help you.

Lucia: I would like to ask you to tell us who you are, and to work a miracle so that everybody will believe that you are appearing to us.

Lady: Continue to come here every month. In October I will tell you who I am and what I want, and I will perform a miracle for all to see and believe. Sacrifice yourself for sinners, and say many times, especially when you make some sacrifice: "O Jesus, it is for love of You, for the conversion of sinners, and in reparation for sins committed against the Immaculate Heart of Mary."

Lucia later reported: The rays of light seemed to penetrate the earth, and we saw, as it were, a sea of fire. Plunged in this fire were demons and souls in human form, like transparent burning embers, all blackened or burnished bronze, floating about in the conflagration, now raised into the air by the flames that issued from within themselves together with great clouds of smoke, now falling back on every side like sparks in huge fires, without weight or equilibrium, amid shrieks and groans of pain and despair, which horrified us and made us tremble with fear. The demons could be distinguished by their terrifying and repellent likeness to frightful and unknown animals, black and transparent like burning coals. Terrified and as if to plead for succor, we looked up at Our Lady, who said to us, so kindly and so sadly:

Lady: You have seen hell where the souls of poor
        sinners go. To save them, God wishes to es-
        tablish in the world devotion to my Immacu-
        late Heart. If what I say to you is done, many
        souls will be saved and there will be peace.
        The war is going to end; but if people do not
        cease offending God, a worse one will break
        out during the pontificate of Pius XI. When
        you see a night illuminated by an unknown
        light, know that this is the great sign given
        you by God that He is about to punish the
        world for its crimes, by means of war, famine
        and persecutions of the Church and of the
        Holy Father.

        To prevent this, I shall come to ask for
        the consecration of Russia to my Immaculate
        Heart, and the Communion of Reparation on
        the First Saturdays. If my requests are heeded,
        Russia will be converted, and there will be
        peace; if not, she will spread her errors
        throughout the world, causing wars and per-
        secutions of the Church. The good will be
        martyred, the Holy Father will have much to
        suffer, various nations will be annihilated. In
        the end, my Immaculate Heart will triumph.
        The Holy Father will consecrate Russia to me,
        and she will be converted, and a period of peace
        will be granted to the world. In Portugal, the
        dogma of the Faith will always be preserved.

Lucia later reported: Then, at the left of Our Lady and a
        little above, we saw an angel with a flaming sword
        in his left hand; flashing, it gave out flames that
        looked as though they would set the world on fire;

but they died out in contact with the splendor that Our Lady radiated towards him from her right hand: pointing to the earth with his right hand, the angel cried out in a loud voice: "Penance, Penance, Penance!" And we saw in an immense light that is God, something similar to how people appear in a mirror when they pass in front of it, a bishop dressed in white. We had the impression that it was the Holy Father. Other bishops, priests, men and women religious going up a steep mountain, at the top of which there was a big cross of rough-hewn trunks as of a cork tree with the bark; before reaching there the Holy Father passed through a big city half in ruins and half trembling with halting step, afflicted with pain and sorrow, he prayed for the souls of the corpses he met on his way; having reached the top of the mountain, on his knees at the foot of the big cross he was killed by a group of soldiers who fired bullets and arrows at him, and in the same way there died one after another the other bishops, priests, men and women religious, and various lay people of different ranks and positions. Beneath the two arms of the cross there were two angels each with a crystal aspersorium in his hand, in which they gathered up the blood of the martyrs and with it sprinkled the souls that were making their way to God.

Lady: Do not tell this to anybody. Francisco, yes, you may tell him.

When you pray the Rosary, say, after each mystery: O my Jesus, forgive us, save us from the fires of hell. Lead all souls to heaven, especially those who are most in need.

Lucia: Is there anything more that you want of me?

Lady: No, I do not want any more of you today.

Again we have the customary greeting: "What do you want of me?" What does your ladyship want me to do? It's interesting that it's always Lucia who speaks first. Brought up as she was, the youngest in an orderly household where manners and small formalities were instilled, it would be natural for her to wait until an elder and clearly superior person had spoken.

"I want you to come here on the thirteenth of next month. . . ."

Our Lady reiterates the thirteenth. This is the third time she has given the precise date. And she will say it again in August. It's doubtful that the children of that time and place thought in terms of exact dates. Seasons, Sundays, market days, liturgical feasts would have been more likely to have stood as measures of time in their young minds. There must, too, have been calendars in the homes of Aljustrel, even if they were only in the form of agricultural almanacs, which give month-by-month advice on crops and vegetables and fruits, well-illustrated for those who could not read.

". . . to continue to pray the Rosary every day, in honor of Our Lady of the Rosary. . . ."

It's not easy to grasp how the Blessed Virgin can refer to herself as "Our Lady" and "she," particularly as the prayer we know as the Rosary is mostly directed to her. Considering that it is Our Lady who is talking, it puzzles us to overhear her telling the children to pray the Rosary "in honor of Our Lady of the Rosary, because only she can help you." It is as if Baroness Smith said, "Ask Baroness Smith, for the sake of the high regard in which we hold Baroness Smith, to do something or other." This is especially confusing as Our Lady herself is appealing to the children in the persona of Our

Lady of the Rosary — even though the children won't be told until October that it is under that aspect that she has been, and is, appearing to them.

In each apparition, Our Lady speaks to the children with such candor and simplicity, such guileless courtesy, that it is unlikely she would make a statement that might baffle them when she could easily rephrase her words to suit. In this instance, she could say: "Pray to me under my title, Our Lady of the Rosary, because it is only in that capacity that I can help you." But she doesn't, and does the fact that she doesn't — that she chooses instead to speak of her various manifestations as if they were other individuals — lie in some ordering of heaven's protocol that is beyond our comprehension?

I certainly don't have an answer and, as always, can only suggest that each person find an answer in prayer. But such answers, while boundlessly satisfying, are usually incommunicable. They can't be flaunted because they melt under all but celestial light. I have one or two suggestions that might be considered.

For instance, it might be that our semantics have not yet developed sufficiently to accommodate the uniqueness of the Queen of Heaven; to appreciate the refinements of her various patents of sanctity, her titles, honors, aspects and crowns , or to understand that each is a mandate for our salvation, for her glory, and for the majestic and unfathomable delight of the divine will.

It is as if there were but one queen ruling many countries, and she wore a different crown for each. If we are rent with strife, we approach the Queen of the Land of Peace; if we are in mourning, it is the Queen of the Land of Sorrows that we petition for comfort. When the heritage of Adam weighs heavy, we invoke the queen who told us she was the Immaculate Conception. When our own misery renders us too blind to know in which direction to turn, we need never despair because we have in our own pockets the key to a staircase, always within reach, a staircase of five, ten, fifteen, twenty flights that leads directly to the private chambers of the Queen of the Holy Rosary.

And should a new, unheard-of obstacle appear, we can simply name the territory and, if we ask her, she will become its queen too. That's how gracious she is.

Or it could be that when Our Lady revisits earth, it is the humble maid of Nazareth who is speaking. Humble enough to know that, after Christ, she is the most exalted being in creation, and humble enough to talk of that exalted person to little children, not pretending that it wasn't herself, but obliquely, so as not to alarm or intimidate them.

". . . in order to obtain peace for the world and the end of the war, because only she can help you."

Peace for the world is what heaven has been anxious about since the expulsion from Eden. Every biblical promise has incorporated it, at least implicitly. Christ was and is the living embodiment of it, and every Christian revelation since has been permeated with a concept of peace. Nor is it solely a preserve of those of us who acknowledge the divinity of Jesus. It is as if heaven is saying "When peace is present, virtue, God's will in man, will flourish." Satan is the implacable enemy of peace.

Peace in the world is the general import of Our Lady's words here. Particularly of concern is World War I, which at that time had been devastating Europe for three years, a continent needlessly sacrificing on an altar of enraged evil. Here in the July apparition is the second time that Lucia records that war was mentioned by the Blessed Virgin. Given the impact it was having, even on remote village life —sons and husbands called to the front, shortages of everyday commodities — Our Lady was clearly aware that it was dominant in people's minds.

Pilgrims had been imploring Lucia to ask the Blessed Virgin when the war was going to stop. At this meeting the heavenly visitor graciously brought up the subject herself, not disclosing the date of an armistice, but spelling out what must be done if it was to happen. Heaven has given us our free will and rarely interposes between us and the outcome of our actions unless we specifically ask for its aid.

So to obtain peace and an end to the war, the children — and, by inference, all of us — must pray the Rosary every day in honor of Our Lady of the Rosary. And then Our Blessed Mother adds a very curious explanation:

" ...because only she can help you."

On a cursory reading this is a simple enough codicil to the main statement; but on reflection, if it weren't Our Lady speaking it might be interpreted as heresy. A Bible-brandishing, six-cylinder Protestant could be forgiven a heart attack if he happened upon it. Indeed, taken at its face value, (and how else could it be taken?), it's the most theologically provocative statement of all the statements Our Lady made during the Fatima apparitions.

Furthermore, deep and prayerful attention will reveal that this clause contains the kernel of the message of Fatima.

". . . Because only she can help you." Softly and sweetly spoken it may have been, but the meaning is plain. "Only she." This means not Christ — not directly anyway — not the Trinity, not a saint or angel. "Only she." When people are godless by choice, not even God can help them. When the villain is suffering the consequences of his crimes, when he has rejected the leniency of the law, and even the compassion of the judge, there is no one but a mother left to plead his cause. That is the extent of our chosen alienation from God. That is how urgent that message of prayer and penance in trustful joy. Only she can help you. Only she can help you *now*.

**"I would like to ask you to tell us who you are, and to
work a miracle so that everybody will believe
that you are appearing to us."**

This is a sort of *non sequitur*. The children have just been
given a monumentally important message that, if acted on, will
mean the salvation of humanity, and they straightaway ask,
through Lucia, who their visitor is and request a miracle. This
gives the impression that either they haven't understood the
importance of what the Lady has just said or they are questioning
her authority to say it. I doubt if anyone can have difficulties in
discounting the second conjecture, and the first seems unlikely,
given the speaker, the grace of the encounter, and the children's
positive reaction to communications of similar depth.

We might wonder why they would ask the Lady who she is,
because in the first apparition she has said that she will tell them
later ("*depois*"). The children might have been expected to leave
the appropriate time to the Lady's judgment; and yet, their curiosity
is understandable. It's not that they didn't know that she was the
Blessed Virgin — as certain as any mortal could be. We have already noted Francisco's exclamation: "Oh dear Our lady! I'll say as
many Rosaries as you want," immediately after the first apparition.
At the end of the "Third Memoir" Lucia writes:

> When we spoke of Our Lady, sometimes we said "Our
> Lady" and sometimes "the Lady." And now I no longer re-
> member which of the two phrases we used at a given time.

Their own sight of her, the impression she made on their souls,
the experience of "the light from her hands," probably told them
that a greater creature than she simply could not exist, so she
must be Our Lady. But they wanted confirmation, too — her
confirmation.

This is a set question. The children have discussed the Lady
exhaustively among themselves and painstakingly arrived at the
most respectful formula. It might be a *non sequitur* after the startling

information that only Our Lady of the Rosary can help obtain peace in the world and an end to the war. But, after all, what answer can possibly follow such a statement? So Lucia asks the devised question, "I would like you to tell us who you are." Not "I would like you to tell *me*" as in her other questions. This was not spontaneous, and that's why it's collective.

In their two months of prayers and sacrifices and talking about the Lady in whispers among themselves, they come to the conclusion that to simply ask the Lady's identity was not enough. They were emboldened to compose a second, much more dramatic, request. With disconcerting ingenuity, they asked her to perform a miracle. The miracle is not for novelty or excitement, or to banish any doubts of their own as to the Lady's ability to perform miracles. They appended their motive, and it was a very reasonable one. They seek credibility. People saw them gazing at and talking to a space in a field. They didn't ask the Lady to show herself to the people, or even to remove the people. Without being aware of how, they knew that the grace of seeing the Lady was theirs alone, but they asked that she manifest her power and save them the anguish of not being believed.

**"Continue to come here every month. In October I
will tell you who I am and what I want, and I will
perform a miracle for all to see and believe."**

The Lady takes the children's petitions seriously. There is no condescension. No "Wait and see." No "My word! You've rehearsed that one, haven't you?" She repeats her instruction that they come to the Cova every month, and in three months she will fulfill both requests.

Although the questions came from the children and were devised over many a conference, they were, perhaps, the ones the Lady wanted them to ask. There is an argument that all true petitionary prayer has its provenance in heaven. Christ impressed upon Julian of Norwich that He Himself was the ground of her beseeching: "First it is My will that you should have it, and then I make you to wish it, and then I make you to beseech it."

"Sacrifice yourself for sinners, and say many times, especially when you make some sacrifice: 'O Jesus, it is for love of You, for the conversion of sinners, and in reparation for sins committed against the Immaculate Heart of Mary.' "

This is the first sentence of the major tenet of the message of Fatima. Our Lady completes the statement during the August apparition, by which time the children have had firsthand experience of sinners. In particular were the sins committed against the Immaculate Heart in the person of Arturo Santos, the local

A rarely seen picture of the seers taken on July 13, 1917.

mayor, whose atheism provoked him not only to terrorize the children but to impede the ordained course of the heavenly visitations, and in so doing to hurl insults at the Immaculate Heart of Mary.

The Lady's call for sacrifice is blunt and unqualified. In the prayer, she taught them that three reasons are given for sacrifice, a trinity of motives. All three children adopt them, but each seems to have championed one of these reasons in particular. The love of Jesus was the primary motive of the seers, but Francisco seems to have held it as his own individual banner — comforting Him as He is disdained and neglected by the world. The conversion of sinners was Jacinta's driving motivation in her prayer, suffering and sacrifices. Reparation for sins committed against the Immaculate Heart seems to have been paramount in Lucia's thinking during her long life.

If we read and meditate on these words of Our Lady with an open heart, we can't help but experience something of the poignant "anguish" of heaven at the blindness and spiritual stupidity of each one of us, whether we be atheistic mayor, cloistered nun, daily communicant or scarlet-clad cardinal. And this being so, how intensely absorbed those children must have been, face-to-face with the Immaculate Mother as she confided in them both the sorrow and joy she has in her appointed role as maternal protectress. One can almost hear them asking permission, like Peter on Tabor, to build altars there in her honor — an extraordinary development, perhaps, of the game they'd been playing with stones just before her first appearance.

But ecstasy is not necessarily all angels and golden clouds. Once more the Lady stretched out her arms, and the children's world was filled with "the light from her hands," the light that was God, but the light did not introduce them to a heavenly banquet. This time the light penetrated the earth, and the gutting flames and filthy stench of hell opened up to their senses. The vision only took a moment; otherwise the children might

have died from the sheer horror of what they saw. Lucia let out a
gasp that alarmed the people who had gathered at the Cova da
Iria that midday.

The oldest seer's description of hell is as vivid a picture as any
pen could supply. It stands complete in itself, only requiring prayerful consideration to release its horrific significance. A lengthy
comment on it would be an impertinence, but if one clause were
to be selected as epitomizing, even justifying, hell, it is "flames
issue from within themselves." It is as if sin — fondled at the
breast and harbored in the heart till it overshadows and becomes
preferable to the love of the Creator — is, itself, the torment of
hell fused with the soul and not imposed from without. It is lim-
itless and eternal because it occupies the spaceless space and time-
less time that God had reserved for Himself in that soul.

**"You have seen hell where the souls of poor sinners go.
To save them, God wishes to establish in the world
devotion to my Immaculate Heart."**

Lucia would later say that Our Lady spoke these words "so
kindly and sadly." The Blessed Mother's kindness was probably
to ease the children's fear. But her sadness may have been for
sinners, to whom she appends the adjective "poor" — poor in
the sense of unfortunate, pitiable, wretched, both in this world
and, should they die preferring their sin, even poorer in the next.
Did her pity even extend to the souls in hell, even though they
had put themselves beyond the power of her mandate?

But it is the poor sinners in this world of whom she speaks
when she states that God wishes to establish devotion to her
Immaculate Heart to save them. This is a repetition of what
she had said the month before. "Jesus wants to establish in
the world devotion to my Immaculate Heart. I promise salvation to those who embrace it. . . ."

A student of Church-approved apparitions — Fatima, Lourdes,
La Salette, Guadalupe and the rest — can't help but observe

certain characteristics of Our Lady: her sadness, her compassion, her exquisite graciousness. In spite of her being filled with, indeed made of, light as splendid as the sun, beautiful beyond our conceiving, she is nonetheless engagingly familiar and approachable. She communicates freely, but no word is superfluous. When we feel she could have said more, subsequent meditation shows that it is all there in the first place. She has already said it, but we have to seek it out and savor it in the heart at prayer. So when she repeats something, what she is saying must be worth a great deal of attention.

"If what I say to you is done, many souls will be saved and there will be peace. The war is going to end; but if people do not cease offending God, a worse one will break out during the pontificate of Pius XI."

The requests that already have been made are the daily Rosary and devotion to the Immaculate Heart. More requests will follow: a formal consecration of Russia to the Immaculate Heart and First Saturday Communions.

A difficulty frequently mentioned is the statement that a worse war would break out during the pontificate of Pius XI. This was not revealed by the children during the interrogations in 1917. Indeed, like everything confided by Our Lady as they knelt enraptured in "the light from her hands," it formed part of what she asked them not to tell anyone, those things that later became known as "the secrets of Fatima."

As it was, Father Ambrogio Ratti, the future Pope Pius XI, was the unostentatious prefect of the Vatican Library in 1917. He was made cardinal archbishop of Milan in 1921 and elected pope in 1922. He died in February 1939, and Pius XII was elected in March. The global conflict that came to be known as World War II was declared in September of that year. So a frequent criticism of Lucia's statement is that Pius XI was not the papal incumbent at the outbreak of the fighting. But Our Lady didn't say that the Second World War would erupt during the reign of Pius XI. She said "a worse war" (*"começerá outra pior [guerra]"*). The civil strife that erupted in Spain in 1936 and won the approval of Satan with the Nazi bombing of Guernica in 1937 merits being called "the beginnings of a worse war" in any listing.

It might be of interest to note here that several weeks before Jacinta's death in February 1920, she said to Mother Godinho, who ran the orphanage in Lisbon where the seer was billeted, "If people don't amend themselves, Our Lord will send upon the world a punishment the like of which has not been seen, and first of all in Spain." She added "that great world events would come about in 1940." It is not known how much notice Mother Godinho took of the very sick nine-year-old at the time. After Jacinta's death she wrote of this to the distinguished author on Fatima, Jesuit Father Gonzaga da Fonseca, then at the Biblical Institute in Rome.

Our dates are helpful signposts, but the history books in the libraries of heaven will, we can be sure, contain more than a few amendments.

"When you see a night illuminated by an unknown light, know that this is the great sign given you by God that He is about to punish the world for its crimes, by means of war, famine and persecutions of the Church and of the Holy Father."

It almost seems a shame that Lucia didn't reveal this prophetic forecast till it had been fulfilled; but, after all, it was revealed to the children with instructions not to tell anybody. The knowledge was for Lucia in particular, because she would be the only one alive to witness what it foretold.

Her revelation in 1941 of a prophecy made in 1917 about something that would happen (although no date was given) in 1938, opens up an arsenal for unbelievers and hands them the weapons. But even if she had made this warning public beforehand, would the world have been brought to its knees when the sky was illumined by the unknown light? Where Moses and the prophets, Christ himself and Fatima's miracle of the sun had failed to convince, would an inexplicable fire in the sky, no matter how dramatic, turn hearts and minds? Would it have been called anything other than an exceptional aurora borealis?

But dramatic it certainly was, and well-chronicled.

As Our Lady had said, it was God's great sign that He was about to punish the world for its crimes: war, famine and persecution of the Church and the Holy Father. It might seem odd to some that the persecution of the Church and the Holy Father should be a means of punishment for the sins of the world. If there is any correspondence with grace on this side of the grave, it is in the Church and in the person of the Holy Father that it is most likely to be found. So why the punishment? There are no words to answer a question like that. One can only point to the incarnate God hammered to a cross, dead.

"To prevent this, I shall come to ask for the consecration of Russia to my Immaculate Heart, and the Communion of Reparation on the First Saturdays."

She indeed asked for these things. Alas, the great sign did appear that let Lucia know that the consecration of Russia had not taken place, and that the response to the Communions of reparation had not been adequate to prevent the war, famine and persecutions.

The request for the Communions of reparation was made to Lucia when she was a novice with the Dorothean sisters in Pontevedra, Spain. (Portuguese law still forbade houses of religious formation on Portuguese soil.) The date was December 10, 1925.

On June 13, 1929, Our Lady again appeared to Lucia at the Dorothean convent in Tuy, Spain, and asked that the Holy Father consecrate Russia to her Immaculate Heart, in union with all the bishops of the world.

Over the decades several attempts at a consecration were made, but Lucia said that they did not meet heaven's requirements. At last, on the feast of the Annunciation, March 25, 1984, in Rome, kneeling before the same statue of Our Lady of Fatima that is venerated in the Chapel of the Apparitions in Fatima, Pope John Paul II renewed the Consecration of the World to the Immaculate Heart of Mary. This same act was realized by a majority of bishops in dioceses all over the world.

"Then, at the left of Our Lady . . ."

This paragraph comprises what was long known as the Third Secret of Fatima. Its being made public in the year 2000 stanched an ever-flowing torrent of speculation. Yet, in Lucia's "Third Memoir" written in 1941, the kernel of the "secret" was there in print, readily available in dozens of languages all along. In that "Memoir," Lucia recalls a siesta that the seers spent by the well of Arneiro. Jacinta sat on the stone slabs on top of the well. Francisco and Lucia climbed up the steep bank in search of wild honey. After a little while Jacinta called out:

"Didn't you see the Holy Father?"

"No."

"I don't know how it was, but I saw the Holy Father in a very big house, kneeling by a table, with his head buried in his hands, and he was weeping. Outside the house, there were many people. Some of them were throwing stones, others were cursing him and using bad language. Poor Holy Father, we must pray very much for him."

Two priests who recommended that they pray for the Holy Father had already explained to them who the pope was. Later, Jacinta asked Lucia:

"Is he the one I saw weeping, the one Our Lady told us about in the secret?"

"Yes, he is."

"The Lady must surely have shown him also to those priests. You see, I wasn't mistaken. We need to pray a lot for him."

Later, in the cave called Lapa do Cabeço, they were prostrated on the ground, saying the prayers the angel had taught them. After some time, Jacinta stood up and said:

"Can't you see all those highways and roads and fields full of people, who are crying with hunger and have nothing to eat? And the Holy Father in a church praying before the Immaculate Heart of Mary? And so many people praying with him?"

Later still she asked, "Can I say that I saw the Holy Father and all those people?"

"No. Don't you see that that's part of the secret? If you do, they'll find out right away."

"All right! Then I'll say nothing at all."

And in the "third secret" (a bishop dressed in white, giving the impression it was the Holy Father), the pontiff passed through a big city half in ruins. Half-trembling, with halting step, afflicted with pain and sorrow, he prayed for the souls of the corpses he met on his way. On his knees at the foot of a big cross he was killed by a group of soldiers who fired bullets and arrows at him. In the same way there, one after another died, bishops, priests, men and women religious, and various lay people of different ranks and positions.

Here again, only personal prayer can make any sense of this apocalyptic prophecy.

**"Do not tell this to anybody.
Francisco, yes, you may tell him."**
It would seem that everything the children saw in "the light from her hands" was, for the time being anyway, not to be re-

peated. It was to be kept, to use the children's word, secret. Unfortunately, the word "secret," like the word "sin," conjures up a formless image, sinister and morbidly exciting. But heaven has no secrets from us, nothing pertinent to our salvation.

By the same token, there are many things we don't know because they are beyond our capacity to absorb. But these are mysteries, not secrets. We shall know them, though never completely. Indeed, we shall spend eternity plunging into the knowledge of these divine mysteries, ever sated, ever hungry. These mysteries are God's gift to us of Himself, and they surpass anything our imagination can encompass. God is not hiding them from us. It is we who are trying to hide from them, in sin.

When Our Lady showed the children the vision of hell, she told them not to tell anyone about it. We can't presume to know our heavenly mother's motives, but they might simply have been practical. That the children were meeting with a being from another world at all was a hefty dose for family and friends to swallow. Now if they returned home full of red hot coals and devils, even those inclined to give them credence might have been disposed to question the origin of the manifestations. Father Ferreira's cautionary aside might have become a general opinion. Even a hell-fire preacher would think twice about exposing small children to his rhetoric. As a mother, and as Mediatrix of Graces, Mary knew precisely what she was doing. She chose to present this terrifying vision to the children and told them not to reveal it, in the knowledge that it would come out over time and work to her purposes.

But neither the existence nor the horror of hell is a secret. The Old and New Testaments are blunt about eternal punishment, and the Church hasn't been coy about endorsing the message either. Hell was hardly a novel concept for Portugal.

As we have seen, the conversion of Russia (and, indeed, the early deaths of Francisco and Jacinta) were prophecies — a remarkable prophecy indeed in the case of Russia, because in 1917

Lenin was still only working on the blueprints for a godless state. That Our Lady didn't want these revelations broadcast immediately makes the *broadcasting* a matter for temporary secrecy, not the prophecy itself. Perhaps "prudent silence for the time being" might be better than "secret."

**"When you pray the Rosary, say, after each mystery:
O my Jesus, forgive us, save us from the fires of hell.
Lead all souls to heaven, especially those who are
most in need."**

The angel taught the children two prayers, and Our Lady taught them two more. This prayer is Our Lady's second. Coming after the profound drama, promises and predictions of this apparition, its very simplicity is loaded. It is a direct appeal to Jesus, who is addressed in the familiar by the use of the personal possessive "my." Then the prayer becomes communal: "forgive *us*, save *us* from the fires of hell." The impact of their vision of hell gives enormous weight to these words.

Our Lady is not simply stressing the negative here. Prayer, true prayer, must be positive because God is positive. "Lead all souls to heaven." The words "all souls" (*alminhas todas*) carries an implication easily missed if one is quickly reading the words. No one is excluded, not even those most in need. In fact, the most hardened sinners are mentioned in this prayer to Jesus, the sacrificed, incarnate God: "especially those most in need of Thy mercy," as we commonly say the prayer in English.

The Portuguese *"alminhas todas"* actually has the meaning of all souls in the sense that we use all souls for the holy souls in purgatory. But this doesn't change the fundamental meaning, because if a soul is saved from the fires of hell, that soul will, we can assume, spend a period of eternity in purgatory. The two shades of meaning, therefore, amount to the same thing.

Since Fatima, this prayer has become a part of the Rosary, said at the end of each of the five decades. After the Our Father, the Hail Mary and the Glory Be, it is possibly the most frequently recited prayer among the Catholic faithful.

"Is there anything more that you want of me?"
"No, I do not want any more of you today."

A literal translation of the question here would read, "Does your ladyship want nothing more of me?" It would be reasonable to suppose that the Lady would take the initiative to indicate when the meeting was over, but each time it seems that Lucia sensed the imminent departure of the heavenly guest and made the closing overture, graciously answered by the Lady.

CHAPTER THIRTEEN

One can't resist wondering whether Francisco's inability to hear Our Lady wasn't perhaps an advantage, a practical gift from heaven.

On one level, it could be seen as a contemplative's asset, as if it wasn't necessary for him to hear because he wasn't being recruited to spread the Fatima message. His task was to live that message in the short year and a half he had yet to remain on earth. He was being burned as fuel for the fire of divine light and warmth that Our Lady had come to ignite in a cold world. He heard Lucia's questions, and Our Lady's answers were repeated to him, but what was said at the Cova da Iria was really only for us. Heaven had much more subtle, much more intimate ways of communicating subtleties and intimacies.

On another level, Francisco was partially protected from the relentless questioning that his fellow seers were subjected to. The young boy, with patience and a courtesy learned, literally, at the knee of his heavenly mother, needed only to tell insistent questioners that he had heard nothing of what the Lady had said to deflect interest from himself. It wasn't a ruse on his part, at least not one for him to chuckle over and feel self-satisfied about. Whatever cunning might have sought a foothold in his character when he stole a coin from his father to buy a music box had long since withered from lack of encouragement and been swept away. It was all of a one with his nature, and now with his grace. As Lucia observed, "He much preferred playing his flute while others danced."

Suddenly word of supernatural happenings moved beyond the bounds of the immediate locality and spread throughout the whole country, leaping from village to town to city like an electrical charge. Father Ferreira's estimation of four to five thousand people at the Cova during the July 13 apparitions increased fourfold for the next. And it must have seemed to the seers' families that each one of those twenty thousand came to Aljustrel during the intervening weeks to seek interviews with their children.

And when these questioners were in the area, they would visit the Cova da Iria, laying waste to the vegetable garden Lucia's father had laboriously created out of the arid, stony land. Then they would look to the holm oak for a souvenir, but by August it was already a stump. Maria Carreira attached ribbons and the like to it and tended the area. But she couldn't prevent the vast number of people and their horses from stomping over the land.

The dos Santos family simply had to abandon their Cova da Iria spot as a source of produce. Its empty spaces were reflected on the family table. "When you want something to eat ask Our Lady for it," Lucia's mother would taunt her before taking up a broom handle or a stick from the hearth and beating her. Although Lucia saw the hand of God in these rejections and spankings, she couldn't help but reflect on the difference between the attitude of her mother and the parents of Francisco and Jacinta. Those parents didn't accuse their son and daughter of lying, and defended them in front of those who did. When Jacinta wished that her parents would treat her with the same harsh disbelief that Lucia's treated her, it wasn't filial ingratitude, but a desire for yet another way of having something to offer up for sinners.

Father Ferreira interviewed the children again on the days after the June and July apparitions. The brevity of his records seems to reflect his own measure of credence. His transcript of the June dialogue reads:

"What do you want of me then?"

"I want to tell you to come here on the 13th and to learn to read so that I can tell you what I want."

"Then you don't want anything else."

"No, I don't want anything else."

The July report is in much the same tone, except for a lengthy paragraph in which the cleric reports Jacinta saying that she had seen a young woman four times, once in her house at night and three times in the Cova da Iria in the middle of the day. Jacinta said that she was about the same size as Albina, a sixteen-year-old girl.

"In the house I saw her beside the trapdoor to the attic. She didn't say anything. My mother and brothers were asleep and it was night. In the Cova da Iria I saw her standing on top of the holm oak…"

The passage describes what the Lady was wearing and so on. Its detail indicates quite a different frame of mind on the part of Father Ferreira, almost as if he had written it at a later date, when he himself was giving more attention, and perhaps even credence, to the children's claims. Also, in the torrents of books about Fatima that have been published, little mention is made of this statement of Jacinta that Our Lady appeared to her in her home before or during the "public" Cova da Iria apparitions.

Very early one morning toward the end of July, Lucia's distracted mother hauled her off to the rectory and into the office of Father Ferreira in a distraught effort to force the ten-year-old to admit that she was lying. "This time," Lucia says, "the attack was so strong that I didn't know what to do."

On the way they had to pass the Marto house, and Lucia ran in to tell Jacinta of the crisis. The younger girl was still in bed. When she heard that Lucia was being forced to admit to lying, it must have seemed to her as if the whole world were cracking up. While Lucia went on toward Fatima with her mother, Jacinta woke Francisco and they made their way to the secluded area around the well of Arneiro. There they fell to their knees and prayed with all the fervor of their young hearts. As seers, the three were as one. There they shared Lucia's mental torment and the agony of all the conflicting forces raging about her, including the pain of being the object of disbelief and ridicule and the heart-rending experience of being faced with fanatical pressure from the mother she loved and wanted to obey. Like Mary at Calvary, the two suffered in prayerful union with their cousin. If she was forced to say that she were lying, the consequences for all three of them, and most importantly their relationship with the Lady, would be earth-shattering.

We can't dismiss these crises lightly; they are not simply the big fears of little children. The pressures these three were under that morning were as real a horror as any of the myriad taking place in the trenches of France and Belgium at the time and, in hindsight, of more far-reaching global importance.

Heaven heard these prayers from the well and, when parent and child reached the rectory steps, Lucia's mother relented. Reflecting an attitude quite at variance with the single-minded insistence she had shown till then, she said: "Just you listen to me! What I want is that you should tell the truth. If you saw, say so! But if you didn't see, admit that you lied."

Here is a graphic illustration of one of those quiet, unfussy miracles, feats of heavenly prestidigitation, that commonly follow prayer, even precede it, so perfectly fusing in with the flow of things that we, ungraciously, wonder if perhaps they mightn't have happened anyway.

The eyes of faith can see that the devil was routed, but within days he was back with hardnosed troops, remorseless guerrillas in the militia of atheism.

The administrative center for the area was the town of Vila Nova de Ourem, about six miles from Aljustrel, down a winding road from the plateau on which the Fatima parish stood, and then across the valley floor.

(On the top of a great outcrop in the middle of the valley is Ourem Castle. This ancient keep is associated with Blessed Nuno, the young general who repelled the Spaniards at the Battle of Aljubartota in 1385. It was here, some centuries earlier in the days of Moorish occupation, that a Christian nobleman brought his Islamic bride, Fatima, whom he'd captured from an enemy stronghold to the south. She had adapted to her husband's faith and changed her name from that of the prophet's daughter, Fatima, to Oureana, the Golden One, which the years chiseled down to Ourem. When she died, she was buried on the plateau and the place was given her original name, Fatima.)

Arturo Santos, the administrator — mayor — of Ourem and a Republican stalwart, sent notice that the three children and their fathers were to present themselves to him at noon on August 11. It's curious that that was a Saturday when most offices would be closed. Perhaps the government leader aimed to keep his contact with the children hidden from his council workers. If that were the case he could, of course, have gone to Aljustrel and seen them himself, but officialdom was his cloak and shield, and he needed to wear it. It was necessary to intimidate these superstitious peasants, show them who was cracking the whip. When they had walked all the way down to Ourem beneath the summer sun, they'd be as easily managed as their own lambs.

Ti Marto bluntly refused to take Francisco and Jacinta. They were too young, he said. But he went himself. So did Antonio dos Santos, Lucia's father, and Lucia herself, riding a donkey. She fell off the animal three times, she tells us, but she didn't expect sympathy. He father had adopted her mother's attitude, that the administrator might be able to frighten her into admitting mendacity and put a stop to the nonsense once and for all.

Before they set out, Lucia was able to tell Francisco and Jacinta where she was going and why. This information threw them back into a state of terrified torment. The godless policy of those with the political power in the land was an ongoing anxiety to most of the Portuguese people. The isolation of places such as Fatima protected them from the direct daily influence of those who had hitched their hopes to the atheistic state. But isolation didn't necessarily equal exemption. Big Brother was alert. A whiff of any threat to the glorious progress of enlightenment and the bloodhounds were unleashed.

Francisco and Jacinta, young as they were, knew these things, in effect if not in detail. Every person they had con-

Arturo Santos, the administrator of Ourem who abducted the seers on the morning of August 13, 1917.

tact with knew the evils of the current government. Such things filter down to children. These were born to it and had experienced no other political climate. True, they couldn't explain the details in any depth, but as children they were awake to disharmony, and felt it keenly. So keenly, indeed, that they thought that Lucia was going to her death. This was a genuine fear. These children weren't alarmists. Their imaginations were sober and controlled. Moreover, they had the rare and inestimable benefit of having looked on Truth, so nothing less than truth could attract them. They had sound reason, according to their intellects, to suppose that Lucia would be killed by the men in Ourem who made no secret of hating God and who worked daily to eradicate all notion of Him from the minds and hearts of the people.

The black cloud that draped their hearts and blinded their minds held the same terror as those black fumes from the furnace that the Lady had shown them.

In Ourem the two men found the doors to the council offices locked and no official about. They inquired where they could find Arturo Santos, but no one could direct or advise them. Eventually they simply stood in the square, uncertain what to do. Perhaps the administrator was watching them from some window. He certainty kept them waiting. That is one of unstable authority's basic stimulants. When one dismisses God, something must take His place, and there is really only oneself. The administrator saw himself as a local god, and his powers as a local god's powers. He had a need to silence any voice that contradicted him. He also had a local divinity's duty to form a trinity with the march of progress and the central government.

Eventually, when the two men were ushered into the mayor's office, his first words were "Where is the child?" Apparently he didn't know, or had forgotten, that there were three children involved. Such confusion is a sad feature of many a local deity.

Santos questioned Lucia at length. There were other men in the office, forming a formidable phalanx of inquisitors. One was taking notes for an article in the local paper that, incidentally, happened to be under the editorship of the administrator. Lucia answered the questions succinctly and truthfully, as we would expect. At one point the administrator turned to the girl's father and asked if these things were believed in Fatima. He replied that they were thought to be women's stories. Ti Marto, however, came to the defense. He said, "Here I am, your worship, and I say the same as my children."

The government men all laughed.

When the matter of the secrets that the Lady had told the children came up, Santos wanted to know what the secrets were. When Lucia declined to tell, he got angry. He insisted, demanded, threatened. He told her that if she didn't reveal what she'd been told he'd have her killed.

Could it have been the devil speaking here through the administrator? The evil one does not know what is happening at the Cova. He suspects it is something important, perhaps that it is the most important intervention of heaven into the affairs of men since the Incarnation. But he isn't privy to what the children see and hear at the Cova da Iria. He uses the staunchly anti-Church administrator to find out for him; hence the barrage of questions, the fixation with secrets and wild talk of death. Devil and pawn are bombastic, arrogant, scathing, cowardly and angry.

However, every player in the drama must be allowed to have his say. The mayor later wrote of this meeting:

> I questioned Lucia about the alleged holy woman she had seen and she continued to state that she had seen her on the oak tree. Everything she said contradicted itself and, having listened to the opinion of two doctors about the strange claim, opinions which confirmed that she was

a sick girl, I asked the Pumpkin what he had to say about his daughter. His response was theatrical. "Senhor Administrator, I do not believe her. She is a great hoaxer."

It wouldn't be long before the Soviets, were developing this convenient diagnosis, that everyone who didn't agree with them was deranged. It accounted for the hundreds of "mental institutions" that sprung up throughout Siberia.

On that summer day after the journey back, which was largely uphill, Lucia ran to the well. She knew her cousins would be there, and she knew the agonies they must have been suffering. The relief, the tears, the emotions of the three when they found themselves together that evening are not difficult to imagine. This was the second time Lucia had been in the arena, the cousins left to pray and suffer out of sight.

It was all for sinners, of course, and to console the suffering Jesus; they consented willingly, but that didn't lessen the dread and the agony. It was difficult for them to envisage greater suffering than this. But their ordeals had hardly begun. That Saturday's trip to Ourem was only a rehearsal.

CHAPTER FOURTEEN

Two days later, on the scheduled August apparition day, Mayor Santos arrived at Aljustrel in a carriage drawn by two black horses. His coachman, João Lopes, pulled up among the crowds who had congregated outside the Marto home. Arturo Santos walked up and down in front of the house several times then, taking off his straw hat, went inside.

"I didn't expect to see you here, sir," said Ti Marto with a touch of irony.

"No, I thought after all I would like to go to the miracle. We can all go together. I'll take the children with me in the carriage. We'll see and believe, like St. Thomas." He appeared nervous, glancing around at the doors of the house but avoiding eye contact with the family. "Aren't the children coming? It's late. We had better call them."

Someone was sent to fetch Lucia, who arrived with her father shortly after Francisco and Jacinta. The two younger cousins hadn't seen Arturo Santos before, but from Lucia's reaction to finding him in the house and his veneer of cordiality — thinly veiling an arrogant and bullying ego — they might have guessed who he was. Not even the rich and influential people from Lisbon and Porto who came to the door had that bearing of sinister officialdom.

When the administrator suggested that they get into the carriage with him and he'd drive them to the Cova, the children said it wasn't necessary. He said it would be quicker, and they would avoid being harassed by pilgrims. They still declined and so, with an abrupt change of tack, he said that they would go to Fatima because he had something to ask Father Ferreira that concerned them all. There was no way to avoid this, so they got into the carriage along with both their fathers.

At the rectory, Arturo Santos bustled the children into the parish priest's office. According to a later statement of Father Ferreira, the administrator had already called on him that morning with a priest from Porto de Mos, Father Manuel Carreira Poças. They had arrived in a car. This priest told Father Ferreira that they had just come from questioning the children in their homes and that the mayor, like himself, believed what the children were saying. Neither of them had any doubts, but they wanted Father Ferreira to question the children about a secret the Lady had told them but they had not revealed. Arturo Santos would then take them to the place of the apparitions, as he himself also wanted to go there.

This is somewhat confusing, because neither Lucia nor Ti Marto mention this first visit to Aljustrel with the priest from Porto de Mos, who seems suddenly to have disappeared from the scene with the car, which is replaced by a carriage. No matter. The details are unimportant. One way or the other the administrator was up to no good.

Once inside the presbytery, Santos asked the parish priest to cross-examine the children. When Father Ferreira asked Lucia who had taught her to say what she had said, she answered that it had been the Lady in Cova da Iria. He reminded her that those who told lies went to hell. She answered that she would not go to hell for that reason, for she was not telling lies. If the people came to the Cova it was because they wanted to, she said. She herself had never invited anyone.

The priest asked her if the Lady had told her some secret. She said that she had, but that she wasn't going to tell it to anyone. She added: "If you want I will ask the Lady for permission to tell the secret. If she gives it, then I will tell you."

At this the administrator exclaimed, "This is something supernatural. Come on! Let's go!"

Arturo Santos stood up and ordered the children into the carriage. The youngsters walked out of the rectory and down the steps. The carriage had been brought up as close as was possible to the stairs, and before the two fathers realized what was happening, the children had stepped into it, Francisco in the front and the girls behind. Jacinta held a rubber ball with elastic in her hands, and Francisco had a little toy that made a cracking sound. Lucia was praying urgently to Our Lady. Arturo Santos, doubtless grinning at the success of his ploy, was right on their heels as the two black horses trotted off toward the Cova. No one had time to register what had taken place until the carriage reached the junction with the main road. Suddenly the coachman was flicking his whip, and the horses were dashing off toward Ourem. As Ti Marto remarked, "It had been most cunningly arranged! Yes, it was well-managed, very well, and there was nothing to be done about it."

We will follow the children in a moment; but meanwhile, in Fatima, it wasn't long before people in cars and on bicycles were arriving at the rectory bringing news of a near riot at the Cova. News of the abduction had reached the estimated eighteen thousand people assembled there. There were some who were trying to incite the others to hang Father Ferreira for being an accomplice to the kidnapping. Happily nothing came of that, but tension was clearly high. Later the parish priest was obliged to write an impassioned letter to the newspaper *Mensageiro de Leiria* in his own defense.

That morning a young seminarian from Santarem, Joel de Jesus Magno, arrived at the Cova by bicycle, locked it up, took a swig of wine (which he appreciated because he was sweating), found a place in the shade and stayed there the whole time. He told later how people came from all directions in cars, on horseback, on bicycles and on foot. The sight of the cars spread over the hillside and along the roadway, the animals in the shade and the enormous number of bicycles everywhere made it clear that there was expectation of a big event. By midday, the actual time for the previous apparitions, there were thousands of people there. The children were already overdue when a fellow seminarian arrived with the news that the Arturo Santos had told the parents he would take their children in his carriage to the field, but fled with them to Ourem. The vast crowds of people were furious.

De Jesus Magno went to Fatima to find out what had happened. He appears to have been shouting something outside the rectory and was called a fool by some priests there. In the middle of this altercation some men arrived, saying Our Lady had appeared at the Cova. Immediately he went back. The roads were already full of people returning, talking about the extraordinary event. There had been two loud explosions like cannon fire coming from beside the holm oak, and the people began to flee as if a riot had started.

Then, not knowing how or why, the people were being pulled toward the holm oak as if by an electric current. It was a moment of terror. Some fainted. Others thought it was their last day on earth, and that judgment was going to take place then and there. Others saw the clouds take on a fantastic sequence of colors : blood red to pink to blue to indigo. Still others said they had seen lightning. There was a devout woman with tears in her eyes who said with the greatest conviction that she had seen Our Lady.

Testimonies of de Jesus Magno and others indicate that Our Lady actually, physically, came down from heaven to earth to keep her appointment with the children. She knew, of course, that they would not be there, that the forces of hate had conspired to prevent their presence. She came nonetheless. There were signs: the thurible smoke, the noises, the coloring of the sky and earth, the supernatural atmosphere — now terrifying, now tranquil. Some spoke of a fall of flowers. Here again, it seems as if every person present saw different things, or different intensities of the same thing.

Despite the claims of one or two enthusiasts, it's unlikely that anyone present saw Our Lady. Yet clearly she wanted the many thousands who had gathered there to know that she had come as promised. There may be other interpretations here, but the most persuasive is that she was emphasizing that her visits were not just for Lucia, Francisco and Jacinta. They were for every single individual present in that barren landscape, and everyone beyond it, over the whole world and on through the mazes of the years. She was underlining the universality of her message: that she is the mother of every soul, not just a chosen few, not just those who acknowledge her; that she is always available even if we, shamed by sin and ignorance, are reluctant to draw near.

In the carriage on the way to Ourem, Arturo Santos covered the children's heads with blankets so they wouldn't be recognized by pilgrims making their way up the hill toward the Cova da Iria.

Before his death in 1955, the mayor wrote: "I took the children to my house, where they were treated as if they were members of my own family for the two days in which they were there."

In her 1924 statement, Lucia said: "When we got to Ourem, we were locked in a room and told that we would not be let out of there, if we did not declare the secret that the Lady had confided to us."

Let's pause for a moment here to take a closer look at the administrator and his household.

In 1917 Arturo Oliveira Santos was a tall, handsome fellow of thirty-three, married to a woman named Adalina, who seems by all accounts to have been a practical, maternal soul. At the time they had six children and were to have two more. The names he gave these offspring tell us something of his role models and political aspirations.

The eldest was a boy called Franklin, a surname name synonymous with revolution and independence. Then came a girl, Democracia, a charmlessly masculine neologism that speaks for itself. Victor Hugo (who believed that man had to liberate himself from religion to achieve truth); Afonso Costa (the fanatically anti-religious prime minister of the time); Henrique and Jaures. Later, Viriato (Celtic leader of a tribe of central Portugal [c. 200–150 B.C.], the Hannibal of the Iberians) and Lusa (presumably an abbreviation of Lusitania, the ancient name for Portugal).

Santos was born in Vila Nova de Ourem in 1884 and brought up under the ideas of the Republic. Before the fall of the monarchy he founded a Republican Center and a Masonic Lodge at Ourem. Although he never had more than a primary education, he also founded two Republican journals. In 1911, at the age of twenty-seven, he became president of the council, a post he was returned to many times. Just as Lucia's father was known as *abobora*, the Pumpkin, so Arturo Santos was called *o latoeiro*, the Tinsmith or Tinker, because he made his living as a metal merchant from an office next to his house in Ourem.

It's not difficult to picture Arturo Santos. He is competent, energetic, driven by that pride of life that despises anything established as being the cause of all evils, a champion of the smooth and sparkling clean "new," however it's defined.

One extant photo of him could be that of a Raymond Chandler detective. In another, he seems to be wearing a monocle. There is also a typical "Edwardian" family pose taken around this time. Arturo is tall and wearing a starched high collar. He sports a curled mustache, and the index finger of his right hand is pointing definitely and ominously earthwards. His fine-looking, smiling wife is seated with Afonso Costa on her lap. Other children stand about, confident and well-dressed. Franklin looks a personable lad. Democracia resembles Belloc's Matilda.

Of Arturo and Adalina's eight children one, Henrique, was still alive in 2000. (He was then eighty-five and living in Lisbon.) Henrique was not a devotee of Fatima, but much of what he had to say when interviewed had the touch of authenticity. In August 1917 he was, at three years and three months, the youngest of the Santos children. Referring to the presence of the shepherds in his house, he had but a vague recollection of them. His memory from that occasion comes mainly from what he was told by his elder sister, Democracia (who was about the same age as Lucia).

Democracia asked Francisco and Jacinta, "What do you see?" and they answered, "Lucia is the one who knows." The Santos girl also told how they all had great fun jumping up and down together on the beds' wire-spring mattresses, a luxury the Aljustrel shepherds had never heard of.

That August afternoon, Francisco and Jacinta's elder stepbrother, Antonio, along with some local lads, biked all the way down the hill and across the valley to see if they could discover anything about the fate of the young seers. They caught a glimpse of them playing on the veranda of the administrator's house, but there was nothing much the young men could do. Any bid to rescue, or even voice an objection, would get them thrown in jail, and that would help no one.

That evening Adalina Santos cooked a meal for the children, her own and the seers, and after they had played together they all went to a neighbor's house to crowd around a window that looked out on to the street. At that time, the feast of Our Lady of Pity was celebrated in the Ourem parish on August 13, marked by a procession. In 1911, when he was minister of justice, the obsessed, anticlerical Afonso Costa had passed a bill forbidding public acts of religious devotion without authorization. The event in 1917 had been approved, but even if the sight of the colorful procession from a neighbor's window pleased the detainees, the effect must have been dampened by the administrator declaiming pompously that "this procession was authorized by me under Article 57 of the Law of Separation."

We mustn't imagine that Jacinta with her plastic ball and Francisco with his cracking toy were simply relaxing at the mayor's house, eating well and enjoying the fun and games between questionings. On the level where it matters, in those compartments of the soul — the mind and the heart — they must have been devastated at not honoring their appointment with the Lady. Also, these children had never been separated from their parents, and now they were abducted, with no indication that those parents were taking any measures to retrieve them.

The loneliness they must have undergone, loneliness compounded by guilt at having failed the Lady from heaven, cannot be exaggerated. If they had not had each other, the pressure, without grace, might have been enough to snuff out the flame of their young lives.

CHAPTER FIFTEEN

Lucia, Francisco and Jacinta went lonely to the beds Adalina Santos provided for them. They woke with probably an even greater feeling of being abandoned. There was no word from Aljustrel, no angry parents knocking on the doors demanding their children, no word from heaven that the Lady knew that failure to keep the appointment was not their fault. Their only consolation was to say the prayer that the Lady had taught them and to believe that she could hear them. "Jesus, this is for love of You, and for the conversion of sinners."

In her 1924 deposition, Lucia includes this stray sentence: "In the morning an old lady interrogated us about the secret." There is no hint of who the lady might be, what she looked like, the approach she used, or indeed anything besides what is contained in the sentence. Indiscreet interpreters of the Fatima story, however, leap on this unfortunate female as if she were some sorceress from the underworld, some fiendish inquisitrix, some vile, repulsive brew-stirring creature intent on turning the children into toads. This is diverting, and it adds a certain filmic color, but we don't come to Fatima to be diverted or entertained.

We come because a silent but insistent intuition has murmured about a love story, a love story so rash, so prodigal, so absolute as to be the only love story worth telling and we, you and I, are the beloved. No concept could be more captivating. Fiction, even exaggeration for literary effect, can only distort the pure intent of the Lover.

This old woman, predictably, failed.

The trio were then taken to the council building, where they were questioned further by Santos and his colleagues. They were even offered gold. Coins and jewelry were placed on a table before them as bait. All they had to do was tell the secret.

We might note here that the mayor and his colleagues weren't, like Lucia's mother, trying to get the children to deny that they saw a Lady from heaven at the Cova. Like the devil, they had no doubts that the children were communicating with a spirit being. What they, like the devil, wanted to know was what this being had confided to them and charged them not to repeat. There is a faith of sorts at work here — even the devil believes in God. It isn't belief that's the problem. It's monstrous, grotesque, implacable pride.

It was a Tuesday, a working day, and the government building was full of officials and citizens on council business. Then, as now, all offices and shops close between one and three each afternoon. Even the bribing and intimidation of small children must stop for lunch. Not even the cavalier Arturo Santos could override the sacrosanct siesta.

They were taken back to the mayor's house to enjoy Adalina's cooking once more, but the strain of captivity and the uncertainty of the outcome was unseating even the veneer of normality by this time. Santos was probably reading the signs, too. How much longer could he keep the children? He must have heard of the near-riot in Fatima the previous day when the pilgrims learned that he had abducted the seers. He couldn't claim official business forever. Soon they would be laying siege to his house. Drastic measures were called for unless he was to lose face in front of the entire municipality.

So — champion of a better world, free of superstition and repression — he placed the children in the same area of the council building where drunks, street brawlers and petty thieves were locked up while waiting to go before the magistrate. There is no record of a formal charge being entered against them. If the administrator had considered charging them, then he saved himself some stress by abandoning the idea. Any charge would have made him a target of scorn. Sedition? Perpetrated by a seven-year-old? Nine- and ten-year-olds provoking public disorder?

Clearly he justified his misuse of official power to himself by reasoning that there was no serious intention of harming the children. This was just a little jolt, a little *soupçon* of fear to let the children know who was boss, and that a boss' order must be followed. It was all in the interest of the People and the State. There were to be no secrets in a socialist republic.

In the prison area of the council building, they were locked alone in a cell while that boss decided what to do. Jacinta couldn't hold back her tears. Lucia tried to placate her. "Neither your parents nor ours have come to see us," the youngest child sobbed. "They don't care about us anymore!"

"Don't cry," Francisco begged. "We can offer this to Jesus for sinners. Come on! Oh my Jesus, this is for love of You, and for the conversion of sinners."

Straightaway Jacinta added, "And also for the Holy Father, and in reparation for the sins committed against the Immaculate Heart of Mary."

Santos called together his like-minded colleagues. The situation was getting desperate, he told them, and desperate situations call for desperate measures. He'd decided to really put the fear of God — that was a timely idiom — into the Aljustrel shepherds. He would tell them that they were going to be hung, or have their heads chopped off. Or boiled in oil. That was a good one. It contained its own hourglass, so to speak. The children would have the time it took for the oil to reach boiling to change their minds and reveal the secret.

So they were given the ultimatum and told that the fire had been lit beneath the cauldron of oil. Then they were taken down a corridor and pushed into another large, rather foul-smelling detention cell. The door was slammed and locked behind them.

In the light from a solitary window, they gradually made out other prisoners, all men, standing, sitting, or sprawling around the room. The men were amazed at first, then curious. If nothing else the appearance of three children must have afforded relief from boredom in the summer heat of a Tuesday afternoon. We can't help but suspect that the presence and manner of the men intimidated the children, but didn't actually frighten them. The rattling of the bolt in the door behind them would have held more terror for them because it locked out parents, home, siblings — all that they knew and loved. And anyway, the threatened future held terrors before which others paled.

It couldn't have taken any more than a few minutes for the men in the jail to work out that these children were the seers of Fatima that everybody was talking about. Their immediate remarks were probably crude, kindly, gruff, sentimental, but whatever each man's level of religious sensitivity his reaction was positive, because these children carried the stamp of the divine on their brows. There was no doubting that they had spoken with heaven. Again the tears came to poor Jacinta's eyes, not because she was going to die, but because she would never see her mother again. Francisco and Lucia consoled her by repeating the promises the Lady had made to them, and the promises they had made to her. Their fellow prisoners' advice was more mundane. "But all you have to do is tell the Administrator the secret! What does it matter whether the Lady wants you to or not?"

Jacinta emerged from her tears like a tigress. "Never!" she asserted. "I'd rather die!"

The understandable angst of a little girl separated from her mother and believing that she would never see her again alternated with the faith the Lady had planted in the child's soul. The prisoners must have been impressed, even if a little embarrassed, when she then joined her hands and prayed with fervor: "O my Jesus! This is for love of You, for the conversion of sinners, for the Holy Father, and in reparation for the sins committed against the Immaculate Heart of Mary!"

Had Arturo Santos (or the devil) been listening at the door, he would have heard in Jacinta's prayer a brief account of the secret for which he was risking his career. (And neither would have suspected it. They wanted solid predictions they could plan ahead for, or evade. Like Adam they wanted the knowledge of good and evil, for with that knowledge they would be equals with God.)

The children then decided to say the Rosary. To create a focal point for their prayers, Jacinta removed a chain with a medal from around her neck. She spotted a nail protruding from a wall, but it was beyond her reach, so she asked a prisoner to hang the sacramental up there for her. The children knelt facing the medal. The prisoners, clumsily at first, but willingly enough, knelt down, too. The children started the prayer and the prisoners prayed with them. "That is," Lucia later recalled, "if they knew how to pray, but at least they were down on their knees."

Francisco had taken off his cap and placed it on a bench. When he noticed that one of the prisoners, though kneeling and joining in the prayer, still wore a hat, the boy respectfully and politely said, "If you wish to pray you should take your cap off." It is not easy for a man, particularly for a man awaiting conviction for a criminal offense, to take instructions from a nine-year-old boy. But with a humility that those not yet charged with criminal offenses would do well to emulate, the prisoner immediately removed his cap and handed it to Francisco. The lad took it over to a bench and placed it on top of his own.

There is much symbolism here for poets, devotion for the pious, textbook reassessment material for penitentiary psychologists and lessons for parents; but nothing, I fear, for Arturo Santos and the political progressives.

After the Rosary Jacinta went to the window, which was barred on the outside and looked out on a corner of the town square.

The prayers had fortified the youngsters against the terror that threatened, but it hadn't removed that terror. When the seven-year-old's tears began to flow again, Lucia and Francisco tried to comfort her. "Jacinta," the older cousin asked, "didn't you want to offer this sacrifice to Our Lord?"

"Yes, I do, but I keep thinking about my mother and I can't help crying."

In a bid to deflect from the intense longing of a child for her mother at this time of crisis, the three agreed that they would apportion their prayers and their imminent deaths for those intentions of the Lady — the causes she had specifically asked prayers and sacrifices for. One child would offer for sinners, another for the Holy Father, the third for sins against the Immaculate Heart of Mary. Francisco and Lucia gave Jacinta the first choice. Like Thérèse of Lisieux some four decades earlier, Jacinta refused to be content with less than everything. "I'm making the offering for all the intentions," she said, but added the one phrase that makes a virtue of avidity, "Because I love them all."

One of the prisoners started playing a harmonica to divert the children, and others started singing. Soon they were dancing, and the girls were dancing with them. Jacinta, as we have seen, had a special aptitude for the arts and would break into dance at the slightest excuse. At one point her partner was a thief who found her so small that he picked her up and held her like a doll as he danced.

We all carry pictures of others, real or fictional, in the albums of our minds. In my own gallery, I reckon no figure emerges radiating the essence of what it is to be human as much as Jacinta Marto in the Ourem prison cell. Surrounded by the social dregs of the town, tears pouring down her cheeks, her heart rent by that truly devastating malady of childhood called homesickness, an excruciating death just minutes away... in the midst of all this, she is dancing.

I find this picture full of pathos, and yet so noble. Admirers can put as many haloes on her head as it will carry, they can endlessly sing of her virtues till their voices croak, but that doesn't tell me anything much about Jacinta. The visible Jacinta, for me, is this picture of her, in love and in prison, seemingly abandoned, crushed and weeping, at the lowest point of human desolation — dancing.

CHAPTER SIXTEEN

After an hour or two in the detention cell, at about five in the afternoon, the children were taken to another room and questioned further. It was their final chance, they were told. The oil was on the boil. They huddled together in mutual trepidation, but ballasted, in the depths of their beings, with a sweet and immovable peace. Not for an instant did they entertain the idea of revealing the secret.

The questioner wrenched Jacinta away from the other two and took her from the room. She was arraigned before the administrator, who again used every trick of flattery, intimidation and bribery on the little child. When it was clear that he was getting nowhere he ordered that she be taken away and flung into the cauldron.

In the meantime, Lucia and Francisco were still in the other room under the eye of a guard. Normally a writer here would be eager to convey the desperate emotional turmoil of the young cousins, but Lucia writes that Francisco confided to her with "boundless joy and peace." All authentic reports on the death of Christ's martyrs, from Stephen to Thomas More to Maximilian Kolbe, affirm that martyrs experience a special embrace of heaven leading up to, and at the time of, death. We have heard it often enough, but on every repetition we must switch on faith to give light to human myopia.

What Francisco confided to Lucia in this exalted manner was: "If they kill us as they say, we'll soon be in heaven! How wonderful! Nothing else matters!" After a little while, he added: "God grant that Jacinta won't be afraid. I'm going to say a Hail Mary for her!" He promptly removed his cap and prayed.

The guard, possibly thinking that Francisco had decided to divulge the secret — deporting himself and giving it utterance after the manner of a Delphic oracle (the superstitious see such things that way) — asked the boy what he was saying. "I'm saying a Hail Mary so that Jacinta won't be afraid." The guard made a scornful gesture and left him to it.

Next, it was Francisco's turn to be taken before the increasingly frustrated Arturo Santos, to be questioned and presumably delivered to the oil when neither honey, money nor malice could wring a word out of him. Then Lucia was subjected to the same routine.

Of course, there was no cauldron of oil. The children simply found themselves together in yet another room. There they were subjected to a last-ditch barrage of threats with talk of a communal immersion in the oil, but that buffalo had blunted horns by this time. Arturo's weapon had backfired. All the exercise had achieved was to reserve martyrs' laurels for the child shepherds.

It must have been a very angry and humiliated (not humbled, alas, just humiliated) mayor who took the children back to his home that evening. He had gained nothing, but lost the respect of the citizens under his administration — if, indeed, he ever had it.

The following day, August 15, was the feast of the Assumption of the Blessed Virgin, a day when Catholics, then as now, are obliged to attend Mass. Santos drove the children back to Fatima and arrived just as the congregation was coming out of the church. The rectory was behind the church and across a road. The administrator took his vehicle there and walked up the steps and onto the porch with the children. Ti Marto spotted them and raced up the steps. He picked up Jacinta in his arms and kissed her with tears of relief. The other two ran to him.

At that moment an official in the service of the administrator approached Ti Marto. He was trembling in a way that alarmed the father. This nervous fellow said, "Well, here are your children." Then a great noise arose in the square. The people were waving and shouting. Ti Marto turned and, with Jacinta still in his arms, shouted, "Be quiet! Some of you are shouting against the administrator and some against the priest, but it all comes from lack of faith and is allowed by God."

After a conversation in the priest's office, the administrator and Ti Marto went back to the porch. The scene below looked as if it might get ugly. The mayor asked the father if he would have a glass of wine with him. Ti Marto refused, but then, seeing a group of youth armed with sticks and clearly out to get the abductor, he relented. Arturo Santos was probably surprised, but nonetheless grateful for the protection afforded by Ti Marto's generosity. He said, "You can be sure that I treated your children well." Jacinta and Francisco's father answered, "It's not me but the people who seem to want to know that."

Just then the children came out from the rectory and, saying that they wanted to pray at the Cova, headed off that way. The crowd began to disperse. Ti Marto went with the administrator to the tavern where Arturo Santos ordered wine, bread and cheese. He started a conversation that didn't interest Ti Marto. At one point he claimed that the children had told him the secret. Ti Marto said, "So they wouldn't tell their father or mother, but it's natural they should tell you!"

Soon Santo's carriage was at the door. Ti Marto said goodbye, but the administrator made him get in and go along till they were clear of the crowd. As they drove by somebody shouted, "There goes Ti Marto! He's talked too much and the Tinker's taking him to prison."

———

One can't help but feel a certain pity for Arturo Santos, so arrogant, so empty, so puffed up with political pride, so dead to the Spirit — a bondsman to the works of darkness. In his own estimation a luminary in the heaven of the secular State; to history the big, bad wolf of Fatima.

He was removed from the office of administrator of Ourem on December 8 (the feast of the Immaculate Conception) of that same year and in 1919 took a post in the colonial ministry in Lisbon. After the 1926 revolution, he was several times taken political prisoner. In 1930, he exiled himself in Spain until the end of the civil war in 1939. Not long before he died, he wrote a document in which he denied imprisoning the shepherds or threatening them in any way.

> My intention was to take them to my house for a little persuasion. And this is exactly what happened, as is known by people who are honorable and unprejudiced.
>
> During the time of my voluntary exile, I always defended, as best I knew how, the name of Portugal. I have hands clean of blood or theft. I was working in hospitals during the war as a vigilante, and in charge of expenses and storage. In the hospital of St. John of God in Madrid, I managed to salvage paintings of artistic and religious value, which would otherwise have been destroyed in the conflict. This can be confirmed by the doctors, the nurses and by the nuns themselves.

This same man never let his family know that he was a Freemason. His son Henrique says he only learned of this affiliation of his father later, from a history book.

An Ourem contemporary stated many years afterward:

> I was well-acquainted with the subsequent life of Senhor Arturo. When he returned from Spain, he came back to the area asking former friends for help and material necessities. All was not well with his conscience. He felt defeated when faced with his failure in the matter of imprisoning the little shepherds — harmless, innocent

children. Later, though, he did become devoted to *Nossa Senhora da Saude*.

These reports are not in accord with the notice of his death, on June 27, 1955, at the age of seventy-one, as recorded in the official Sanctuary monthly, *Voz da Fatima*. The paper said he had a most important role in the unfolding of events:

> Fair-minded history will be the judge of his actions. He himself, to the end, refused to defend himself and the silence he maintained until he died was not the least of his strange attitudes. It does not seem that he in any way made his peace with God, humbly receiving His forgiveness at the hands of a priest. Nevertheless we recommend his soul to the Father of Mercy, in the hope that he will obtain in the next life the peace that for the most part he lacked in this.

In the end, perhaps this "big bad wolf" was not so bad, really, despite Francisco's comment, "Most likely Our Lady didn't appear on the 13th, so as to avoid going to the administrator's house, maybe because he is such a bad man." Perhaps more sad than bad. A fellow of his time, of his upbringing. And who is to know how anyone stands in the inscrutable designs of God? One who only receives a thimbleful of grace and responds to it might touch the heart of our Savior more than those who receive gallons and use only a pint.

There is no record of the few days after that Wednesday. The children were clearly the most famous, most talked-about individuals for a great many miles around — for all they cared! In the Marto home, all would have been the same as before, but intensified. Their parents and older siblings were, perhaps, a little more indulgent with Francisco and Jacinta, as their absence would have spotlighted their value. But, as is necessary with a current of energy, this was earthed by the nuisance of the constant flow of callers, the same old questions, the havoc the intrusion brought to daily life. Nowadays people would flatly discourage uninvited visitors, erect a notice threatening prosecution, install a ferocious hound. But hospitality and courtesy were concepts as entrenched in the mentality of the Portuguese peasantry as the need for a roof over the head and food on the table.

Yet the family routine didn't change, even if it was regularly interrupted. The men worked the fields, the women cooked and spun and the younger children tended the sheep.

The following Sunday, August 19, was, appropriately, the feast of then-Blessed John Eudes, the first and greatest propagator of the Immaculate Heart of Mary. He was canonized just eight years after the Fatima apparitions. In the morning, Francisco and Jacinta went to Mass in the parish church, then to the Cova da Iria to say the Rosary. After that, Jose Alves (who later became a generous benefactor of the shrine) took them to his house in Moita for lunch. When they arrived back in Aljustrel, Francisco and his brother João, who was eleven at the time, went with Lucia to Valinhos, barely one-third mile from Aljustrel, to pasture the sheep. Jacinta stayed indoors because her mother wanted to wash her hair.

Around four o'clock, Francisco and Lucia experienced the approach of the supernatural, that cooling of the air as if it were suddenly rinsed clean, the heralding flash. Their immediate thought was for Jacinta. They told João to run home and fetch her, but he wanted to stay to see the Lady. Lucia had a small coin in her pocket, a vintem. She offered it to him if he would go to get his little sister. João doesn't seem to have been gifted with that spiritual sensitivity that is alert to the supernatural. He had been with Lucia the third time she had seen "the figure in a sheet" in 1915. Lucia saw it. João didn't. And, to give him credit — for peer conformity is a powerful pressure for children — he didn't pretend that he had. Material things, however, he could understand readily. A vintem had an immediate value, and if he was to fetch Jacinta, he could come back with her and still see the Lady.

At the Marto home, his mother told him, "Now, what do they want Jacinta there for? Isn't there enough in Valinhos to play with?" João's manner must have betrayed him for his mother caught hold of him and said, "Either you tell me why they want her, or I won't let you go either!" João told her that Francisco said the Lady was coming, and Olympia answered that Jacinta was in her godmother's house. She said to get the child and bring her back home because the mother, too, wanted to go with them to see — if not the Lady, at least something of what happened at these apparitions. But, such was the urgency of the moment, that when João found Jacinta he whispered something in her ear and she sped off along the beaten path between the oaks and the olive trees. João had forgotten about his mother and was panting at his sister's heels.

Where the land begins to rise slightly, Francisco and Lucia were kneeling with their beads between their fingers, their heads bowed and their hearts and minds praying with fervent anticipation. Just as Jacinta joined them, her hair still wet and wrapped in a towel like a turban, another of the celestial flashes of glorious light beamed the signal. A moment later, the Lady of Light stood above another holm oak sapling. Francisco, Jacinta and Lucia were immediately folded into her radiance and, to the unseen angels if not to João, they became light themselves, because anything exposed to light will be illuminated, and anything illuminated turns to light.

It was Sunday, August 19, 1917.

Lucia: What do you want of me?
Lady: I want you to continue going to the Cova da Iria on the 13th, and to continue praying the Rosary every day. In the last month, I will perform a miracle so that all may believe.

Lucia: What do you want done with the money the people leave in the Cova da Iria?

Lady: Have two litters made. One is to be carried by you and Jacinta and two other girls dressed in white; the other one is to be carried by Francisco and three other boys. The money from the litters is for the "festa" of Our Lady of the Rosary, and what is left over will help towards the construction of a chapel that is to be built here.

Lucia: I would like to ask you to cure some sick persons.

Lady: Yes, I will cure some of them during the year.

Pray, pray very much, and make sacrifices for sinners; for many souls go to hell, because there are none to sacrifice themselves and to pray for them.

The exchange here is disarmingly short. There are no preliminaries about the abduction. No "Where were you on Monday?" or "I'm sorry we couldn't meet you at the Cova on Monday as planned, but the mayor cheated us and took us to Ourem." No "We tried to offer it all for the offended Jesus and for the Immaculate Heart." No "You did well, my children, Jesus is touched by your love and loyalty." It seems abrupt, but how do we know? Given the Lady's absolute openness to the children's sensitivities on previous apparitions, it's unlikely that the conversation was as formal as the "Memoirs" and records suggest.

"What do you want of me?"
"I want you to continue going to the Cova da Iria on
the 13th, and to continue praying the Rosary every
day. In the last month, I will perform a miracle
so that all may believe."

The answer is a repetition of three statements already made during previous apparitions: two requests and a promise. Is it used in this instance to reinforce the importance of the statements, or because it's children who are being addressed and, for children, repetition is part of the learning process?

The request to keep coming back to the Cova da Iria might well hinge on the word "continue." As the sequence of the assignations — on every 13th for six months — has been broken, the children might suppose that further meetings were automatically canceled, and that even the promised October miracle might have been shelved. But this apparition at Valinhos dispels such ideas. The Lady's promise holds good no matter what human, or diabolical, agencies do to thwart them. She is constant, just as the children must be to the daily praying of the Rosary.

"What do you want done with the money the people
leave in the Cova da Iria?"

This is another rehearsed question. In her first deposition when she was not quite fifteen, Lucia wrote this question as "The woman who has the money asked me to ask what you want her to do with that money." Maria Carreira had been taking custody of the cash. She didn't want to, but there was nobody else to take it. She offered it to the parish priest, but he refused to touch it. Carreira insisted that Lucia ask Our Lady herself what to do with it.

"Have two litters made. One is to be carried by you
and Jacinta and two other girls dressed in white; the
other one is to be carried by Francisco and three other

boys. The money from the litters is for the 'festa' of Our Lady of the Rosary. . . ."

The litters'— floats or portable platforms (*andores*) — were wooden trays with handles like a stretcher. A statue was secured in the center, often on a small dais. The litter was covered with flowers and carried in procession. The custom was for people to throw coins onto it and this money would be used for Church purposes. The Lady is referring to these coins when she says, "The money from the litters is for the 'festa' of Our Lady of the Rosary" — presumably for flowers and candles and the white clothes for the young litter-bearers. In the interview with the parish priest two days after the apparition, Lucia said that Francisco and the other boys were to wear white, including white capes.

". . . and what is left over will help towards the construction of a chapel that is to be built here."

This is the first mention of a chapel in the "Memoirs," but Lucia might be allotting memories to the wrong apparitions. By now the parish priest was questioning Lucia after each apparition and writing down her replies against any episcopal inquiry. Those notes were also to arm himself in preparation for confrontation with the swelling thousands who were descending on the Cova from all over Portugal, to say nothing of the agents of the adamantly anti-religious government.

After the September apparition, Lucia told Father Ferreira that the Lady had said, "With half the money that has been collected so far have litters made and take them to Our Lady of the Rosary, the other half may help towards a chapel." (Apparently Lucia had just told the Lady, "The people would dearly love a chapel here.")

Perhaps Lucia, writing from memory more than twenty years later, mixed these things up in her mind, but it is of no great consequence. What comes across to us is the exquisite interest the Queen of Heaven shows in the minutiae of their daily lives and devotions, from the color of their clothes to how donated money is to be spent.

The parish records say that in August the Lady told Lucia, "I want you to return to the Cova da Iria; if they hadn't abducted you to the village" (that is, Aldeia da Cruz, the Village of the Cross, the old name for Vila Nova de Ourem).

A parenthetical observation here. Why would Our Lady use the old name for the town? It doesn't appear to have been in use at the time. Could it be that if there is a choice between the religious and the secular, she chooses the religious? If she uses a secular name it is for the want of a better. Everything, absolutely everything, even the daily trivia, is centered on and tends toward heaven and things of heaven, Christ and things of Christ. (St. Petersburg loses its substance and takes on the patina of a black hole when it calls itself Leningrad; the lackluster Michaelmas daisy suddenly has a unique fragrance and is fit to adorn the throne because its name aligns it with the angels.)

Catholic devotions, which are often incomprehensible even to other Christians, can be justified when seen in this light. The Hearts of Jesus and Mary, the Stations of the Cross, indulgences, Holy Hours, litanies, the Sign of the Cross, medals, scapulars, even the Rosary itself can easily be dismissed as weak, sentimental, obtuse, superstitious. But viewed in the light of faith, they are none of these things, They are the currency of love, the arias of the eternal opera, because they are movements of a will struggling to express conformity to the will of its Creator, Lover, Redeemer. These whispered pieties will be the paving stones of the Kingdom — brilliant stones of jasper and onyx and emerald — long after the fatuous bubbles of this world, the myriad oracles, the erotica, the fashions, have burst to disclose that they are nothing at all.

"I want you to return to the Cova da Iria; if they hadn't abducted you to the village, the miracle would have been better known. St. Joseph would have been seen with the Child Jesus blessing the people. Our Lady of the Rosary would have come with an angel on either side, and Our Lady of Sorrows surrounded by an arc of flowers."

This extract is from the parish records written by Father Fereirra within two days of the August apparition, so we have no reason to disregard it simply because Lucia didn't mention it in her "Memoirs." The difficulty is not in believing it, but in understanding what it signifies. "The miracle would have been better known" means what? In October, St. Joseph with the Christ Child, Our Lord, Our Lady of the Rosary and Our Lady of Sorrows were seen in the sky, but only by the children. Could the implication be that, had Arturo Santos not abducted the seers, the crowds in the Cova would have seen Jesus, Mary and Joseph in the sky along with, or maybe instead of, the Miracle of the Sun?

"I would like to ask you to cure some sick persons."
"Yes, I will cure some of them during the year."
Lucia was always conscientious about asking the Lady for specific favors on behalf of people who had approached her to intercede for them. There were even times when she went out of her way to avoid petitioners because she was afraid of forgetting their requests. Here she seems to have bundled them all together in the hope that the Lady would be able to sort them out. This the Lady did and her answer, as always, was succinct, comprehensive, and with a kind of transparent integrity that left nothing essential unsaid. It was as if she were confiding in equals, even though she kept her own counsel as to the details.

Then, Lucia later said, the Lady's expression became sadder as she spoke these words, now engraved on a stone marking the spot where the Valinhos apparition took place.

"Pray, pray very much, and make sacrifices for sinners; for many souls go to hell, because there are none to sacrifice themselves and to pray for them."

Here is another simple statement of stunning import, delivered without preliminaries and without explanation. Again, it is an aspect of the next life, which is altogether alien to our supposing, one we can only graft onto our consciousness by pondering it in our hearts. We have been given free will, and heaven does not interfere unless asked to. Only a fool would deny that the prospect is terrifying. Sad to say, most of us seem to be fools. Only the humble can transform the terror into holy fear and loving gratitude.

Chapter Seventeen

Among the witnesses' statements studied for the beatification of Francisco and Jacinta was that of reliable Maria Carreira. She told Father Formigão that during the August apparition in Valinhos, at her request, Lucia asked the Lady if she had appeared to anyone else at the Cova da Iria besides the three children. The reason for this question was that Maria Carreira's youngest daughter Carolina, twelve, had seen a figure near the holm oak on July 28. The small figure was very beautiful and had blond hair. Carolina later saw it above the holm oak. Apparently the Lady told Lucia that it had not been her but an angel.

No one is urged to give credence, or skepticism, to such statements. Even the most genuine and devout of folk can be misled — or, indeed, mislead themselves. But if we accept the possibility we must also accept two other propositions,

First is that there could have been a number of supernatural happenings apparent to many people besides the seers, indicating and attesting to the "public" nature of the six apparitions. (And quite distinct from those that Our Lady made to each individual seer in private and Lucia mentions in her "Memoirs.")

Second, there was probably much more dialogue between Our Lady and Lucia than is recorded in the "Memoirs." What Lucia has written down is what she has definitely remembered as being for everyone, the message that she was to pass on. What she did not record, perhaps even couldn't remember, were the exchanges between a spiritual mother and her daughter that, if they had been memorized and set down, might serve to confuse rather than emphasize the message.

On the evening of August 19, Ti Marto was heading home when a neighbor said to him, "Our Lady appeared to your kids again in Valinhos. I have to tell you that your Jacinta has something very special about her. It seems that Our Lady didn't appear till she arrived. Our Lady actually waited for her!"

Ti Marto continued on home, but Jacinta wasn't there. He sat on a stool in the kitchen thinking about life. Suddenly he saw Jacinta on the road, skipping, very happy with herself. She had a twig of holm oak in her hand. As soon as she came into the house there was a smell of perfume, the likes of which he said he had never experienced before. He asked what she had in her hand. Jacinta said, "It's a twig from the holm oak in Valinhos where Our Lady appeared just now."

For the children, the great significance of the unscheduled August apparition was the confirmation that the Lady had not abandoned them for not keeping their appointment at the Cova. They had no doubts about their own innocence in the matter, and they knew that the Lady, who was the embodiment of sweet love and tenderness, was incapable of embracing a negative concept and wouldn't hold them responsible. Nevertheless, without the Lady's own reassurance, their minds were a mire of questions and contradictions.

So the Lady's appearance at Valinhos inspired a return of confidence. It was a surprise visit to the nursery when the night light was burning low, rousing alarms in little hearts.

This exquisite kindness of the Lady rekindled those hearts till they were ready to burst with love, the sort of love that would trek to the frozen North Pole and forge a path through torrid jungles to declare itself. Children, particularly, are restricted in aiming at such feats, but these three knew what the object of their love wanted. She wanted them to say the Rosary. This wasn't simply a mental exercise. It was both a way of learning how to communicate with heaven, and communicating with heaven while learning, because heaven was the teacher. It was both the lesson and the application, the ladder and the climb, the yearning and the kiss. It was rarely difficult, and even when it seemed so, the Lady would be there, not visible as at the Cova, but closer still, leading, teaching, feeding, wrapping them in swaddling clothes and pressing them to herself.

The Lady had also asked for sacrifices, and the children had formed a pattern of these. There were the physical sacrifices that limited their food and drink, exchanging the tasty for insipid stuff, foregoing water during the hot, dry afternoons. But — and it is an important "but" — they never took these privations to excess. The Lady had asked for sacrifices, not marathons of self-denial. The solid good sense of the peasantry established a meter at the pulse of their devotions, and grace kept the mercury beneath that red line beyond which religious sacrifice becomes culpable masochism. Godly sacrifice offers itself in union with the Crucified; masochism crucifies itself to admire its sacrifice.

Then there were the interior sacrifices. Francisco and Jacinta didn't have the disbelief of their parents to contend with, but there were taunts, often savage, from adults in the village, in the parish and beyond. The jealousy of some of their peers could be hurtful too, as the attention of all of Portugal seemed to focus on them. Fortunately, Francisco, Jacinta and their cousin had no sense of self-importance. Their center of being was the Jesus they had seen in "the light from the Lady's hands," and the Lady herself whose beauty and goodness were a reflection of His. The Lady's majesty was clothed in humility. The majesty dazzled them. It was inimitable, but the humility they adopted as their own. To love the Lady and at the same time advertise oneself simply wasn't an option.

This humility of the Lady was the garment they borrowed to offer their interior sacrifices, particularly the endurance needed for that tedious sacrifice that continued from the rising of the sun till its going down — the procession of people queuing to question them. A number of contemporaries attest to the unwavering courtesy of the children. They gave plain, brief answers to the questions, never altering them for effect, or to show contempt for questioner, or exasperation. True, when they saw people coming they often hid, in barrels, in cupboards, in the loft. Sometimes on the local roads, strangers would ask them for directions to the seers' homes. They would politely supply a detailed route, then set off in an opposite direction themselves.

They were ever on the lookout for new sacrifices. This wasn't a morbid abnormality. It was love. The object of their love was hurt — not piqued, not upset — hurt; literally brokenhearted on a cosmic scale. Only by sharing the hurt could a lover hope to assuage it to any degree at all. The pains of childbirth are not abnormal, nor is a parent's agony over a wounded child, nor a child's over a stricken or humiliated parent. They are pangs of love.

After the August apparition, as they were taking their sheep to pasture, the children saw an old piece of rope that had fallen off a cart. Lucia picked it up and, as children will in associating the unfamiliar with the familiar, tied it around her arm. In effect she made a tourniquet, and the interference with the flow of her blood caused a certain pain. Immediately this registered as a sacrifice in the minds of the young lovers. "We could tie it around our waists and offer this sacrifice to God."

They lay it across the surface of a rock and pounded at the fibers with a sharp stone to divide it into three parts. Each child did as suggested, tying a portion around his or her waist underneath clothes so it wouldn't be seen. The rope was thick and rough. They tied it tightly, and the pain was intense and constant. They wore it day and night. No one suspected what they were enduring; but sometimes, when they were alone together, Jacinta would give vent to her suffering with tears. The others, of course, pleaded with her to remove it — the mercury was dangerously near the red line. But Jacinta wouldn't do that. She would say, with a sincerity that makes the words dance like sunlight on rippling water, "I want to offer this sacrifice to Our Lord in reparation and for the conversion of sinners."

This need for sacrifice, the holy joy and satisfaction the children found in it, increased during these weeks before the September apparition. Jacinta accidentally stung her fingers with some nettles. In no time they were beating their bare legs with the plants when they found them. They also began giving the lunches their parents had prepared for them to the children of families in Moita who lived on very basic rations. Yet more pains, yet another forfeit to be offered, tokens of a love that was determined to burn for the beloved.

There was another sacrifice, not of their choosing but imposed upon them. The uninvited visitors had become such a regular feature of the Marto household that around this time their parents kept Francisco and Jacinta at home while João was sent out with the flock. This was easier than dispatching someone to call them every time a set of pilgrims knocked at the door. This, of course, split the trio of seers, which must have caused anguish on both sides, even though they still would have had some hours of each day together. Eventually Ti Marto sold the family flock, just as Lucia's family was shortly to sell its. The Cova was now as crowded during the day as a airport terminal, and the land that had fed the dos Santos family might as well have been flooded by the sea for all the use it was to them. Lucia's father had even been knocked down in front of a crowd when he'd protested their trespassing.

All these inroads into regular family life were burdens enough for those who believed that the supernatural was declaring itself in the area, but for those such as Lucia's parents, who had doubts, all the upheavals must have seemed as bitter and futile as war. At this point, though, Lucia does report that her father had revised his opinions enough to say, in tune with the basic principles of philosophy, "We don't know if it's true, but neither do we know if it's a lie."

It was around this time, too, that Lucia refers to three unpleasant men who came to speak to the children. After their sour questioning, they took their leave with the remark, "See that you decide to tell that secret of yours. If you don't, the administrator has every intention of taking your lives!"

There are terribly sinister undertones here. It would be no surprise to discover that these three men had no acquaintance whatsoever with the Arturo Santos. From what we have seen of the mayor, it is certainly doubtful that he ever seriously considered killing the children. This is the devil at work in malicious minds. The horror is that they should say this to the children. The evil here would seem to be more culpable than Santos, who made exaggerated threats that the children believed but he himself didn't. It was a foolish, irresponsible hoax, but a hoax for all that. These men, it seems, actually believed their own fabrication. If that is true, then their hearts were blacker than the administrator's and — this is the real horror — there were probably thousands more with identical malice snooping around the Fatima periphery as that summer moved toward the promised climax. It took the angels and the faith of the people to keep them from having their way.

When these three "gentlemen" had made their ominous threat, Jacinta, "her face lighting up with a joy she made no effort to hide," said, "How wonderful! I so love Our Lord and Our Lady, and this way we'll be seeing them soon!" It would have been worth triple the price of an opera ticket to have been there and studied the faces of the three in the wake of that short and splendid declaration.

On September 13, as the apparition hour approached, Francisco and Jacinta set out for the Cova with Lucia. The roads were packed with people. Everyone wanted to see the children and speak to them. Importunate people struggled to break through the crowd. Those who managed to reach the seers threw themselves on their knees, begging the three to place petitions before Our Lady. Others shouted from a distance, "For the love of God, ask Our Lady to cure my son who is a cripple!" Or ". . . to cure mine who is blind!" Or ". . . to cure mine who is deaf!"

It was Thursday, September 13, 1917.

> Lady: Continue to pray the Rosary in order to obtain the end of the war. In October Our Lord will come, as well as Our Lady of Sorrows and Our Lady of Mount Carmel. St. Joseph will appear with the Child Jesus to bless the world. God is pleased with your sacrifices. He does not want you to sleep with the rope on, but only to wear it during the daytime.
>
> Lucia: I was told to ask you many things, the cure of some sick people, of a deaf-mute . . .
>
> Lady: Yes, I will cure some, but not others. In October I will perform a miracle so that all may believe.

This is the encounter as recorded in the "Memoirs," but if we look to the early interrogations and depositions, we find that further exchanges passed between the Lady and Lucia. However, let us attend first to the words Lucia wants to draw to our attention:

"Continue to pray the Rosary in order to obtain the end of the war."

If the Great War, hungry as it was for bodies and thirsty for blood, occupied a large part of the mind of the people, it was no less the concern of heaven, which longed for the souls of the combatants and the peace of their families. The Lady, without any preamble at all, without even a formal greeting if the "Memoir" is to be taken as a definitive text, comes straight to the point.

She knows the horror and devastation the war is causing, and she knows how it can be stopped. The world is too swollen with its own complications to think that she speaks any more than trite pieties — but the children listen. Continue to pray the Rosary, for very few others will. They lament the grip that evil has on the world, but are too dazzled by its darkness to see they are the cause of it. Stretch out your arms and be Moses for the end of these battles. Continue to pray the Rosary.

"In October Our Lord will come, as well as Our Lady of Sorrows and Our Lady of Mount Carmel. St. Joseph will appear with the Child Jesus to bless the world."

In light of what the Lady had said in August concerning these heavenly appearances, the promise now can mean one of two things. What had been in the subjunctive the month before was now a statement of definite promise. It is curious, though, to note the use of the word "come." "Would have come" (*havia de vir*) is now plain future indicative (*virá*). (The word "appear," as in the clause "St. Joseph will appear," is not used in the Portuguese — *virá* is the only verb in the sentence.) The word "come" implies that the person concerned was somewhere else and made a journey to arrive at the place at which the speaker is speaking. "Appear," in this context, suggests being seen in another dimension or in a recorded form, such as by laser or on film; being visible without any physical effort. "Come" is concrete, a personal visitation. "Appear" is a representation. Ghosts appear. Friends come.

This could be interpreted as meaning that Our Lord, the various personas of Our Lady, and St. Joseph with the Child were simply scheduled to *appear* before the August abduction; but now that the enemy has stolen a move, they themselves are actually going to *come*.

When the October event came, Our Lord, with St. Joseph and the Child, gave a blessing. Lucia doesn't tell us whether or not Our Lady in white with the blue veil, or Our Lady of Sorrows, or Our Lady of Mount Carmel also gave a blessing.

"God is pleased with your sacrifices."

In May, the children had agreed to offer themselves to God and to bear all the sufferings He would send. In July, the Lady asked them to sacrifice themselves for sinners. She used the same words in August. Compliantly they had been sharing their lunches, thirsting, binding their bodies with rope and such. Now, with a courtesy truly regal, she encouraged them, with an acknowledgment greater than which there could not be.

"God is pleased with your sacrifices."

Few mortals have had that sort of assurance direct from the inner sanctum of heaven — a sort of celestial knighthood. And it is followed by a manifestation of the attentive kindliness and exquisite consideration of the Almighty.

"He does not want you to sleep with the rope on, but only to wear it during the daytime."

The deposition Lucia gave to Father Ferriera on September 15 had more to say. In the following exchange, even in those passages that are more or less the same as above, notice how the wording opens the way to wider interpretations.

Lucia: What is it that your ladyship wants? [There is the usual greeting, but no "want of me" this time. Then she gives five immediate intentions to pray the Rosary for.]

> Lady: I want you always to continue praying the Rosary to Our Lady of the Rosary: that she might assuage the intensity of the war and that it might come to an end, that on the last day — meaning the last day of her visitations — that St. Joseph will come to give peace to the world and that Our Lord will come to give a blessing to the people, and that you, too, will come here on the 13th of October.

The armistice wasn't until November 11, 1918. The peace treaty was signed at Versailles on June 28, 1919.

Note that there was no guarantee that the children themselves would make it to the Cova for the October apparition. The forces of evil had been stirred to a pitch by these manifestations of the divine, and if they could find a way to prevent the promised miracle, they would. Only prayer could prevent them, urgent prayer.

> Lucia: That little deaf and dumb girl is here. If only your ladyship would cure her.
> Lady: **Within a year she will find that she is getting better.**
> Lucia: I have here many petitions, some for conversions and some for cures.
> Lady: **I will cure some, others no, because Our Lord doesn't trust them.**

Here is another of the Lady's straightforward statements, which stings us to attention: "Our Lord doesn't trust them." What a devastating indictment!

Lucia: The people would very much like a chapel here.

Lady: With half the money collected so far make the litters and take them to the Lady of the Rosary; the other half will help towards the chapel.

Then Lucia offered the Lady two letters and a bottle of scented water someone had asked be presented to her.

Lucia: They gave me these, if your ladyship would like them.

Lady: This is not needed in heaven.

This response could also be translated as "This would be out of place in heaven." I wonder how Our Lady, who is the Mother of Truth and could only express herself in a way conformable with that truth, said it. With kindness, and maybe a tinge of humor. But with apologies for refusing a gift? No! Lucia was a child, used to obeying adults even though doing so might have embarrassed her. But one wonders at the level of thinking of the person who reckoned that the Queen of Heaven might esteem such a gift. As for the two letters, we are told no more about them.

CHAPTER EIGHTEEN

The month between the September and October apparitions saw such an upheaval in the Fatima parish that it must have seemed to the parishioners that the old way of life had gone forever. In many respects, they were right. An uninhabited dip of land in their midst was suddenly a vast and busy amphitheater. Every day, and indeed throughout many a night, enough people swarmed over it to constitute a city, albeit a city without infrastructure. There wasn't even a building to be seen in any direction, except perhaps, from the high point to the east, the steeple of the Fatima parish church.

As October 13 drew nearer, more and more people arrived from all over Portugal: by foot, donkey, horseback, carriage, bicycle and motorcar. There were no signs indicating the direction, no information center when they arrived, no accommodations (not even a stable), yet they were drawn there by a questing faith and a hunger for the divine. Once in the Cova, they knelt on the dry, stony earth — there had been no rain all summer — in front of a tree that had been stripped of its branches, and they prayed the Rosary.

During these weeks, Maria Carreira set up a table during the day where people could leave the donations they insisted on making. That gifts should be made at all seems a little curious, because nobody solicited money. The seers themselves, would not touch it, nor would their parents or the parish priest. Maria Carreira didn't want the responsibility either. As we have seen, the Lady said it was to be used for a statue "float" and for children's outfits, but an awful lot more had accumulated than would be needed for these articles.

The building of a chapel had not yet been organized, so there was nothing for Maria to do but to accept the money and keep it at her home in Moita, just up the hill to the north. Between the September and October apparitions, Maria also arranged for a simple scaffold of wooden beams to be erected over the apparition site to mark the spot, because the holm oak sapling was now no more than a dying stick in the ground. A lantern was hung from a crossbeam as a beacon for those who came after dark to pray and sometimes even to spend the night.

One important aspect of this scene that we can easily overlook in our age of instant media coverage is that the thousands making their way to Fatima had learned of it solely by word of mouth. Some of this oral communication might have been by telephone between the cities, but this was before television, even before the wireless. There was virtually no public transportation. The nearest railway station, Chão de Maçãs, (literally "Floor of Apples," the name was changed to "Fatima" in the 1920s) was some ten miles away. There were coaches and carriages between the main centers, but none passed anywhere near the Fatima parish. There was no prospect of accommodation, no restaurants and no bathroom facilities.

Normally there was no reason for a stranger to go there, yet wave after wave of people, from all directions — seventy thousand is the accepted number for the October apparitions — came almost blindly, urged by a compulsion we can barely guess at. That in itself was miracle enough.

The buildup to October 13 was harrowing for just about everyone in Aljustrel. The seers' confidence in the Lady's promise to perform a miracle that month was unshaken. Ti Marto, too, kept a calm born of credence, but most of Aljustrel and the outlying villages and towns were confused and apprehensive. That was the case because, apart from fearing that there would be no miracle and the pilgrims might stampede, a rumor had spread that "they" were going to plant bombs in the Cova and at the seers' houses. A disastrous "war to end wars" was being waged even as they spoke, and "they" were talking of bombs to restore peace. Surely there was a lesson here, but without prayer such lessons are never learned.

Who "they" were is not specified, but the government agents or the Freemasons would have been the faceless perpetrators in the minds of the villagers. The devil was nervous, and his nervousness was transmitting itself to the people in the same measure as their lack of faith invited. Lucia's mother was particularly harassed. The neighbors were blaming her in advance for the havoc the bombs would cause. (As already observed, this admirable woman's "lack of faith" in the apparitions seems to have been a design of heaven — the grace to forego grace, so to speak.) As for the children, all they wanted was the peace and privacy to make sacrifices. They were learning to adjust to the great paradox, the primary lesson every contemplative must learn, that the deprivation of these faculties is the greatest sacrifice of all.

A few days before October 13, the parish priest of Porto do Mós, Father Manuel Carreira Poças, and one of his parishioners came to the Marto home to try to make the children deny what they had said. They questioned Francisco, but without result. They wanted to talk to the girls, but they had gone to Boleiros with a donkey to get some lime. When they returned, Father Poças attacked Lucia, saying, "Look here, child, you're just going to tell me that all this is stuff and nonsense and if you don't I will say so myself and tell everyone else, too. People believe me and, besides, they are going to the Cova to destroy everything and you won't escape either."

Lucia didn't say a word. Ti Marto turned to the visiting priest and told him, "Well, then, better telegraph the news everywhere."

"Yes," the cleric replied, "that's just what we ought to do and then nobody will come here on the 13th. It would be the best thing that could happen."

Jacinta, disturbed at the anger shown by the priest, left the room. Then the parishioner who had accompanied Father Poças said furiously, "This is nothing less than witchcraft. The same thing happened with a servant of mine some time ago and when she got the idea into her head nothing on earth could rid her of it!"

Later they found the youngest seer on the doorstep playing with a child about her own age. "Listen, Jacinta," Father Poças tried again. "Haven't you anything to say? You know Lucia has told us everything and now we know that it's all a lie."

The little girl was unimpressed. "Lucia never said that!" He insisted that she had, but Jacinta repeated that Lucia had said nothing. Others who were watching the exchange were surprised at Jacinta's firmness. The parishioner then pulled a coin out of his pocket and tried to give it to Jacinta. She ignored the offer and her father told the man that he mustn't do that. When they were leaving, Father Poças turned to Ti Marto and said, "Congratulations, you have played your part well!"

"Well or ill, that's my way," Ti Marto answered. "You haven't succeeded in making the children deny their story, but even if you had I should still believe in them!"

This is a perfect little vignette. Lucia never said anything superfluous. She hadn't actually been asked a question, so she said nothing at all. Francisco in the wings, the contemplative, the hermit, remained silent and unconcerned. Presumably he was questioned, but there was no one present to report his answers. The only comment we get (the incident was related by Ti Marto) is "without result."

Jacinta had the star quality. The tendency she had a couple of years before to be stubborn and willful at games has been turned by grace to pure gold. She was still willful, but the Will was heaven's; she was still stubborn, but the stubbornness was against sin, untruth, deception. The priest was lying. He was treating her like a seven-year-old. She *was* a seven-year-old. She was playing with another seven-year-old because that's what seven-year-olds do. She knew the priest was lying, but she didn't tell him so. She contradicted him, but obliquely. She was not angry. She was not contemptuous. She didn't sulk because her intelligence was being belittled. She was supremely, gloriously willful and continued playing with her seven-year-old friend. Her world had not altered one jot.

The rain had held off all summer, and the people of the plateau had almost forgotten what it felt like. But on the night before October 13, and all morning of that day, the great stadium of the sky was crammed to capacity with rain clouds, which opened up together and turned the dust and baked clay of the Cova into a basin of mud. This deluge, however, didn't discourage the pilgrims who converged on the parish from every direction. They came by every mode of transportation though most were walking; many, in penitential spirit, in bare feet carrying the necessities for the journey on their backs or their heads. Not since the Israelites passed over the mud on the bed of the Red Sea, with the walls of water banked up beside them, had such vast numbers moved through water, united in faith in an undisclosed eventuality.

The Marto home was jammed full of people — strangers for the most part. They had brought the mud of the streets in with them and were plastering the floors and the furniture with it. A lady from a nearby village had made white and blue garments and floral coronets for the girls. They refused to wear the clothes, but it would seem from the photo with the chauffeur that Jacinta wore her veil and crown. Whether there was similar attire for Francisco no one recorded, but it seems doubtful the boy would have noticed what he wore. It would have been all the same to him if they'd put him in a burnoose or a poncho. He himself was incidental here. Nothing material could distract from the Lady. Furthermore, because this was the final apparition, he probably thought it very likely that today he and Jacinta would be taken to heaven. It didn't matter what clothes they wore. It wasn't their bodies that were going to heaven. Their bodies and their clothes might be blown up by the bomb. It was themselves, their souls, that would sail into that sublime harbor, their souls as the Lady had shown them in "the light from her hands."

And no matter how they were dressed, the seers would have been as soaked as everyone else by the time they reached the Cova.

Ti Marto and the children maintained an equilibrium among all the commotion and dissension that afflicted their family, neighbors and strangers. The threat of the bomb, now scheduled to explode alongside the children at the apparition site the moment they went into ecstasy, fired speculation — varied and contrary, whispered and trumpeted. Another great fear was that the

The chauffeur—possibly the Baron Alvaiazere's—posing with Jacinta after the October apparition.

people, placid pilgrims now, might turn into an infuriated mob, stampeding and wrecking the village, if no miracle occurred.

By the time the family left the house, the rain was falling so heavily and the crowds were so dense that Francisco, Jacinta and their parents could barely see the road. As they made their way slowly toward the Cova, people were kneeling in the mud shouting petitions to be delivered to the Lady. Others were falling over each other to attract the children's attention or stretching out just to touch them. This was the first time that Ti Marto and Olympia had accompanied their children to the Cova.

Lucia and her parents also joined the procession: Antonio held her hand, and Maria, thinking that her daughter might be killed, let her maternal love override her disbelief.

As they approached the Cova, the multitude was so tightly packed around the seers that there was a fear that the little ones might be trampled to death. Antonio was the only parent of any size, but even he wasn't big. Ti Marto was decidedly small and both mothers were tiny. The children were even tinier. Suddenly, a burly fellow among the throng, a chauffeur in his uniform, swooped Jacinta up in his arms and shouted, "Make way for the children who saw Our Lady!" This twentieth-century Christopher forged a path to the apparition site. Ti Marto, just behind him, remembered Jacinta calling out to those around, "Don't push my father, don't hurt him."

(The photograph on page 193 shows a man in a chauffeur's outfit holding Jacinta in his left arm. She has her right arm around his neck and is huddled close to him. Her left hand is held up close to her chin. She wears a gingham blouse and dark skirt. The white veil and floral tiara are still on her head (unless of course these were simply put on her head for the photograph). An unconscionable and undetected pilgrim bearing scissors had snipped off Lucia's plaits at some point during the afternoon, so a coronet on Jacinta's head might be counted as a security item after that. There are about twenty people

standing around the man and child, none of them recogniz-
ably family. There is a mere handful of people in a vacant
space in the background. Nobody appears to be moving forward toward a common goal; indeed the picture looks posed,
though not self-consciously. It is not raining. There is no suggestion that the picture is a fake but it certainly wasn't taken
in that torrential downpour before the apparitions with seventy thousand people milling about. However, Lucia says that
she, Francisco and Jacinta were around the Cova that afternoon for a long time after the apparitions. Many people wanted
to see and speak with them and it's quite probable that Jacinta
was asked to pose with the chauffeur after most of the people
had moved on. She's clearly not afraid of the man; indeed,
she appears to have developed a certain affection for him.)

When Jacinta was set down at the site, the pressure of people
was so great the little girl began to cry until Lucia and Francisco
arrived. Then a man started to wield a stick about in all directions. At first this was thought to be a provocation to disorder
but, in fact, he was clearing the area. Soon the crowds had stepped
back, and the seers had their own space in front of the cairn that
enclosed the bare holm oak trunk, now decorated with ribbons
and protected with palm fronds.

As midday by the sun approached, Lucia — moved, she says,
by an interior impulse — told the people to shut their umbrellas
and to say the Rosary. And the seventy thousand obeyed her.

A priest who had been at the site all night checked his watch
and said, "Look! It's midday now. Our Lady doesn't lie, eh! Well,
well!" Then after a few more minutes, he noted, "It's past midday. You see, it's all a delusion! Run along now, all of you!" and
he began to shove the three children.

The priest's action in this incident, related by Father Formigão,
is embarrassing. As many people as it takes to constitute a city were
present. They were focused on Lucia, Francisco and Jacinta and

this man was shunting them off with a "run along now," as if the ingenuous charms of the young at play were beginning to wear thin.

Lucia, who was almost in tears, sensibly told him that others might do as they wished. She would stay where she was because the Lady had said she would come at the other times and she would come now, too. Then, suddenly, and with urgent gravity, the child called out, "Francisco, Jacinta, kneel down. Our Lady is coming. I saw the lightning!"

CHAPTER NINETEEN

Pilgrims at the apparition site on October 13, 1917.

It was Thursday, October 13, 1917.

Lucia: What do you want of me?

Lady: I want to tell you that a chapel is to be built here in my honor. I am the Lady of the Rosary. Continue always to pray the Rosary every day. The war is going to end, and the soldiers will soon return to their homes.

> Lucia: I have many things to ask you: the cure of some
> sick persons, the conversion of sinners, and other
> things . . .
> Lady: **Some yes, but not others. They must amend
> their lives and ask forgiveness for their sins.
> Do not offend the Lord our God any more,
> because He is already so much offended.**

This conversation is even shorter than that of the previous
month, but like all exchanges it contains abundant treasures for
those with the patience and facility to mine for them.

Lucia offers her customary greeting, which is at the same time
a prayer and an act of submission. The Lady answers it fully by
repeating part of the question. This is a nuance that suggests a
degree of intimacy; it is a signal that there is full comity between
them, that the majestic Queen of Heaven is not overawing illiterate peasant children. Indeed it could be read as if there was a
benign and dignified conspiracy between them.

Already the people had expressed a desire for a chapel,
and the Lady had endorsed that when she instructed the children that half the money collected could go toward its construction. Now, however, she is formally giving the idea her
permission and offering herself as its patron under the name
of the persona she had promised to reveal to her young seers
on this day. And this revelation she makes in a singularly
modest way, linking it to the chapel's name rather than making a grand announcement of it. (No "I am the Lady of the
Rosary. Seek me out and speak to me in your heart every day.")
Immediately she makes a promise that the war will end, almost as if it shouldn't. On this one occasion she will relent,
but people must amend their lives and seek forgiveness for
sin.

Then, as Lucia wrote, the Lady looked very sad as she said:

"Do not offend the Lord our God any more, because He is already so much offended."

Elsewhere in the "Memoirs," Lucia comments on this sentence: "How loving a complaint, how tender a request! Who will grant me to make it echo through the whole world, so that all the children of our Mother in heaven may hear the sound of her voice?"

Our Lady then began to ascend toward the east. But while doing so she opened her hands — as she had done in the first three apparitions — and made them reflect on the sun. As she moved back to heaven, the reflection of her own light continued to be projected onto the sun itself.

At this point Lucia cried out, "Look at the sun!" She gives no account of the famous "Miracle of the Sun," because she, like Francisco and Jacinta, was absorbed with the images beside the sun rather than with the sun itself. As no one person's experience of the miracle seems to have been the same as another's, perhaps we can assume that for the children, the sun's activity was very secondary to the appearances alongside it. (Francisco and Jacinta's brother João, in stark contrast, was at home hiding under a bed in fear of the lynching that he imagined was to come when there was no miracle to satisfy the people.)

Lucia reported that as Our Lady disappeared into the immense distance of the firmament, and the assembled seventy thousand watched the solar marvels, she and Francisco and Jacinta saw — next to the sun — St. Joseph with the Child Jesus and Our Lady robed in white with a blue mantle. St. Joseph and the Child Jesus appeared to bless the world, tracing the Sign of the Cross with their hands. A little later, when this apparition disappeared, the children saw Our Lord and Our Lady of Sorrows. Our Lord appeared to bless the world in the same manner as St. Joseph. This apparition also vanished, and then Lucia alone saw Our Lady once more, this time as Our Lady of Mount Carmel.

Lucia said that the main purpose of "the light from the Lady's hands" in June was to infuse within the three children a special knowledge of and love for the Immaculate Heart of Mary. She explained that on the other two occasions — May and July — it was to immerse them in the things of God and the mysteries of the Most Holy Trinity. So how, one wonders, would she categorize this day's, when the Lady opened her hands and made them reflect on the sun, and as she ascended, the reflection of her own light continued to be projected onto the sun itself?

Lucia later confided that an interior impulse influenced her to cry out "Look at the sun." At the time, she was not even aware of the presence of the crowds. So maybe we can hazard that this fourth manifestation of "the light from her hands" was to directly involve us, the people. It was to demonstrate the power God has given her, a power that she yearns to use for our own good, to nurture us in the fulfilling of the purpose of our creation in the womb and our re-creation in the waters of baptism: assimilation into the very being of her Son, the God-Man.

We say that people saw the sun "dance" that day. Lucia said she saw it spinning around. Francisco and Jacinta saw the cartwheeling and color-changing of the sun, though they don't refer to its apparent falling to Earth, a phenomenon that impressed — indeed terrified — the crowds. The three children saw various tableaux in the sky, but the Marto children didn't see Our Lady of Mount Carmel — whom Lucia innocently referred to as "the Lady of the Two Cards," by which she meant the scapular.

Now, this disparity of what was seen, both among the children themselves, and between the children and the seventy thousand pilgrims, and the fact that the rest of the world continued unaware of any irregularity in the solar system, suggests that the sun did not, in reality, move.

Nor can we suppose mass hypnosis. The Lady promised a miracle, not a display of vaudeville legerdemain, no matter on how grand a scale. What the people probably saw was just what Lucia saw: the reflection of the Lady's own light projected on the sun itself. This was a wonder of far nobler significance, a prodigy far more worthy of heaven than the old "eye in the sky" doing a spirited jig around the stratosphere.

If there is any substance in this argument, then there's another point that might be tentatively offered for consideration. Lucia said that in May the light's "rays penetrated our hearts and the inmost depths of our souls, making us see ourselves in God, Who was that light." This is something beyond our unaided comprehension. But if the same held true of each manifestation of "the light from her hands"—if that light was God—then what the pilgrims saw that Saturday was in some ineffable way, which is a mystery to us on this side of eternity, a reflection of God.

Be that as it may, what is known as the "Miracle of the Sun" in the Cova da Iria is very well-documented, and eyewitness accounts can be found in any number of books. Even so, no two accounts concur exactly. With such a phenomenon this is not surprising; astonishment, fear, exaltation and plain old imagination must have all played conspicuous roles in both the observing and in the retelling. At the same time, the suspicion that every individual saw something different is inescapable. The template was the same, but each experience of it was unique. It's the same with prayer. No two people have the same approach to God in prayer, or the same experience as a response. There will be as many explanations for the October 13 phenomenon as there are people.

Of the many published impressions, I offer only one here. Although disarmingly simple, it summarizes what all the witnesses said. It was made by Mabel Norton, a young Englishwoman then in service in Portugal. At the time she was not a Catholic, though she later converted and became a staunch Fatima champion.

Suddenly the rain stopped and the sun broke through, casting its rays on the earth. It seemed to be falling on that vast crowd of people and it spun like a firewheel, taking on all the colors of the rainbow. We ourselves took on those colors, with our clothes and even the earth itself. One heard cries and saw many people in tears. Deeply impressed, I said to myself: "My God, how great is your power!"

CHAPTER TWENTY

After the September apparitions, Lucia told Francisco that the Lady had promised they would see Jesus again in October. Francisco was lost in joy. Lucia says that he exclaimed, "Oh, how good He is!" In the young boy's mind, the distinguishing characteristic of Christ was goodness. With the Lady it was beauty, which is the reflection of that goodness. Goodness is the attribute of God that could be said to encompass all His attributes. Christ himself said, "No one is good but God alone." So Francisco was, in the manner of toddlers, affirming the divinity of Jesus with this exclamation of wonder at His goodness.

Francisco then added, "I've only seen him twice, and I love Him so much!" The "twice" was during the June and July apparitions, when the seers were enraptured in "the light from her hands." During September he said several times, "Are there many days left till the 13th? I'm longing for that day to come, because then I will see Our Lord again." This simple expression of longing shows that the nine-year-old had arrived at the summit of human knowledge. To reach that height is not the same as knowing everything a human is capable of knowing. It is stepping through the clouds and onto the summit, the importance of human knowledge beneath the feet, and the sun of God illuminating the boundless and unimpeded territory of the unknown. Simplicity was Francisco's license, faith his transportation, and prayer his fuel. He traveled light. Once the summit was reached, love took over from human learning.

"But listen!" Francisco said, feeling the pain of the lover. "Will He still be sad? I'm so sorry to see Him sad like that! I offer Him all the sacrifices I can think of. Sometimes I don't even run away from all those people, just in order to make sacrifices." Being beyond the importance of human knowledge isn't tantamount to being beyond the knowledge of humans, or beyond human experience. If anything, human sensitivity is maximized. Francisco had been above the clouds, and his heart and soul lived there, but his body spent most of its time back in the valley below the clouds, with all the mists, ailments and shortcomings that are humanity's lot east of Eden. Christ had lived there, too, and was sharing his pain with Francisco.

After October's events, the boy told Lucia, "I loved seeing Our Lord, but I loved still more seeing Him in that light where we were with Him as well." So, if I'm reading this correctly, the October apparitions were splendid and satisfying in a number of ways: The seers learned that the particular persona of their heavenly visitor was Our Lady of the Rosary, and the people got their miracle. But, even so, it was something of an anti-climax for the seers. The appearance of the adult Jesus Himself (was there any significance in His being visible only from the waist up?), St. Joseph with the Christ Child, Mary as the Mother of Sorrows and as Our Lady of Mount Carmel — though privileges beyond expectation — didn't have the personal, absolute intimacy of that encounter when they were drawn up into "the light from her hands." The various aspects of Jesus, Mary and Joseph — the protagonists of the mysteries of the Rosary — as they appeared on either side of the sun that Thursday midday were royalty on the balcony. But for Francisco, his sister and their cousin, who had been inside the palace and who had been kissed by the King, these displays of the ones they loved blessing the world only whetted their appetites, unharnessed their hearts.

Francisco went on to say, "It's not long now, and Our Lord will take me up close to Him, and then I can look at Him forever." This is proof that the boy had reached the summit, when a sentence spoken to a peer in spontaneous exchange is, at the same time, a perfect prayer.

"It's not long now...." We must mark that phrase. Death for Francisco and Jacinta is imminent. The Lady of the Rosary would not appear in the Cova anymore. She had promised to come and take them. It should have been yesterday. It might be today. It could still be a little while, but it would be soon. The Marto children showed no particular fear of the act of vacating the body, because they weren't exactly going into the unknown.

Being a seer has responsibilities, some crushingly heavy, which is why children are usually chosen. They aren't yet carrying much baggage of their own. Being a seer doesn't guarantee personal sanctity; indeed, some may have merited damnation. But for those who allow the grace they receive to form their spiritual perceptions, their foretaste of heaven must do much to temper the mystery of death. One knocks on a door with confidence when one personally knows the master and mistress of the house, has dined with them, and it is they who have issued the invitation.

The message of Fatima, in fact, is just such an invitation. We have already dined on the Eucharist, and we are expected. There is no need even to knock. The mistress is so eager for us to join them that, along with the invitation, she has sent the key: the Rosary.

Every action of the two children was tempered with the knowledge that they were shortly to die. With hindsight we can be more specific. Francisco was to live for 538 days longer and Jacinta another 861. But it was to be a whole year before they both fell ill.

———

The completion of the cycle of the apparitions didn't mean an end to interest in Fatima or in the seers. On the contrary, the procession of people, each with a list of questions for the children, each believing that he or she had the right to be interrogator and judge of the undertakings, grew longer. The word from seventy thousand returning to their homes spread the news to every town and village in the land. For those inclined to discredit the testimony of neighbors or those who considered their own intelligence above the mean level, the leading Lisbon newspaper (*O Secula*) carried extensive and objective coverage of the event October 15-19, including many photographs. The articles were written by a well-respected journalist, Avelino de Almeida, who, on the day of the October apparition, published an article deriding the superstition that could lead people to what he saw then as an elaborate piece of gimmickry. In the words of the governor of Santarem, "Fatima is a stage of reaction in the country, which seeks a support point as a base for its resistance."

The Martos, as we have seen, sold their flocks and kept Francisco and Jacinta at home so that they would be available to speak with those who stopped by. It had become impossible to constantly fetch them home from the pastures. Of course, many of the questioners would have been genuine, or at least open to accepting the children's claim as true. That wouldn't have made the grilling any easier. The piety of many of these folk could have been suffocating. Conversely, a number could have set themselves up as fingers of God to warn the seers of the dire consequences to themselves if they misinterpreted the proclamations of heaven, and so forth. The questions of each inquisitor often contained the answers he wanted to hear, along with reams of egocentric twaddle. The questioning must have been, in its way, a bizarre realization of the threat of Arturo Santos, a slow boiling in the oil of inquisitive egos.

The seers would escape whenever possible. The cave hollowed out of the rock, the place of the first angelic apparition, was a favorite refuge. Lucia, still shepherding the dos Santos sheep, would join them there when possible. They would say the Rosary together and recite the angel's prayer. Over and over, they would discuss and savor the things the Lady had said during the apparitions, encouraging each other in prayer and sacrifices, deepening their own perceptions of those things close to the heart of the Lady. They never mentioned to anyone what had been revealed to them concerning the Immaculate Heart — there would be no public word of this mystery until Lucia wrote of it under obedience, and even that wasn't published until 1942. But they spoke of it among themselves and how she would come again to ask for the conversion of Russia. They had no idea when this would be. It wasn't even explicit to whom she would come: to all of them, only to Lucia if the others had been taken to heaven, or to someone else altogether. In any case, they didn't know what Russia was. Lucia later told how they thought it was the name of a wicked woman.

The "First Saturday Communion of Reparation" was frustrating for Jacinta, who lamented, "I'm so grieved to be unable to receive Communion in reparation for the sins committed against the Immaculate Heart of Mary." Lucia, as we know, had made her First Communion at the age of six, an exception even at that time, which was shortly after Pius X's *Quam Singulari*. But as yet, neither Francisco nor Jacinta had received first Communion at the parish. They had been given the Precious Blood from the hands of the angel, but this didn't entitle them to come forward in the church. Francisco received the Blessed Sacrament on only one occasion: the day before he died. Jacinta received Holy Communion a number of times in Lisbon during the weeks leading up to her death.

The inquisitors who gave the seers the most trouble were priests. These clerics — sainted, but tactless — clearly felt they had a vested interest in the goings-on, whether these goings-on were genuine or products of delusion. Most set themselves up as attackers and attacked, prosecutors and defendants, and the children suffered. Lucia noted, "Whenever we found ourselves in the presence of a priest, we prepared to offer to God one of our greatest sacrifices. They would put us through the most rigorous of examinations, and then return to question us all over again." Even Father Ferreira complained sternly of the children's avoidance of priests.

The seers did except several from the category of clerical bogeyman. Two of these have causes for canonization being considered in Rome. One was Father Formigão, whom the children soon came to trust and appreciate. It's largely due to his disciplined approach to the apparitions — his detailed record of his interviews with the seers and published investigations — that scholars are able to reconstruct the early history of Fatima. One can't help but sense that he was heaven's appointed one for this task. His subsequent life was entirely devoted to Fatima. As early as 1926, he founded the Congregation of Sisters of Reparation of Our Lady of Sorrows of Fatima. These are the religious who, among other duties, maintain the twenty-four-hour vigil of adoration before the Blessed Sacrament chapel at the Fatima shrine. Father Formigão died in 1958.

The other favorite was Jesuit Father Francisco Cruz (1859–1948), who taught the children a litany of short prayers. They are the sweet, spontaneous expressions of affection that lovers delight in whispering and those who are beloved can never hear enough of. Even in 1917 Father Cruz was well-known in Portugal for his piety and was always referred to as "the saintly Father Cruz." By one of those accidents devised in heaven, it was this same priest who was present when the six-year-old Lucia was told by the parish priest that, although she knew her catechism, she was too young to receive her first Holy Communion. The holy Jesuit intervened. He asked that she be allowed and said he himself would take responsibility. She must have recognized him when he came to Fatima after the apparitions and told Francisco and Jacinta of his role.

On a visit to Aljustrel after the October apparition, Father Cruz questioned the children and asked them to show him the place where Our Lady appeared. Lucia remembered that the priest rode a donkey so tiny that his feet almost touched the ground. "O my Jesus, I love you!" he taught them as they walked on either side of his animal, and "Sweet Heart of Mary, be my salvation!" Jacinta adopted these and repeated them ever after. Those who have no feeling for God, or those who cannot understand why he is not Superman writ large, will wince with embarrassment at the naiveté of these religious utterances. But for those who know, those who love like this seven-, nine- and ten-year-old, each endearment has a force more powerful than any atomic bomb. Father Cruz' litany, if employed to its full capacity, could subdue the world and lead humanity to that Paradise more splendid than the one from which Adam was evicted.

Another time when clergymen gave the children more than they took was when two nameless priests (mentioned in chapter twelve) told them about the Holy Father and of his great need for the faithful's prayers. These clerics were planting in fertile soil. Even so, they made an enormous impression because, from that time on, the children never offered a prayer or sacrifice that didn't embrace the office, person and intentions of the Holy Father. As the Fatima snowball grew, Father Ferreira told Lucia's mother that her daughter might have to go to Rome to be "questioned," as he put it, by the pope. Lucia, quite unconscious of any cachet international travel might give her, clapped her hands with delight at the prospect of actually seeing Christ's vicar on earth. Francisco and Jacinta were sad; but even the very deprivation of an encounter with the Holy Father became a gift of great value that they could offer as a sacrifice for him.

Father Jose Ferreira de Lacerda also interviewed the children shortly after the October apparition. He had just returned from the front, where he had been serving as a volunteer chaplain and founded a weekly magazine in Leiria called O Mensageiro. He went to Aljustrel to interview the children, but found a very cool reception from Olympia Marto. Later, a neighbor explained to him that two days previously "the devil in the form of a man," the arsonist of the church in Alcanena, had been there to question the children and threaten them. This was the reason for the mother's unwillingness to extend the customary hospitality.

Father de Lacerda got his interview two days later. It appeared in his magazine over four weekly issues in November 1917 and is a rich source of material. On the matter of the pressure of interviews, he writes that Olympia:

> ...had every reason for the coolness she had shown on first meeting me. There had been so many people appearing in Aljustrel to hear the three children that they no longer knew what to answer. Some of these people had gone there just to force contradictory answers out of the children.

The reference to "the devil in the form of a man" proved to be not quite as literal as it appears. The neighbor was referring to one of a group of people from Santarem, where an infuriated Satan was injecting venom into willing Republican breasts. "The arsonist of the church at Alcanena" is a reference to the burning of the church in that town, which is about ten miles from Fatima on the Lisbon side of the Candeeiros range of hills. The church was closed by the governor under the 1911 Act of Separation, but was scheduled to reopen on April 15, 1915. At two in the morning on the 14th, it was set on fire and burned to the ground. Six suspects were arrested. Three days later Father Ferreira lodged a protest "against the vandalism of the enemies of religion who are intent on destroying our temples, setting them on fire as they have done these past days to the church of Alcanena."

It was probably members of that same cadre who drove right up to the site of the apparitions at the Cova da Iria late October 23 or early October 24. They dismantled the arch and took it, along with the lanterns, altar, statue, candles and donation box. Before they left, they chopped down a sapling that they thought to be the tree of the apparitions and dragged it behind the car all the way to Santarem. They had the wrong bush, of course. The original was a dying, if not already dead, stick. Maybe it was providential that so many of the faithful had carted off souvenir leaves and twigs over the early months, so that the resting place for the feet of the Queen of Heaven didn't fall into the hands of these desecrators.

A day or two later, an exhibition featuring the stolen goods opened in Santarem. An admission fee was charged. When the perpetrators of this disgrace made a show of public spirit by offering the money collected to the Misericordia charity, it was pointedly refused. That evening the arch, lanterns, altar, statue and tree were paraded through the streets to the accompaniment of a blasphemous version of the Litany of Our Lady. This silly, evil activity can only be attributed to the fury of Satan losing souls. But, as the psalmist sings "they conceive evil, and are pregnant with mischief, and bring forth lies."

A backlash of indignation swept through the Portuguese people. Crowds made pilgrimages of reparation to the Cova, and the publicity that resulted triggered a sensational display of faith that the Republican authorities could only deal with by threatening violence under the guise of keeping order. It was either do that, or organize more silly, evil profanities. One of these was an invitation in the paper O Mundo for all liberal-minded people opposed to "Jesuitical inventions" to assemble outside the Fatima parish church after Sunday's Mass. They would "unmask the comedy of Fatima and its actors."

This symposium came to nothing, because the parish priest switched the venue for the Mass to the chapel at Ortiga. However, in case the children should be in danger, he arranged for them to go to a *quinta*, a large farmhouse in the area, where Mass was celebrated in a private chapel. Ti Marto's retelling of the excursion gives a miniature glimpse into the doings of Francisco and Jacinta during those days.

An hour before sunrise we set off for the Quinta, flee-ing from persecution like St. Joseph and the Holy Family. When we arrived the chapel was already chock-full of people. Lucia and Jacinta had their shawls over their arms and Francisco carried his cap in his hand. We asked if Mass had begun and were told that it was already the Offertory. At this moment the servant of the house arrived and took us into the chapel by way of the house, which led into a choir where the whole family was assembled. We heard Mass right by the altar.

When Mass was over we had something to eat and the servants showed us over the house, room by room. Such huge rooms, my word! Lucia amused us very much be-cause each time she went into one she said astonished, "Oh, what a barrack!" And the servants kept on saying, "Lucia, do you want to see another barrack?" And the "bar-racks" went on until we had seen the whole house.

Then Dom Pedro Caupers, their host, sent for three lambs and took the children's photographs with the lambs on their shoulders. After that we had something more to eat, and then Dom Pedro said to me, "Oh, Senhor Marto, will you stay here with Francisco because I have to go to Vargos and I have only room in the car for two little ones." So they went to the Quinta on the way to Torres Novas, while Francisco and I went for a long walk around the property. The others were away a long time, but they came back that day. We went home late and it was night when we arrived.

If those photographs came to light now, I wonder if they would show the children smiling as they carried the lambs on their shoul-ders. They are so somber in the pictures we have, but one can't believe that melancholy is representative, particularly in 1917. That year they could have spent every day smiling, because despite their sufferings, indeed in part because of their sufferings, the angels were pointing them out as the most blessed of living mortals.

CHAPTER TWENTY-ONE

One of the most dramatic events during this time after the October 13 apparitions was Francisco's encounter with the devil. Whenever the boy prayed or offered sacrifices, he preferred to go apart without warning and hide, even from his sister and cousin. They would search for him, calling out his name. He would answer from behind a wall or a clump of brambles, and there he would be on his knees, praying.

"Why didn't you tell us so that we could come and pray with you?"

"Because I prefer to pray alone."

This is not individualism asserting itself. It is the exact opposite: a soul so lost in the contemplation of God that contact with creatures only reminds it that it is an individual. The soul is not ashamed of being an individual, because if it wasn't it could not love or be loved. But in love that very individuality is exchanged for the beloved's — like rings, like vows, like blood — and the only place the individual wants to see itself is as a reflection in the lover's eyes.

Francisco was passive by nature. His attitude toward games ("You think you won? That's all right! I don't mind!"), his resigned acceptance when his gift from Nazere was stolen by another boy ("Let him have it! What does a handkerchief mean to me?"), and the like are among the records of events before the apparitions.

Grace built a cloister on these foundations, a sanctuary where an unloved God could find silent solace. Mary herself taught Francisco to pray. He couldn't hear her words, but it was the observed example of her own character, the type of person she showed herself to be — for she is a person; not a statue, but a person of flesh and blood, albeit glorified, transformed into light and exalted above all others. The Maid of Nazareth shaped Francisco's passivity after her own, and so brought it to perfection.

But we mustn't confuse passivity with inertia or speechless acquiescence. Any human characteristic carries in itself the potential for good or bad. Francisco's passivity could have developed into self-absorbed, world-weary nonchalance or worse, but it didn't. It became, when aligned with Christ's passivity, a shield, a weapon and an embrace wide enough to encompass God. (That passivity drove Him into the solitude of the desert, the solitude of the cross, the solitude of the Eucharist.)

It was this passivity of total commitment that brings Francisco to life for us — and, at the same time, hides him. He is like a firefly among the trees, a glowworm in a cave. He doesn't ask us to seek him out. We want to. His very elusiveness intrigues and draws us. When we catch the occasional glimpse of him, it is not because he wishes to show himself, but because he knows the way deeper into the forest of prayer, further along the unlit path into the cave of contemplation. If we promise to ignore him, he will be our guide.

Lucia tells us that Francisco was anything but fearful. He'd go anywhere in the dark alone at night, without the slightest hesitation. He played with lizards, and when he came across snakes he'd get them to twine themselves around a stick. He'd even pour sheep's milk into their holes for them to drink.

On day was different. While the girls played among the rocks, Francisco went off to be alone. After some time, they heard him shouting in distress. He was calling urgently to Our Lady to help him. The cries, electric with fear, echoed among the rocks and alerted the girls. They thought that maybe he had fallen and injured himself. At last they came upon him, trembling with fright, still on his knees, and so upset that he was unable to rise to his feet.

"What's wrong?" they asked. "What happened to you?"

In a voice half-smothered with fright, he replied, "It was one of those huge beasts that we saw in hell. He was right there, breathing out flames!"

Neither Lucia nor Jacinta could see anything, so they laughed and said, "You never want to think about hell, so as not to be afraid; and now you're the first one to be frightened!"

The fiends always seem to dance in protest at any exhibition of God's love for mortals. The degree of fury appears in some measure to be proportioned by heaven's benevolence. One effect of heaven's loving, though admonitory, presence in Fatima was that the hornets of hell were roused to apoplectic frenzy, bursting, on occasions, through the very membranes of time and space that separate us from their eternal dungeon.

In the meantime, as heaven and hell fought for the children's attention, the relentless questioning continued. Lucia said that by nightfall on the day of the last apparition, she was so exhausted by "the multitudes who wanted to see and observe the curious creatures" that she simply dropped down and fell asleep on the floor. In a telling aside that could apply equally to her cousins, she adds, "Thank God human respect and self-love were, at that time, still unknown to me. For that reason I was as much at ease with any person at all, as I was with my parents."

But such delightful naiveté wasn't short on self-protective cunning if dishonesty and rudeness weren't involved. The children would dive under beds or climb into trees and nest there silently, trusting to Providence and to the wide brims of the ladies' hats that they wouldn't be seen. No sooner had the danger passed, than they would be slithering down the trunks and racing off across the fields out of sight and hearing.

Jacinta developed her own approach to discouraging unwanted questions. She would often hang her head and fix her eyes on the ground and say nothing. She explained, "I always do that when I don't want to tell the truth and I don't want to tell a lie either, because lying is a sin."

Francisco, probably influenced by the success of Jacinta's ploy, adopted a similar tactic, but with a justification entirely his own. Lucia wanted to know, "When you are questioned why do you put your head down and not want to answer?" He explained, "Because I want you to answer, and Jacinta, too. I didn't hear anything. I can only say that I saw. Then, supposing I said something you didn't want me to say."

In her "Memoirs," Lucia exclaims, while reminiscing on Francisco: "What a fine priest he would have made!" She was undoubtedly right, but if priesthood hadn't been an option then he might have found success in the diplomatic service. His passivity might have been seen as exquisite tact, and he wouldn't have hesitated about saying "no" just because it didn't please.

One day a woman with a foul disease approached the seers. She started to weep and fell to her knees in front of Jacinta. Why the seven-year-old , we can't be sure, but I suspect it was because she was the youngest and smallest, and therefore mightn't be so repelled by the supplicant's odious ailment.

The woman implored the child to ask Our Lady to cure her. Jacinta was disturbed by this humiliating posture and physically tried to lift the woman back onto her feet. Finding she was too small to manage the maneuver she, too, knelt on the ground and said three Hail Marys with her. Jacinta then told the poor woman, with a certainty we can only wonder at, that she would be cured, as indeed she was.

There's a similar story told of Francisco.

He was walking with Jacinta and Lucia on their way to the Cova. As they turned a corner, they found themselves face-to-face with a group of people coming to question them. There was no escape. The interrogation started. Then, because there were stone walls on either side of the path, the people lifted Jacinta and Lucia up and set them on top of the nearest one, the better to see and hear them. Francisco, however, would not allow the people to set him up there. His excuse was that he was afraid of falling; then, when attention was centered on the girls, he quietly slipped between the people and stood against the wall behind them.

There is a beguiling, surreptitious quality to the humility of the boy, humility by disappearance. There are shades here of Christ slipping through the mob in the Temple, or from among His fellow Nazarenes when they were intent on hurling Him over a cliff. With Francisco, as with Jesus, there is no fanfare to mark the event. He simply folds in on himself, serene and unseen, until he is elsewhere.

Among the crowd that day was a peasant woman from São Mamede with her son. They couldn't get anywhere near the girls seated on top of the wall and had no chance of addressing them. However, seeing Francisco in the shadows of the opposite wall, they crossed over and knelt on the stony path before him. They begged him to ask Our Lady to cure her sick husband and not to let him be conscripted into the war because they had no other support.

Francisco showed no sign of anger or even embarrassment at seeing this woman and her son kneeling at his feet. His reaction was to kneel down too, remove the cap from his head, take out his beads and ask if they would care to pray a Rosary with him. Before long the questioners were shamed into curbing their curiosity and their tongues and kneeling to pray alongside the two boys and the mother. That's not just humility. Even a world besotted with fashion and attitude would exclaim with awe, "That's style!" The world would be missing the point, of course, but at least it would have been acknowledging the integrity of those at prayer.

There is an interesting contrast of attitudes between the siblings here. They face similar situations and resolve them in the same ways. Even so, there's a distinct difference. Jacinta's initial reaction was to raise the woman to her level. As soon as she saw that it couldn't be done, she assumed the woman's. Francisco didn't pause to consider, he simply joined the supplicants because he saw that their level is his rightful place, too. In one summer Jacinta had come a long way from the little girl who would pout and "tether the donkey" if games were not to her specifications. Francisco, too, had advanced from "You think you won? That's all right. I don't mind" to recognizing the cross as the goalpost and Christ's poor as the crucified winners. Now he must be a winner, too, if he is to console Jesus. So he doesn't simply identify with the poor suffering sinners as a missionary or a conscientious social worker might. He *was* a sinner. And he was winning.

On that day along the road, the whole group finished the Rosary, then went off happily with the children to the Cova, reciting another Rosary on the way. Later, the lady from São Mamede returned several times with her son and with her husband, full of thanks to Our Lady for granting both her requests. Perhaps if all the people who came to see and question the children had stayed to pray a Rosary, the seers would not have felt besieged.

Many visitors accompanied them to the Cova where the Rosary was recited, but often, prayer was far from the minds of a number of the questioners. This was as true of priests as of the people. The youngsters were often summoned to the Fatima rectory to undergo a grilling from curious clergy who assumed that ordination bestowed expert discernment in regard to visionary prodigies. These interviews were particularly grueling, as the children's sense of religious respect and obedience was often in conflict with what the Lady had told them as "secrets." Lucia, particularly, suffered from scrupulosity in this, even to the point of blaming Jacinta all over again for having broken silence on the apparitions in the first place. Jacinta's reaction was to cry and beg forgiveness. In time, their minds were put at rest by Father Faustino, the vicar of a parish past Ourem, called Olival. He taught them how to keep their secrets peacefully intact within their consciences.

The local parish priest, Father Ferreira, had acted throughout "the birth of Fatima" with a restraint and practicality that is rarely praised but that, in hindsight, can be seen as heroic. That's particularly so in view of the besieged mentality that the politics of the time forced on the Church. Of course, the cleric didn't know that he was, to stretch the metaphor, the midwife at this momentous birth. He was simply a hard-working, unsung, diocesan clergyman, and as such it is worth noting a theologically sound complaint he made. It's one with which Lucia concurred. He said, "Why are all those people going to prostrate themselves in prayer in a deserted spot like that, while here the Living God of our altars, in the Blessed Sacrament, is left alone, abandoned, in the tabernacle?"

Lucia's comment, which would have been her cousins' too, was: "I understood perfectly why he spoke like that, but what could I do? If I had been given authority over the hearts of those people, I would certainly have led them to the parish church, but as I had not, I offered to God yet another sacrifice."

Mary of Nazareth, too, would have led them to the parish church but, as the glorified Queen of Heaven, that is what she was doing, on a scale that neither Father Ferreira nor the seers could have imagined at the time. She was using the deserted spot to lay foundations for an altar to the Living God, which would have the whole world for its parish, an altar where the Blessed Sacrament would never be alone, day or night. The Immaculate Heart, the Mother of the Eucharist, would draw children there and teach them about the centrality of that Eucharist. Fatima was to become the Lady Chapel of the Universal Church.

As the year between October 1917 and 1918 progressed, Lucia's mother talked things over with Olympia Marto, and they agreed to send the children off to school. Lucia uses the word "us" here, and a reader tends to think Lucia is referring to both her cousins, but perhaps she was only thinking of Jacinta. It may be that Francisco had already been going to the schoolhouse near the Fatima parish church throughout 1917. Lucia says nothing whatsoever about Francisco going to school during that year, and there is almost no reference to it in the official documents except Father de Lacer's article in O Mensageiro. It refers to Francisco "arriving home from school" shortly after the October apparitions.

In Father De Marchi's Fatima From the Beginning, a nameless correspondent is quoted. At the time of quoting, the 1940s, the correspondent had moved on to be director of the seminary at Leiria. This man claims to have been at school with Francisco, and as his is the only evidence we have of Francisco's education, the quote is worth repeating because it confirms and adds to the picture we have of the boy:

> I had the good fortune to attend the same school as Francisco Marto from February to June of 1917. Francisco distinguished himself from the others by reason of his humility and kindness, virtues that, however, caused him much suffering, thrown as he was among companions under the influence of a teacher without Christian formation.
>
> He was very backward at his lessons and was still in the lowest form, a misfortune which drew upon him the strictures of his teacher and school-fellows. It is obvious, however, that he was occupied with the sublime thoughts which the angel had brought to birth in his mind and that

he cared little or nothing for the ordinary instruction of the school. Francisco would humbly bow his head and receive the censures of his master and companions.

At the break, which we had at midday, he would eat his lunch and stay quietly with a few other boys until the teacher gave the sign to go into school again. I remember playing with him and enjoying it because Francisco was always pleasant and friendly with everyone.

In the evening he went his way and I mine, which was in the opposite direction, and for this reason I do not know how he passed the rest of the day. From February to May, the life of Francisco in the school at Fatima was more or less as I have described and such was the attitude of his teachers and fellows toward him. In the last half of May the news of the apparitions spread through the village and the attitude of the school towards him began to alter. The teacher, a good professor but a bad educator, took advantage of Francisco's scant interest in his lessons to dub him a fraud and a liar. He never ceased to point out his defects, I don't know whether with the intention of shaming him into greater efforts, or to induce us to take his part against the little seer.

We, mere children as we were, naturally followed the teacher's lead and often joined with him in humiliating poor Francisco. The worst of it was that our words were sometimes translated into actions, and he sometimes had to spend the recreation period pinned against the wall unable to free himself from the ill treatment meted out to him by certain stronger boys among us. This all took place during the last half of May and the whole of June. After the long vacation I entered the seminary and lost touch with the seers.

There is a ring of authenticity to this testimony, but one wonders why Lucia's "Memoirs" gives us the impression that Francisco spent most of his time with her and Jacinta shepherding
the sheep.

Anyway, if Francisco did spend much of his day at school during
term time, Jacinta certainly didn't, because girls were not admitted
to this school before 1918, when their mothers decided that Lucia
and Jacinta should attend. One suspects, though, that Jacinta at
least was taking the Lady's injunction to advance in literacy seriously. In December she was already telling Dr. Carlos Mendes, a
young graduate from nearby Torres Novas who was a witness to
several of the apparitions, with a justifiable pride that she "was almost up to the letter 'H'."

The thirteenth days of June, July, August and September 1917
were all weekdays. Was Francisco let off school to attend apparitions? Were school days more flexible then, as often now in Portugal, with some children attending in the morning and others
in the afternoon? Was he playing truant? Was schooling voluntary and, if so, why did he bother to go at all? It's confusing, but
of no particular importance.

At playtime, the girls would skip off to the church to visit the
Blessed Sacrament. But fame often sought its payment there. They
were no sooner inside than the crowds arrived, asking their questions. "They seem to guess," Jacinta would say. "I wanted so much
to be alone with the Hidden Jesus and talk to him, but they never
let us."

In Father Ferreira's parochial deposition of August 6, 1918,
he stated that Jacinta reported the Lady had appeared to her on
Ascension Day in the church during Mass and taught Jacinta
how to pray the mysteries of the Rosary (*"rezar as contas"*). This
intriguing statement was not developed by Jacinta and, eager as
we might be for some elucidation from her or comment from the

priest, there is none forthcoming. At the same time, however, she did say that the Lady also had appeared standing by the door of the attic when the family was asleep (Father Ferreira had already written about that in his notes on the July apparitions), and on another occasion under a table. Apparently the Lady said nothing on either of these appearances in the house.

The child's mother was there on the last occasion, and Jacinta said, "Look! Don't you see the Lady, the one we see on the top (of the tree), is here below?" Olympia confirmed that Jacinta had said this. If it's difficult to picture Our Lady under a table in a kitchen, it might ease the strain of visualization to reflect that the Lady might well have been showing her infinite resourcefulness by lowering herself to Jacinta's height, and even to her age, and making a grotto of the furniture. Heaven has a charm that Hollywood wouldn't dare imitate.

We can only lament that Jacinta wasn't urged to share what insights Our Lady gave her into the mysteries of the Rosary during the "incidental apparition" in the church. But those who take the message of Fatima to heart and actually recite the prayer daily well know that she gives private lessons that are not easy to share. Indeed, it might be said that it is easier for us to learn firsthand from the source ourselves than to hanker after Jacinta's report.

Before leaving the matter, there is one small reservation about this "incidental apparition." It's the statement that it happened during Mass (*"durante a missa"*). Perhaps before Mass or after Mass or even during the sermon — but one can't believe that the Mother of God would distract a soul from the celebration of the Eucharist. The Mass is the confirmation in time of the supreme act of love in eternity — the triumph of the courage of God — that virtue that not even the angels knew existed. The Lady of Fatima could not turn her attention from the enactment of that supreme sacrifice even for something as important as to instruct a little girl. It would be like a bride neglecting her wedding to sew her gown — a weak simile, I grant, but that is because there is little to compare with such an unthinkable proposition.

The Rosary serves the Mass; the Mass doesn't serve the Rosary.

Francisco didn't tell Father Ferreira that he had seen the Lady in the church or anywhere else (or if he did, the priest left no record of it). However, Francisco, too, would slip into the church whenever he could, sometimes hiding in the choir loft or climbing the semicircular staircase that led into the pulpit, halfway down the aisle on the Gospel side. If he knelt there, he could not be seen by the questioners or worshipers but, like a sailor in a crow's nest, he could remain solitary and aloft from the world. With the eyes of his soul intent on the tabernacle, he could gaze on horizons far beyond the scope of those below, laboring on deck.

(During this period, the Fatima church was being renovated. The parish had been founded 1568. When the Diocese of Leiria had been dissolved in the persecutions of 1882, it had been annexed to Lisbon, under whose authority it had been during the apparitions. In January 1918, however, the Leiria diocese had been restored and the new bishop, José Alves Correia da Silva, clearly thought that some of his churches needed restoring too. There was no connection between the apparitions, from which the Church wisely stood apart in the early days, and the restoration of either the diocese or the Fatima parish church. Near the baptismal font — on the left of the entrance, i.e. the Gospel side — the altar with the tabernacle for the Blessed Sacrament had been installed while the main sanctuary was being renovated. During much of 1918, work was suspended because of shortage of money, and the temporary altar remained near the font.)

Carnival time in Fatima was the same pre-Lenten three days of feasting and dancing it was in the rest of Portugal; indeed, in any

Latin country. Locally, an area was set aside for those younger than fourteen, and in 1918 it was a house in Casa Velha, a tiny village very near to Aljustrel. Lucia was coerced into preparing food and decorations and joining in the festivities. Joyous as these celebrations were, they had lost their attraction for Lucia, who had tasted the sweets of eternity. It was Francisco who challenged her: "Have you forgotten that we promised never to have anything to do with parties and games anymore?"

"I didn't want to go. But you can see that they never stop begging me to go and now I don't know what to do."

Francisco's advice was practical: She could tell her friends that at the Cova da Iria she had promised Our Lady not to dance anymore. Then they could go and hide up in the cave where no one could find them.

Francisco showed the same resolute determination when the villagers were together and got to singing the local songs about shepherds enchanted by shepherdesses and so forth. He would urge Lucia and Jacinta to go off with him to the cave or the well. "Let's not sing that song anymore. Our Lady certainly doesn't want us to sing songs like that now." This uncompromising attitude might have appeared priggish and puritanical to those with no sense of the supernatural, but Francisco didn't have the worldly experience or psychological equipment to indulge in such quirks of vanity. He was a lover refusing to countenance an inferior attraction. A person accustomed to diamonds cannot be fobbed off with paste; a taste of riding first-class sours any inclination a traveler might have had toward going coach. Anyway, it is doubtful whether he would have spoken to anyone other than Lucia and Jacinta in that manner. We saw that when he suggested to a fellow prisoner in the jail in Ourem that the man remove his cap, the adult's reaction suggested a smiling, nonconfrontational inducement.

The boy gave his fellow seers no leeway. One day, Lucia came to the Marto home with a group of young people and said goodbye to them at the door. Francisco told her bluntly, "Don't go with them, because you might learn to commit sins. When you come out of school, go and stay for a little while near the Hidden Jesus, and afterwards come home by yourself."

For Francisco, Lent — with its prayer and sacrifice — was carnival enough.

When the seers passed by the church on their way to school, he would often say, "Listen! You go to school, and I'll stay here in the church, close to the Hidden Jesus. On your way home, come in and call me." It's also reported the children, either individually or together, would take advantage of the rare times when no one was in the building looking for them to walk on their knees around the perimeter aisles beneath the Stations of the Cross. Here was yet another sacrifice to console the offended Jesus and to save from damnation the souls poisoned by sin.

At that time, a woman from a nearby village who knew Lucia's sister, Teresa, kept nagging her to ask Lucia to intercede for her son. He was facing banishment or a lengthy imprisonment for some crime, probably political. Lucia mentioned it to Francisco and Jacinta as all three were making their way to school one morning. When they reached the church, Francisco said, "Listen! While you go to school, I'll stay with the Hidden Jesus, and I'll ask him for that grace." Later, on their way home, the girls stopped by the church and asked, "Did you pray to Our Lord to grant that grace?" Francisco answered, "Yes, I did. Tell your Teresa that he'll be home in a few days time."

There is no prying into another person's prayer, but the confidence of the reply can't help but make us wonder at the manner in which the Hidden Jesus communicated His response. Apparently it was only a few days later that the matter was resolved, and the son returned home. On the next 13th, that entire family came to the Cova to thank Our Lady. Notice it was not to thank Teresa, Lucia or Francisco, whose mediation in the matter they may not have known about anyway, but to show their gratitude to Our Lady. That's Faith with its compass primed.

Even though the cycle of appointed apparitions was completed, the children still observed each 13th as a sacred day. Lucia records Francisco as saying to her on the evening of the 12th of one of the months during that year, "Look! Early tomorrow morning, I'm making my escape out through the back garden to the cave on the Cabeço. As soon as you can, come and join me there." This cave, sheltered from sun and rain by oaks and olives, the Lapa de Cabeço, the place of the first apparition of the angel, was their private retreat. It was the one place where the crowds could never find them, their secret oratory. "How many were the prayers and sacrifices offered there to our dear Lord," Lucia exclaimed.

During the summer of 1918, the cousins seem to have been invited to stay by a number of ladies from the greater area around Fatima. There were places near Torres Novas and in Leiria and as far away as Valado, between Alcobaça and Nazere. But if these visits were made, there is very little documentation about them.

One journey to the home of the priest of Olival, north of Ourem, seems to have been confined to Lucia and Jacinta. It was already night, and they had been finding their way by the light of lanterns, when they were coerced into stopping at a house along the way. A young woman came out to meet them. Weeping, she knelt down, and begged them to enter her home and say at least one Hail Mary for the recovery of her father. For three years he had been unable to get any rest because of continual hiccups.

Lucia helped the twenty-year-old to her feet and told Jacinta to remain at the house while she went on ahead to the priest's home to pray the Rosary with the people there. Jacinta agreed. When Lucia came back, she found the young girl seated facing the man. He was not very old, but he looked emaciated, and he was weeping. Members of his family were gathered around him. On seeing Lucia, Jacinta got up, said goodbye, and promised that she would not forget him in her prayers.

Three days later, they passed the place on their way back to Fatima. When they reached the house, they found the girl and her father. He now looked much better and had lost all trace of nervous strain and weakness. They came to thank Lucia and Jacinta for the grace they had received; he was no longer troubled by the annoying hiccups.

Immediately after this, Lucia tells another story featuring Jacinta. It, too, has a miraculous element, but is also eerie. An aunt's son was a true prodigal. He had left their Fatima home, and no one knew what had become of him. In her distress, the woman came to Aljustrel to ask Lucia to pray to Our Lady. Not being able to find Lucia, she asked Jacinta instead. A few days later the young man suddenly returned home, asked his parent's forgiveness, and came to Aljustrel to tell his sorry story.

After spending all he had stolen from his parents, he wandered about like a tramp until, for some reason, he was jailed in Torres Novas. After he had been there for some time, he managed to escape one night and fled to the hills, where he completely lost his way. Torn between the fear of being captured and the darkness of a stormy night, he found that his only recourse was to fall to his knees and pray.

A few minutes later, Jacinta appeared to him, took him by the hand, led him to the main road that runs from Alqueidão to Reguengo, and pointed out which way he should head. When morning dawned, he found himself on the road to Boleiros. Recognizing where he was, he was overcome with emotion and hurried to his parents' home.

Lucia asked Jacinta if it was true that she had gone there to guide him. She answered:

... she had not, that she knew nothing of the area where he had been lost. "I only prayed and pleaded very much with Our Lady for him, because I felt so sorry for Aunt Vitoria."

The last of the stories worth quoting doesn't cry "miracle," but illustrates that prayer itself is the greatest miracle of all: A soldier had been ordered to leave for the front even though his wife was sick in bed and they had three small children. When asking for help, he wept like a child and pleaded that either his wife would be cured or that his orders would be revoked. Jacinta invited him to say the Rosary with her, and then said, "Don't cry. Our Lady is so good! She will certainly grant you the grace you are asking."

The little girl never forgot her soldier. At the end of the Rosary she always tacked on one Hail Mary for him. Some months later, he came to Aljustrel with his wife and three small children to thank Our Lady for the two graces he had received. Because he had come down with a fever on the eve of his departure, he had been released from military service. And his wife, he said, had been cured by Our Lady.

One trait of Francisco's that isn't always associated with beati — those one step from canonization — is his reluctance to be in the presence of the sick and suffering. "I can't bear to see them, as I feel so sorry for them! Tell them I'll pray for them." For example, although he was invited along with the girls, he wouldn't visit a man in the nearby village of Montelo because the man's mother couldn't hear or speak. "I'm not going there because I can't bear to see people who want to speak and cannot." This is not "that secret horror and effeminate loathing which those given to sin always have for blood and wounds" as Catherine Emmerich said of Salome, but a sensitivity that cannot gaze on the suffering Christ but must close its eyes and bow its head and suffer alongside in blind silence.

Francisco took any food that was offered to him on his sick-bed, to the extent that his mother could never discover which things he liked and which he didn't. This indicates that the compassion was for the suffering of others. For himself, his body would be Christ's puppet, to do with as the Savior wished, so long as his soul could remain cradled in His peace.

Given the crowds that pursued the seers and the ailments that many brought with them in the hope of intercession for a cure, this sensitivity of Francisco's must have been sorely tried on a daily basis. One afternoon when the girls had gone off elsewhere, a contingent of the faithful arrived to question the children. There's no reason to suppose that they were ill or disabled; nevertheless, when he saw them coming, Francisco hid. His mother searched in vain for him, until the crowd eventually left. When Lucia and Jacinta returned in the evening and were alone in the house, Francisco's voice came through a hole in the ceiling. He had climbed up there through that same trapdoor where Jacinta had seen Our Lady. "There were so many people!" he exclaimed. "Heaven help me if they had ever caught me by myself! Whatever would I have said to them?"

Just being himself would have been impressive, but the questioners, for the most part, don't seem to have been the sort of folk who could learn through silence. Imagine if, instead of asking their stereotypical questions ("What did the Lady look like?"), they had wanted to know something similar to Lucia's query. ("Francisco, which do you like better — to console Our Lord, or to convert sinners, so that no more souls will go to hell?" To which he had responded: "I would rather console Our Lord. How sad Our Lady was when she said that people must not offend Our Lord anymore, for He is already much offended? I would like to console Our Lord, and after that, convert sinners so that they won't offend Him anymore.") That questioner would have gone home with incalculably more to ponder on than whether or not the apparition wore shoes or earrings.

Or had Francisco told them, "We were on fire in that light which is God, and yet we were not burnt! What is God? We could never put it into words. Yes, that is something indeed which we could never express! But what a pity it is that He is so sad! If only I could console Him!" And Jacinta further upheld the flame: "I like to tell Jesus that I love Him! Many times, when I say it to Him, I seem to have a fire in my heart, but it doesn't burn me." Had that been the tenor of the dialogues between children and visitors, those inquisitors might themselves have returned to their homes with their own hearts ablaze.

But miracles are paid for by the medium. Christ was reimbursed for his compassionate cures with insults and, ultimately, a criminal's death. Those through whom He continues to work can expect no different. Francisco and Jacinta were still wearing the cords around their bodies every day throughout this year. Sacrifices were multiplying to an extent that a cautious confessor would never permit: things such as drinking water from a stagnant pond, eating bitter nuts and berries while giving away the food their mother had prepared, swallowing insults from people and clergy, and even enduring physical attacks such as the kicks and blows from local "pious" women.

There was also one woman who was not so pious who hurled abuse at the seers every time she saw them. During the summer of the apparitions, half-drunk outside a local *tasca*, she spotted them and launched into a torrent of obscene invective. Jacinta told the others, "We have to plead with Our Lady and offer sacrifices for the conversion of this woman. She says so many sinful things that if she doesn't go to confession, she'll go to hell." A few days later the children were running past this woman's door when suddenly Jacinta stopped dead and, turning round, said, "Listen! Let's not play anymore. We can make this sacrifice for the conversion of sinners." Then she raised her hands and eyes to heaven and made her offering, quite unaware that the woman was watching her from behind a shutter. That action of Jacinta, the intensity of love and trust with which it was made, so impressed the errant woman that she saw, in an instant, the truth of the seers' claims and resolved to reform her life. All this she later told to Jacinta's mother.

CHAPTER TWENTY-TWO

The year 1918 saw the end of the Great War, and the Allies, to use the accepted word, were victorious. In fact, the armies had fought themselves to a standstill. Disease stalked both camps, rendering soldiers useless and taking lives at random. The terrible Spanish flu seems to have been heaven's way of halting a calamitous war and combining a punishment and a warning with the instrument of abrogation. This virulent pandemic ranks with the Black Death as one of the most terrible outbreaks of disease in history. It claimed more than twenty million lives and an estimated a half-billion people suffered through the illness. At least one in four Americans fell ill and about a half-million died. (It was called Spanish flu because Spain was its first serious point of attack. The British called it Flanders grippe, and the Germans *Blitz Katarrh*.)

While patients showed the ordinary symptoms of influenza (headaches, severe cold, fever, chills and aching bones and muscles), the disease also generated complications such as severe pneumonia, with purplish lips and ears, a pallid face, purulent bronchitis, mastoid abscess, and heart problems. It occurred frequently in children ages five to fourteen, but those who caught it between the ages of twenty and forty were most likely to die from it.

After the armistice was signed on November 11, 1918, the pestilence subsided dramatically. Within a year, it was no longer a menace. It later vanished completely — a strong argument for seeing it as a divine instrument to stop the war.

What concerns us here, however, is that in late October 1918, both Francisco and Jacinta succumbed to the dread curse, as did many others in the area, children and adults. Francisco, who seemed to have developed the simpler form of the disease initially, was to suffer for just more than five months before it proved fatal. Jacinta's illness took a different course. She would be ill and then appear to recover before falling ill again. Eventually she developed the purulent bronchitis that caused her such intense suffering before it took her from this world, just six weeks short of a year after the Lady had fulfilled her promise and taken Francisco to heaven.

The evening before she first became ill, Jacinta said to the others, "I have a terrible headache and I'm so thirsty! But I won't take a drink because I want to suffer for sinners." The next day she said to Lucia, "My chest hurts so much, but I'm not saying anything to my mother! I want to suffer for Our Lord, in reparation for the sins committed against the Immaculate Heart of Mary, for the Holy Father and for the conversion of sinners."

Around this same time, as they were leaving the village for the school at Fatima, Lucia asked Francisco, "What's the matter? You can hardly walk!"

"I have such a bad headache, and I feel as if I'm going to fall."

"Then don't come! Stay at home!"

"I'd rather stay in the church with the Hidden Jesus while you go to school."

The Marto children were immediately confined to their beds in two of the tiny rooms toward the front of the small family house in Aljustrel. At the time, many households had two or more people sick in bed. There was no family who had escaped the scourge of this sword. At one point Ti Marto was the only one in the whole household who hadn't fallen to the "three-day fever." When someone knocked on the door, João would call out, "There's no use coming here, we're all sick!"

On her way to school, Lucia would stop by to see her cousins. One morning she asked Francisco, "Are you suffering a lot?" He nodded, then from beneath the covers he smuggled out the rope he had worn for the past year and handed it to her. "Take it away before my mother sees it. I don't feel able to wear it around my waist anymore."

Jacinta did the same. She was lying in bed picking the petals from the irises that Lucia had brought her from Cabeço. "Keep it for me," she said quietly. "I'm afraid my mother may see it. If I get better I want it back again!" Lucia confides that the cord had three knots in it, and was somewhat stained with blood. She kept it hidden until she was finally leaving Aljustrel, when she burned it and Francisco's, too.

Often Francisco would say things like, "Lucia, on your way to school, go into the church and give my love to the Hidden Jesus. What hurts me most is that I cannot go there myself and stay with him a while." On one occasion she found him smiling with happiness when she arrived and asked, "Francisco, are you better?"

"No, I feel worse," he answered with paradoxical blandness, but the explanation was not long in coming. "It won't be long now till I go to heaven. When I'm there, I'm going to console Our Lord and Our Lady very much. Jacinta is going to pray a lot for sinners, for the Holy Father and for you. You will stay here, because Our Lady wants it that way. Listen, you must do everything that she tells you."

This initial period of the illness lasted until around Christmas. The rest of the family quickly rallied, though two of the girls were to succumb again and die. (Jacinta died in February 1920, and her two sisters passed away later that same year.) With the seers, however, the illness settled in for a lengthy run. There were spasmodic improvements, especially with Jacinta, but never a suggestion of a cure.

During one of these remissions, the little girl was sitting on her bed. She sent her sister to call Lucia. On her arrival, Jacinta made a statement that Lucia relates with a casualness that obscures the wonder: that the celestial Lady of Light was at the sickbed of peasant children in a rural village. The almost-eight-year-old told her cousin:

"Our Lady came to see us. She told us she would take Francisco to heaven very soon, and she asked me if I still wanted to convert more sinners. I said I did. She told me I would be going to a hospital where I would suffer a great deal, and that I am to suffer for the conversion of sinners, in reparation for the sins committed against the Immaculate Heart of Mary, and for love of Jesus. I asked if you would go with me. She said you wouldn't, and that is what I find hardest. She said my mother would take me, and then I would have to stay there all alone. Maybe the hospital is a big, dark house, where you can't see, and I'll be there suffering all alone! But never mind! I'll suffer for love of Our Lord, to make reparation to the Immaculate Heart of Mary, for the conversion of sinners and for the Holy Father."

On some days, when Jacinta was on her feet and thirsting for sacrifices, she would even refrain from visiting Francisco for a whole day. She would remain in her iron bed, with its hay or horsehair mattress, enduring the pain in her chest while making sure that no word or movement of hers betrayed the intensity of that pain.

Francisco rallied once or twice, but rarely was well enough to leave the house. In January he got up for a bit, but he never believed he was better and always repeated that Our Lady would soon come to fetch him. Once or twice he even managed to get to the Cova to say a Rosary, but soon he was back in his bed. Then the suffering that was to consume him really set in. It was his share of the burden of the ignored and deeply hurt Jesus, and it weighed on the boy like a mountain. Every pain-wracked breath took him a further step into black and inescapable loneliness.

Visitors saw none of this. People, often strangers, were frequently heard to make remarks like "I don't know what it is about Francisco, but it feels so good to be here." Or "It seems that when we go into Francisco's room, we feel just as we do when we go into a church."

The boy was put in his parents' room in the front of the house, and Olympia and Ti Marto moved their bed out into the pen with the sheep. Children, apparently, were free to run in and out of his room, and to talk with him through the window, though he never sought the company of any but Lucia and, of course, Jacinta, who exerted the same inexplicable attraction over people. As women from the village told the mothers of the seers, "It's a mystery one cannot fathom! They are children just like any others, they don't say anything to us, and yet in their presence one feels something one can't explain, and that makes them different from all the rest."

A woman from nearby Casa Velha came to Francisco's sickroom one day asking him to pray that her husband and son might be reconciled. The father had banished the young man from their home, and his mother was distraught. Francisco said, "Don't worry! I'm going to heaven very soon, and when I get there I will ask Our Lady for that grace."

Doubtless this statement will fail to astonish us, set as it is among so many explosions of piety and wonders, but in fact it is as perfect an expression of faith, hope and charity as any mortal ever uttered. The faith and hope are not just faith and hope in eternal life, not just Francisco believing and hoping in eternal life. He loved enough, and was consequently humble enough, to believe that eternal life believed and hoped in him, too. He could readily have sent a message ahead and it would have been granted, but he had been waiting so long, his Mother so anxious to receive him, that he wanted to give her the pleasure of doing everything to welcome him as soon as he arrived.

The father and son were reconciled on the very day that Francisco died.

Another story says that during one of the short periods of reprieve, Francisco had gone with Lucia to the Lapa do Cabeço. When they returned, the Marto house was full of people, in the midst of them a woman blessing Rosaries, medals, holy pictures and the like. With a pious cry, the self-appointed dispenser of benedictions urged Francisco to join her in this ritual. The boy remained calm, but as fixed as stone. "I cannot give a blessing," he said. "And neither should you. Only priests can do that!" Lucia comments that his words went round the room like lightning. The crowd turned on the woman and demanded their objects back. She fled from the house.

Another day, Lucia and Jacinta were at Francisco's bedside when they were warned of a throng of questioners coming into the village. The girls ran out and hid in barrels in the back garden; Francisco had to face the inquisitors alone. He was able to say with perfect truth that he didn't know where his fellow seers were and claim to be a mere bystander at the apparitions because he had heard nothing.

During his last weeks, Francisco's pain was so intense that he couldn't even pray. Considering the boy's whole being was bound up in prayer, it was terrible to hear him complain that he could not pray. And yet no soul who has the habit of prayer is a stranger to his meaning. There are times when the repetition of a simple "My God, I adore you!" can envelop the mind, the soul, the being in an impregnable divine security. At other times, the same aspiration is as dry as old oats, the effort to get from one word to the next a tedious slog across a parched wilderness.

The person who disdains prayer will tell us that there is nothing inexplicable here, that it is all straightforward psychology. And he would be perfectly right, because the God "Who makes mountains and veins violets" established the principles of psychology, too. He did that all from the abundance of His own being. Original sin might have engrossed the primordial limpidity of what we call psychology, but it's still within the workings of that science that He approaches us and we approach each other. Even mysticism, that privileged glimpse into the Kingdom, is psychology in a mini-climate.

A study of the life of Christ should make no fuss about His miracles. They are simply incidental indicators of the compassion of the Second Person of the Trinity. A study of the God-Man is a study of God Himself functioning within the bounds of human psychology. It culminates in the dreadful cry "My God, My God, why hast Thou forsaken me," in the Sacred Humanity's inability to pray, which itself was the greatest prayer of all, the object of the divine plan, the redemption of mankind and, paradoxically, human psychology's greatest comfort.

For Francisco, as for any soul, prayer is a raft. In the fury of a midnight storm, one might well be washed overboard and despairing among the waves. But when calm comes with the dawn, the raft is still there, its lifeline strapped securely to the floundering sailor. Archbishop Fulton Sheen used this same image to better effect: "Pain can become so intense that it possesses us like being drowned by the sea; no possibility exists of laying hold of it as one does an object outside of the hand. Sequence of thought is impossible; memorized prayers are never finished, they are so invaded by this crucifying assault."

Two days before Francisco died the fever rose, his chest contracted, and he lay in a state of sweating exhaustion. He told his father that he wanted to receive Communion before he passed away, and Ti Marto went directly to ask this of the priest. Father Ferreira wasn't there at the time, but Father Moreira, from nearby Atouguia, agreed to come and hear the boy's confession, then make a decision about the boy's receiving Communion the next day. On the way to Aljustrel, they said Rosaries. Ti Marto had forgotten his beads, so he counted the Hail Marys on his fingers.

Meanwhile, alone with Lucia, Francisco said, "I am going to confession so that I can receive Holy Communion. Then I shall die." He asked her to repeat to him any sin she had seen him commit. Lucia reminded him of several instances of disobedience. Then, on his behalf, Lucia went into Jacinta's room and asked the same thing. Jacinta said, "Well, tell him that, before Our Lady appeared to us, he stole a coin from our father to buy a music box from José Marto of Casa Velha, and when the boys from Aljustrel threw stones at those from Boleiros, he threw some too."

When these rather charming misdeeds were brought back to the offender, he said, "I've already confessed those, but I'll do so again. Maybe it is because of these sins that Our Lord is so sad. But even if I don't die, I'll never commit them again."

The priest heard Francisco's confession and returned to Aljustrel the next day to bring the Blessed Sacrament. It was Francisco's first Holy Communion from the hands of a priest. Lucia and Jacinta spent the day at his bedside. He spoke of his happiness at having the Hidden Jesus within his heart and of being with Him soon in heaven. But the final burst of the disease was turning his body, as on a spit of pain, and he could not pray. The girls recited the Rosary in his stead.

Francisco managed to say, "I'm sure I'll miss you terribly in heaven. If only Our Lady would bring you there soon also."

Lucia answered, "You won't miss me. Just imagine! And you right there with Our Lord and Our Lady. They are so good!"

With devastating pragmatism, he reflected, "That's true! Perhaps I won't!" Multiple consciousness and other mysteries that pertain to heaven would be sorted out when he got there.

The girls thought he would die during the night. The leave-taking was, in its way, more heart-rending than the death itself.

During the night, Olympia sat with her dying boy. At one point Francisco said, "Mother, look at that lovely light by the door." Later he said, "Now I can't see it anymore."

Francisco Marto, son of Ti and Olympia Marto, died at ten o'clock on the morning of April 4, 1919. His mother described how he gave a smile and remained like that. Then he breathed no more. His father said, "He died smiling."

⁂

There were so many deaths around Fatima at the time that one more wasn't particularly noted. When the simple wooden coffin arrived, it was too small, and the body had to be rearranged to fit into it. A fifteen-decade bone rosary was entwined between his fingers. The lid was secured and tied with a yellow braid. Francisco was buried in a grave in the Fatima cemetery, one he shared with several other children from the parish.

He was just shy of his tenth birthday, a few days younger than Lucia had been at the time of the first apparition not quite two years before.

Jacinta had just turned nine and had more than nine months longer to live; but even at her death she, too, was younger than Lucia had been at the first apparition, and younger than Francisco at the time of his departure for heaven.

Jacinta felt Francisco's death keenly. Lucia says she was often lost in thought and, when asked what was occupying her mind, would answer, "I'm thinking about Francisco. I'd give anything to see him again." Her last words to him had been, "Give my love to Our Lord and Our Lady and tell them I'll suffer as much as they want, for the conversion of sinners and in reparation to the Immaculate Heart of Mary." The youngest seer had meant it; but compounding physical pain was this further agony of the heart.

Although Jacinta had given up the rope belt, she was still thirsty for sacrifices. When not observed she would get out of bed, kneel, touch the ground with her forehead and say the prayers the angel had taught them. As the illness progressed she found that she would lose her balance while performing this prostration and topple over, so she confined herself to kneeling on the floor. When Lucia repeated this to the vicar — she doesn't specify which vicar, probably the understanding vicar of Olival — he said Jacinta was not to get out of bed. She was to pray lying down but only so long as it didn't tire her. Jacinta's reaction bypassed questions, objections and explanations. She straightaway tackled essentials. "And would Our Lady be pleased?"

Lucia replied, "Our Lord wants us to do whatever the vicar says."

"That's all right then. I won't get up anymore."

But with an enthusiasm that might have been called devious if the motive had been less than love, Jacinta took her sacrifices to bed, refusing to turn over during the night to relieve the pain, and offering it for sinners. The result was that she didn't sleep at all.

During the day she would find little sacrifices, such as drinking milk, which she disliked. At the same time she would forego eating the tempting fruit that well-wishers brought to her bedside. This sort of mortification is the stuff of the "improving" school of hagiography. It's laudable but, in Jacinta's case, unnecessary. The bronchial pneumonia provided suffering enough. Compounding the pain, a purulent abscess was setting in around the pleura, the membrane that surrounds the lung. Jacinta's main concern was to hide the extent of her continuing agony from others, particularly from her grieving mother.

But there was no concealing the visible effects. The disease was clearly reducing her body to a stick-thin vessel of raw pain. The local doctor suggested a hospital in Vila Nova de Ourém. Jacinta knew that no physical benefits would come from such hospitalization, but Our Lady had told her it would happen, and that it would be a means of saving souls from hell and making reparation to the Immaculate Heart.

So, less than three months after the death of Francisco, transportation was arranged and the dying girl was taken to what she feared would be a dark, empty place where she would be left to suffer alone. In fact, it was a hospital with rows of beds in clean white wards like any other, and she seems to have settled in without any Mephistophelian disruptions.

Unfortunately we have almost no record of Jacinta's two month stay in St. Augustine's — it was a secular hospital — except that Lucia and Olympia managed to visit her twice, and Lucia's comment was that she was "living her ideal," which is admirable for anybody, but momentous for a nine-year- old. Presumably she had good relations — cordial if not close — with the nursing staff and her fellow patients. Well-wishers and the ubiquitous questioners would certainly have found their way there. Others, braving the risk of infection, would have come to beg some cure or other. It is unlikely that Arturo Santos would have penciled a corporal work of mercy into his diary, but his wife, Adalina, might well have stopped by for a maternal word as the Santos home was but a stone's throw from the hospital, diagonally across a small square. Jacinta's elder brothers, surely, would have come to visit on their bicycles, and there would be other Aljustrel people in town for the Thursday market. Yet overall it mattered little whether people stopped by to chat or not. The being alone that Our Lady had predicted was a different level of loneliness; the loneliness of being alone with God, and Him sleeping. The apostles had experienced it on the lake, and it was terrifying.

As the summer of 1919 wore on, it was clear that the hospital treatment was ineffective. Besides, the family could no longer afford the expense. At the end of August, Ti Marto had his little girl discharged and brought her home. She had an open wound on her left side, over the rib cage, which, in addition to emitting a very unpleasant odor, was continually producing pus. The wound had to be dressed every day, but that could be done at home. So, after the two-month hospitalization, Jacinta was back in her own bed, in her own bedroom in Aljustrel.

As the suffering intensified, it's reasonable to assume that heavenly favor did, too — not necessarily in the form of visions and sweet caresses for the chosen child, but deeper, less easily cataloged favors: an infused grasp of the contradiction of a God suffering and the implausible, but real, role she had in that radical but awesome drama. The monumental things that the Lady had divulged with such simplicity during her visits came back now, not as pleasant memories, gladsome reminiscences of happier times, but as great burning truths, smelting the child in fires of pain until her love ran as pure as untarnished gold, as flawless crystal.

All the things Jacinta had seen in "the light from her hands," she could now witness intermittently in the light generated by the fires in her own flesh: the Trinity; the ache of the heart of the outraged Redeemer; the Holy Father; hell; sin; death; and that banner of heaven's last and most gracious campaign to win humanity back to the ways of God by the goad of goodness, that magnet of love, the Immaculate Heart of Mary.

Chapter Twenty-Three

Lucia said that a book on Jacinta should have one chapter devoted to hell and another to the Immaculate Heart. She said further that a consciousness of hell and devotion to the Immaculate Heart was not her idea, but that God Himself made it clear that it pertains to His glory and to the good of souls.

Jacinta would have been appalled that any book would have been written about her at all. Still, if there must be books, then many chapters should be about hell because so many people were lured there to be tormented and unloved for eternity.

"Tell them not to do that!" she admonished questioners when they told her details of others' errors. That kind of talk was a sin. "They offend the Lord our God, and later they could be damned." This was an eight-year-old speaking, not a maiden aunt or a fiery sermon, but an eight-year-old, whose eyes had actually seen the infernal furnace and whose ears had heard the howls of despair. The horror almost had her, in Lucia's graphic expression, withering away with fear. "Oh hell! Oh hell!" She would exclaim from the midst of deep thought. "How sorry I am for the souls who go to hell! All the people down there, burning alive, like wood in the fire! Oh my Jesus, forgive us our sins, save us from the fires of hell and lead all souls to heaven, especially those most in need of Thy mercy."

This last prayer, which Catholics have slotted into the Rosary after each decade, is "The Jesus Prayer" with footnotes, a distillation of the thinking behind the liturgy, a catechism. It is worth a library of books itself, but souls stampeding to hell don't read such books. Such souls obstinately refuse to apply the mind to the language. It is more convenient to remain illiterate; that way we can all manage to avoid the letter "H."

Preoccupied after the July apparition with the eschatological fact of hell, Jacinta told Lucia that she must tell Our Lady to show hell to all the people at the Cova. "You'll see how they will be converted," she added naively.

After the next apparition, she asked, "Why didn't you tell Our Lady to show hell to those people?"

"I forgot."

"I didn't remember either," she said, looking very sad.

That's an exchange we can all understand, even though we might be hard-pressed to analyze it to universal satisfaction. Had they remembered to ask Our Lady to show the people hell, what would her answer have been?

"What are the sins that people commit for which they go to hell?" Jacinta then asked Lucia.

"I don't know! Perhaps the sin of not going to Mass on Sunday, of stealing, of saying ugly words, of cursing and of swearing."

"So for just one word, then, people can go to hell?"

"Well, it's a sin!"

"It wouldn't be hard for them to keep quiet, and to go to Mass! I'm so sorry for sinners! If only I could show them hell!"

It appears that later, in Lisbon, Jacinta asked Our Lady what sins sent most people to hell. She was told "sins of the flesh!" and, unsure what the phrase meant, she thought they might have something to do with eating meat on Friday. For the rest of us, the thought is sobering.

The other chapter in a book on Jacinta would be on the Immaculate Heart. To human thinking, it is odd that the time had come for Our Lady, under God's plan, to assume most of the posts in heaven's government of the world. She did so under the aegis of the Immaculate Heart — heaven's unabashed exposure of love, so foreign to our own hearts, tiny and imprisoned between bone and flesh. She came to earth and told three illiterate children that she would use them to make her Immaculate Heart known to the world. Soon two of them die. The other kept as silent as she could on the matter, and only under religious obedience revealed what she had been told. Such a schedule might produce heart attacks if presented to the board of an advertising agency. But what rich grazings for prayer!

―――

"It will not be long now," Jacinta said to Lucia, "before I go to heaven. You will remain here to make known that God wishes to establish in the world devotion to the Immaculate Heart of Mary. When you are to say this don't go and hide. Tell everybody that God grants us graces through the Immaculate Heart of Mary; that people are to ask her for them; and that the Heart of Jesus wants the Immaculate Heart of Mary to be venerated at His side. Tell them also to pray to the Immaculate Heart of Mary for peace, since God has entrusted it to her. If I could only put into the hearts of all, the fire that is burning within my own heart, and that makes me love the Hearts of Jesus and Mary so very much."

How did Jacinta know that God had entrusted peace to Mary's Immaculate Heart? Precise answers are suspect in these areas, but an early paragraph from Lucia's "Memoirs" is telling: "God usually accompanies His revelations with an intimate and detailed understanding of their significance...Jacinta seemed to have this understanding to quite a remarkable degree."

Along with chapters on hell and the Immaculate Heart in a biography of Jacinta, Lucia might have suggested another on the Holy Father. We have already looked at the importance of the papal role in Jacinta's thinking. This must have been infused in some measure. She had witnessed the vision of a papal assassination in the July apparition, but heaven must have accompanied both this and her interior sighting of a pope kneeling at a table weeping, with an intimate and detailed understanding of their significance. This chapter in Jacinta's book would be a long one, and it would require a big mind and heart, well-steeped in prayer, to write it. It would need the detachment of true humility, too, along with a belief in the preeminence of the Immaculate Heart in these latter times. Then, too, there are the eschatological verities. The survival of mankind, not simply as a species on this revolving planet, but his survival into eternity, into the Kingdom of Christ, is a subject that only the humble can have an inkling of.

From September through December 1919, Jacinta lay on her sickbed in Aljustrel. The interminable procession of questioners sought her out and found her because she could not hide. But it was no longer a matter of simply barging in. More often than not, they would collect around the door, waiting to enter the bedroom following Lucia or some member of the Marto family. They seemed to be held back by a sense of diffident respect.

Lucia's visits were the youngest seer's main consolation. One of the few in the area who hadn't been affected by the flu epidemic, Lucia was going to school in Fatima and often to Mass and Holy Communion in the parish church across the road. On those occasions Jacinta would ask her to come closer to her bedside "because," she said, "you have the Hidden Jesus in your heart. I don't know how it is, but when you do I feel Our Lord inside me and I understand what He says though I can't see Him or hear Him, but I love to be with Him."

In the middle of January 1920, a medical practitioner, Dr. Eurico Lisboa from Lisbon, was breaking in a new car, so he and his wife decided to set out for the Cova. On the way, they stopped at Santarem to see Father Formigão, an old friend, who agreed to accompany them. After reciting the Rosary at the Cova with Lucia ("an unforgettable experience of faith and devotion" he was later to write), they moved on to Aljustrel to visit Jacinta.

Dr. Lisboa found the little girl extremely pale and thin. The family told him she was very ill, but that her only ambition was to go to Our Lady. The doctor censured them for their lack of effort to save their daughter. He impressed upon them that to be certain that Our Lady really wished to take Jacinta, they must not neglect any of the normal aids of science to save her life. Father Formigão supported the doctor's opinion, and Ti Marto and Olympia were convinced by the doctor and the priest that it was their duty to send Jacinta to Lisbon. When they told her of the plan, Jacinta said to Ti Marto, "Father dear, even if I recover from this illness I should get another straightway. If I go to Lisbon it means goodbye."

Her father commented, "Indeed, she was a sorry sight. Her heart was enlarged and her digestive organs were ruined." Was there a medical reason for the enlarged heart, one wonders? Or was it identification with the Hearts of Jesus and Mary that made her own heart literally swell with love? This is not a flight of pious speculation, but a genuine question as to whether the will, generating an intense emotion, can expand the heart.

We have no way of knowing exactly when, where or how many times Our Lady appeared to Jacinta in Aljustrel during those last months, or in Lisbon, but such appearances were not isolated occurrences. Her heavenly Mother had already informed the girl she would go to two hospitals. Jacinta reported this to Lucia, "She told me that I am going to Lisbon to another hospital, that I will not see you again, nor my parents either, and after suffering a great deal I shall die alone. But she said I must not be afraid, since she herself is coming to take me to heaven." She hugged Lucia and wept. "I will never see you again! You won't be coming to visit me there. Oh please pray hard for me because I am going to die alone. Oh Jesus, now you can convert many sinners, because this is really a big sacrifice!"

"What does it matter if you die alone, so long as Our Lady is coming to fetch you?"

"It is true, it doesn't matter, really. I don't know why it is, but I sometimes forget Our Lady is coming to take me. I only remember that I'll die without you near me."

It was arranged through a benefactor, the Baron Alvaiázere who lived in Ourem, that Jacinta would travel to Lisbon by train with Olympia and Antonio, Jacinta's half-brother who had just turned nineteen.

Early in the morning of January 21, 1920, Jacinta left Aljustrel for the last time. She traveled in a mule cart. The leave-taking was poignant; Jacinta clung to Lucia with her arms around her cousin's neck. "We will never see each other again," she wept. "Pray a lot for me until I go to heaven. There I will pray a lot for you. Never tell the secret to anyone, even if they kill you. Love Jesus and the Immaculate Heart of Mary very much, and make many sacrifices for sinners."

On the way, the cart made a detour so Jacinta could visit the Cova. Three weeks after the death of Francisco the previous year, the parish council had started to erect a small Chapel of the Apparitions on the site. Two months later, on June 15, 1919, it had been inaugurated but not blessed.

On the day she left Aljustrel, Jacinta managed to get down from the cart to kneel and pray in this chapel for a short while. When her mother was helping her back onto her feet, Jacinta said to her, "When Our Lady went away she passed over those trees and went to heaven so quickly that I thought she would get her feet caught in them."

The railway station, then called Chão de Maçãs and now called Fatima, was some ten miles from the Cova, so the journey by donkey cart would have taken all the morning.

Once on the train, Jacinta remained standing and looked out the window. Before she left, Ti Marto told Olympia that when they got to the train, she must ask the other people to excuse them because her little girl was very ill and that was the reason for the unpleasant smell. "Unpleasant" here may have been something of an understatement. Jacinta had purulent pleurisy, one of the more severe forms of the epidemic, which had resulted in osteitis of the seventh and eighth left ribs. The putrid smell was flesh and bone literally rotting on the living body. So Jacinta, on top of her extreme physical and spiritual sufferings, had to endure the social ignominy of being the source of a fetid odor.

This would certainly be a challenge to pride, which gives it a sort of dubious merit, but at the same time it could cause a person to lose all self-esteem, that motivation for living, the spark plug that fires the will to continue from one moment to the next. At an age when most little girls are discovering the lure of perfumes and scents, Jacinta smelled like a rotting corpse. There is no single record of a complaint coming from her, or even an excuse. It would have been typical of her, young as she was, to reason that if a small body could smell so foul to other people, how much more nauseating must souls rotting in sin smell to heaven. Her own hurt and embarrassment would be the medicine, taken in silence, to heal those wounds on the Mystical Body of Christ.

Ti Marto, who had traveled as a young soldier, also told Olympia, "Be very careful that she doesn't lean out of the window when another train is passing." The Baron Alvaiâzere had arranged for some ladies to meet them in Lisbon, and the Martos were to wrap scarves around their arms to identify themselves when they arrived at Lisbon's Rossio station. Ti Marto pointed this out, too. "When you are going through the Rossio tunnel don't forget to tie on the white handkerchiefs, and don't worry."

Antonio Marto found the ladies at the station. They took the travelers to various houses to find accommodation but, in Olympia's words, "nobody would take us in." One would have thought that these matrons, known to the baron, would have prearranged rooms for a sick girl and her mother rather than simply showing up at the station to go traipsing around the streets of the hilly city knocking on doors. Perhaps they made those plans and the prospective landladies backed off when they saw peasant folk, one of them a tiny girl who smelled awful and looked as if she might die before morning. Then again, the ladies might have thought that there was some social cache in being the Lisbon contacts for one of the Fatima seers. They might even have planned to put them up in their own homes, but reasoned much the same as the landladies, once they had met the little group.

Walking those steep streets, confronted with rejection after rejection as the early winter night was setting in, must have been heartbreaking for Olympia and an excruciating torment for Jacinta. Perhaps Antonio carried her, but even so, the cold and the slamming of the doors was too close to the experience of Bethlehem to be missed.

At last, in the Estrela district down toward the river, they found a warm welcome in an orphanage run by a plump, kindly woman known to all as Mother Godinho. In a building on the Rua da Estrela, which is now a Poor Clare Convent, she cared for between twenty and twenty-five orphans in a Catholic atmosphere. Next door was, and is, the charming Chapel of the Miracles. From the first floor of the orphanage a tribune, or choir balcony, looks down into the sanctuary. For Jacinta, this was worth all the pain and anguish of getting there. To be able to sit for as long as she wished and gaze down at the tabernacle of the Hidden Jesus, untroubled by intemperate questioners, was a little preview of heaven. Mother Godinho gave her and Olympia beds in a room near this window.

At that time, Maria da Purificação — "Mother" — Godinho was forming a congregation of Poor Clares of the Reparation. Most Poor Clares, though not all, are enclosed contemplatives. In Portugal, all communities of female religious began to die out after 1834 because in that year the government prevented them from receiving novices. In 1901 this was relaxed somewhat, but not for contemplatives. Religious sisters were required to be active in some form of what we would now call social work, and this particular sister had founded the orphanage of Our Lady of the Miracles in Lisbon in 1913. At the time Jacinta was with her, Mother Godinho, or Madrinha (Godmother) as she was known to her charges, was around forty-three years of age. She lived till 1960.

Antonio returned to Aljustrel, but Olympia stayed on in Rua da Estrela for the first of the two weeks that Jacinta spent there while preparations were being made for her to be admitted to Dona Estefânia Hospital on the other side of town. Each morning they attended Mass in the Chapel of the Miracles, where Jacinta was carried to the front by Olympia or Mother Godinho to receive her Hidden Jesus. She doesn't appear to have made a formal first Communion. Mother Godinho certainly believed in the authenticity of the Cova da Iria apparitions and could discern that the little seer had reached a degree of union with God that obviated catechetical questioning. The very old Indian priest

Mother Godinho shortly before she died.

who celebrated Mass in the chapel, Father Santa Rita Sousa, presumably concurred with her judgment, and the dying girl was received the Eucharist six times while she was there.

Jacinta also went to confession. Diagonally across the busy Praça da Estrela stands the great eighteenth-century Basilica da Estrela, originally a church of the Carmelite Fathers. Among the niches on the façade is an imposing statue of St. Teresa of Ávila. She looks wise, bemused and uncompromising, much as we would expect her to look, and in her crossed hands she is holding a knotted rope discipline. Early one morning, Olympia took Jacinta across the Praça to go to confession in the church. Jacinta might have known of the Spanish saint because one of her sisters bore that name. But even if she didn't, she would have identified with the discipline and, for a moment perhaps, have missed her own knotted cord. For her part, Teresa of Ávila, that most human and pragmatic of saints, must surely have smiled from heaven to see such love for her "Divine Majesty" consuming one so young. After her confession, Jacinta said to her mother, "What a good priest that was. He asked me so many things." Later Olympia commented, as most of us would, "I would have given anything to know what the good Father had asked her, but one can't pry about confessions."

Olympia had obviously spoken of her family at the orphanage, and one day Mother Godinho asked her if she had ever considered the possibility of her elder daughters, Florinda and Teresa, entering religious life. Olympia's spontaneous, "Heavens no!" was a reaction clearly not of irreligion but of a peasant woman for whom holiness of life is centered around the hearth. In all probability she had never had any experience of nuns. The nearest convent, if there was one the government had neglected to close, would have been in Leiria, and there were seldom reasons for Aljustrel folk to go that city, let alone to its convents.

Jacinta was not privy to this exchange, but soon after it she astounded Mother Godinho by saying in the course of their conversations, "Our Lady would like my sisters to be nuns but mother wouldn't like it, so she is going to take them to heaven before long." As previously mentioned, the two girls were stricken with the flu later that same year and died within a few weeks of each other.

———

Not infrequently, a pattern of prophetic utterances emerges toward the end of the lives of saints who have been willing victims of sacrificial suffering. It's as if their spirits, though still suffering, have entered a realm not unlike Eden, where the Divine friendship has been restored in full, along with an abundance of gifts, supernatural and preternatural, that puzzle and astonish everyone but the recipient.

Two doctors examined Jacinta at the orphanage. One asked her to pray for him, and she said she would, but added bluntly that he would die soon, which he did. She told the other doctor

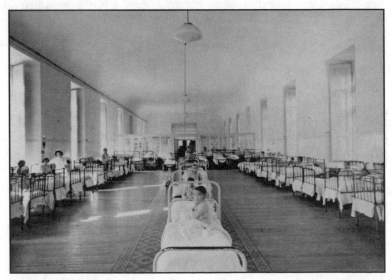

The children's ward in Dona Estefânia Hospital in Lisbon where Jacinta spent her last weeks.

that both he and his daughter would die. That, too, happened shortly after her own death, exactly as she had foretold. She also intimated to Father Formigão and Mother Godinho that they were to be instruments in founding religious houses devoted to the spirit of Fatima. Father Formigão later founded the Congregation of Sisters of Reparation of Our Lady of Sorrows of Fatima, and Mother Godinho changed the orphanage into an enclosed Poor Clare convent.

Two other instances of Jacinta's prescience from those days at the Estrela orphanage are often quoted. One concerns a sermon given by a young priest, perhaps in the chapel, or perhaps in the Basilica across the Praça. Apparently his homily was forceful, articulate and doctrinally sound, and everyone who heard it was full of praise for the preacher. Everyone, that is, except Jacinta. Later, in private, she told Mother Godinho, "That priest will turn out badly, though you wouldn't think so now." Mother Godinho remembered those words after the child's death when the young man abandoned the priesthood and took up living in open scandal.

Jacinta also told Mother Godinho that she would visit the Cova da Iria. The good woman had wanted to make that pilgrimage since she had first heard of the apparitions, but there was little likelihood of her ever having the opportunity. As it happened, she was on her way there before the month was out, accompanying Jacinta's coffin on the train.

After Jacinta's death, Mother Godinho related how the youngest seer, with the unselfconsciousness of innocence, told her that if she wished to make reparation to Our Lord, she and one of her nuns — Mother Godinho had already gathered a small community about her — should "go to the tabernacle and kneel at each side of it, and pray as the angels do in heaven."

"Have you ever seen the angels adore Jesus?" Mother Godinho asked.

"I have heard them sing, but it is not the way people sing. I don't like that sort of singing."

One day, quite out of the blue, Jacinta told Mother Godinho to ask the priest to have a medal coined with Our Lady on one side and an angel on the other. Nothing came of this request at the time, but in the 1930s, after the apparitions had met with official Church sanction, a Franciscan friar, Father Estavão Maria, had one made. It was very small, about half the size of a penny and not quite stamped to Jacinta's specifications. The priest's medal had an image of Mary on one side, but the reverse simply carried the words "Souvenir of Our Lady of Fatima." Of course, at that time nothing had been made public about the angelic appearances in the Aljustrel area in 1916, so angels weren't linked with Fatima in the minds of the faithful.

Mother Godinho said that on several occasions she overheard Jacinta say, "Oh, hell, oh, hell! Mother of God, have pity on sinners!" Here again, the fact that the child had actually seen hell wasn't made known until 1941, so at the time the full significance of her anguish couldn't be assessed by the good nun.

One day a well-to-do lady and patient of Dr. Lisboa's, Maria Sande e Castro, came to the orphanage. She was delighted to hear that Jacinta was there. She asked to see her. Jacinta, though in great pain, sat in the parlor and said nothing about it. The woman enthused piously, no doubt, and asked Jacinta to pray to Our Lady for her intentions. Jacinta made no reply. The poor visitor was understandably disconcerted and left, but before she did so she placed a fifty-escudo note, the equivalent of about fifty dollars in our own time, onto Jacinta's lap. When Jacinta realized it was there, she handed it to Mother Godinho. That good woman wasn't anxious to accept something given to the little girl and suggested that Jacinta give it to her mother. "No, it's for you because I give you a lot of trouble" was Jacinta's response.

Later, Mother Godinho gently asked her why she had ignored the lady, particularly when she had asked for prayers. Jacinta answered, "I did pray, but I couldn't say so at the time because I was in such pain and that made me afraid that I might forget."

In the meantime, arrangements were being made for Jacinta to be admitted to Dona Estafânia Hospital and to undergo an operation that would entail the removal of part of her two diseased ribs.

Olympia decided to return to Aljustrel because Florinda had fallen ill, and she wanted to consult with Ti Marto over the advisability of allowing Jacinta to be operated on in her delicate state. She had intended to return as soon as she was able, but heaven had decided otherwise. When Olympia said goodbye to Jacinta at the orphanage of Our Lady of the Miracles, it was the last that mother and daughter were to see of each other in this life. Jacinta evinced no great show of emotion. She simply said, "Goodbye, Mother, until we meet in heaven!" She was learning from Mary beside the Cross.

Lucia says that Jacinta sent word to her from Lisbon that Our Lady had appeared to her there and told her the day and the hour of her death. In all likelihood, Mother Godinho wrote a letter for Lucia at Jacinta's dictation, and her mother took it back to Aljustrel. Mother Godinho had Jacinta's confidence from the outset of her stay at Estrela. The seer wasn't secretive with her about Our Lady appearing to her in the orphanage. Indeed, after the child's death, Mother Godinho said that Our Lady had visited Jacinta more than once. She said that on one particular occasion when the little girl and the nun were together, Jacinta said, "Dear Madrinha, please leave me for a little while, I am waiting for Our Lady." She also relates that Jacinta made a revealing remark concerning such visits: "She didn't come like she came in Fatima, but I knew it was her."

What was the form Our Lady took for these visits to her chosen child? It could have been a direct communication with the soul or the intellect. A comment of Jacinta's reported later by one of the nurses in the hospital suggests that, on that occasion anyway, there was a visible presence. Perhaps every communication took a different form. The resources of the realm are infinite, and parents delight in expanding the perceptions of their children.

Father De Marchi, in his colorful and informative book *Fatima: From the Beginning,* lists a number of aphorisms that Mother Godinho heard from Jacinta during her stay in the orphanage. So does G.L. Baker in her equally admirable book, *The Finger of God is Here.* Here is a small selection, "clothed," Father De Marchi points out, "in Mother Godinho's own words."

> "The sins which cause most souls to go to hell are the sins of the flesh."
>
> "The world is perishing because the people do not meditate."
>
> "Many marriages are not of God and do not please Our Lord."
>
> "Wars are the punishment for sin."
>
> "Priests must be very, very pure."
>
> "Confession is a Sacrament of Mercy and we must confess with joy and trust. There can be no salvation without confession."
>
> "The Mother of God wants more virgin souls bound by a vow of chastity."

"Who taught you these things?" Mother Godinho is said to have asked Jacinta.

"Our Lady, but some of them I thought myself. I love to think."

But we mustn't picture Jacinta seated in the rooms of the large house on Rua da Estrela dispensing maxims and prophecies while awaiting heavenly visions. That suggests a very spoiled little girl.

Let's make no mistake about it: She was still a little girl with a little girl's delights and ways. But not spoiled. Holiness doesn't spoil, or smother, or negate personality. It works on it just as a jeweler works on the compressed carbon, polishing and cutting the raw material to bring forth the diamond. Jacinta was no more the precocious little miss than these sayings could suggest, than the twelve-year-old Jesus was a precocious little provincial when He beguiled the learned Jews in the Temple with His wisdom. They were captivated as much by His lack of pretension as by the maturity of His vision. That maturity had nothing to do with age; it was the maturity of the soul radiating through the human form. It was the Second Person of the Blessed Trinity, shy and delicate and ablaze with love, eager to dispel fear and make itself known.

Religious dedication doesn't alter personality, not Francisco's nor Jacinta's nor any saint's, canonized or unsung. It might refine aspects of it, but any wisdom, any radiance, any virtue, any miracles that come from that person are facets of Christ, shimmering glimpses of His banner unfurling on conquered territory, the cannon-fire of love's victories. But these manifestations of spiritual growth don't inhibit an eight-year-old from acting eight — whether the eight-year-old be Jesus or Jacinta. After a period of ecstatic union, a funny hat is still a funny hat — in fact it's probably funnier.

On February 2, Jacinta was admitted to Dona Estafânia Hospital wearing the blue frock she had been wearing at the time of the September apparition, even though it was now a little short for her. Although she could scarcely walk, she had to climb two flights of stairs to get to the spacious, high-ceilinged children's ward, where she was allotted bed No. 60. For Jacinta this was the foyer for heaven, the waiting room. She had agreed to suffer more for souls, and suffer she did. If a person is buried alive, or burned at the stake, or chopped up by laser we can, in a measure, identify with his pain. But spiritual annihilation compounded with physical suffering concentrated inside the body cannot be readily imagined. The doctors and nurses were doubtless kind, and Mother Godinho and Amalia Sande c Castro visited every day. Ti Marto, too, managed to get away from Aljustrel to lighten the burden of his youngest, but his other children had again succumbed to the flu, and he returned home immediately.

But it wasn't consolation Jacinta needed. It was courage. Courage from one moment to the next, and each moment lingered long before passing. It was as if she were on a tightrope stretched taut across hell. She, who could barely walk and who toppled when she knelt to say the angel's prayer, was forced to step onto it. To cross it was impossible, but that was the paradox of the Cross. Only grace could sustain her courage and move her feet on the narrow thread. Grace was generated by love and, though she loved and knew she loved, her love seemed to her more like an effrontery to the invisible and omnipotent God. Jesus was not only hidden in the Blessed Sacrament, He was hidden altogether. Perhaps He had lost interest in little girls who were rotting away and had gone off to someplace interesting. When you gave it some thought, there wasn't all that much about her to be interested in. If the Immaculate Mother visited during those interminable hours in bed No. 60, she came out of the darkness, and took her light with her when she returned to it. If she left a memory, that memory itself served only to torture love.

What Jacinta couldn't see as she balanced there alone and terrified, was that behind her, a door was being held open by her own relentless act of will, and that through that door souls bound for the pit were escaping in great numbers.

None of the hospital staff or patients were aware of Jacinta's identity. She was admitted as Jacinta de Jesus of Ourem and her father's name on the admittance form was given as Manoel Marques. Only her visitors, Mother Godinho and Amália Sande e Castro, knew that she was one of the seers of Fatima.

On February 10, little Jacinta was wheeled along the corridors to the operating room. She was too emaciated to be anaesthetized, though she was given a local anesthetic. The surgeon, Dr. Leonardo de Sousa Castro Freire, made an insertion in her body large enough to drain off the pus and dry off the two ribs. Then he took a surgical saw to the ribs and removed a two-inch section from one. The hole that was left in Jacinta's side was as large as a fist. The operation was considered a success. The wound was dressed and the patient was ready to be returned to the ward. Jacinta had been awake throughout.

Many years later, as part of the process toward beatification, the doctor gave his testimony. When asked if he knew that his patient was one of the seers of Fatima when he operated, he said:

> No, I didn't. It was much later that the nurse, Nadeje, told me. She [Jacinta] always gave me the impression — left me with the impression — of a child with much courage, and because she wasn't under general anesthetic she wasn't immunized from the pain involved in the opening of the fistula. She was certainly heroic, considering all she suffered and the way she suffered it. And also the fact that she was a child because, you know, an adult has more capacity for suffering than a child. The only words I heard from her during the operation were, "Oh Jesus! Oh my God!"

She was now in bed No. 38 in the surgical ward, but the tightrope was as taut. Every day the ghastly wound was dressed by the nurses. Many of them in that time and place weren't the hospital nurses we of later decades are used to. For one thing, they wore their own clothes beneath an apron. As often as not this clothing bordered on a streetwalker's outfit, and Jacinta said sadly to Mother Godinho when she came to visit, "What is it all for? If only they knew what eternity was."

Mother Godinho said the child mentioned to her that Our Lady had appeared on February 17 and told the little girl the constant pain would leave her for a period before Mary came to fetch her. It did, in spite of the gaping hole in her side, the fact that part of two bones had just been extracted and that disease had so eaten away at her flesh that her body looked like a little marionette. At one point Jacinta was out of bed in the middle of the ward, talking to the other children and maybe even laughing at funny hats. This was a reprieve from pain though not from sacrifices. There was no reprieve from sacrifices. Reprieve suggests a cancellation, temporary or permanent, of something unpleasant, something dreaded. Sacrifices, like prayer, are the verbs in the language of love. A soul could not be reprieved from prayer and sacrifices, only deprived of them. Pain was preferable.

Mother Godinho also later said Jacinta told her Our Lady repeated on February 17 what she had told the seers at the first apparition in the Cova: She would appear there a seventh time. This may have already happened, or it may be an event to come. One way or the other, it's intriguing. But speculation avails nothing and, blown up, it could become a media byword like the "third secret."

———

During the, hours of physical well-being, Jacinta's chief delight was a holy picture of the statue of Our Lady of Sameiro someone had given her. This sacramental is prominent in a very popular shrine on the outskirts of Braga in the north of Portugal. (A sign at the shrine reads: "Our Lady never appeared here; she *is* here.") The statue is, as statues go, rather beautiful. And Jacinta said the features resembled the features of Our Lady as she had seen her at the Cova.

During one of Mary's visits, Mother Godinho stood in a particular place near the foot of Jacinta's bed when the seer said quickly, "Oh, please move from there, Madrinha; that is where

Our Lady stood." In spite of Jacinta's anonymity, word must have got around the ward, because years later, one of the nurses admitted that she had deliberately lingered on this spot to gauge Jacinta's reaction. The girl said nothing when she saw the nurse there, but the expression on the child's face was so unnerving that the nurse moved without waiting to be asked.

Suddenly, on the evening of Friday, February 20, Jacinta began to feel her pain returning and asked for the priest. Father — later Monsignor — Pereira do Reis from the local parish, the Church of the Angels, came and heard her confession around eight. Jacinta asked, pleaded, for the Blessed Sacrament, but to the priest she looked so well that he felt there was no urgency for the viaticum or the anointing of the sick. ("Extreme unction" was the term in those days.) He stroked her gently on the cheek and promised to bring Holy Communion when he did his rounds in the morning. She knew that she would die that night and told Father Reis so, but he was used to exaggerated claims by overwrought patients. He was kind but adamant that he would not bring her Communion till the morning.

An hour or two after he left — without a family member or Mother Godinho or the Hidden Jesus, with only the night duty nurse, Aurora Gomes, keeping a professional eye on her patients — Jacinta Marto died in bed No. 38 of the surgical ward of Dona Estafânia Hospital at ten-thirty in the evening. When questioned some years later, Nurse Gomes stated that she couldn't recall any details about of the death of the seer, indeed she couldn't even remember the child herself. All we know of Jacinta's death is that Our Lady's prediction of her dying alone proved true.

Should we wonder if there was any letup of the child's suffering in the final hours, we might note the chilling evidence of Mother Godinho who, with Dona de Castro, came to wash the body in the hospital mortuary. The nun stated very positively that there were tears of dried blood on Jacinta's dead face. This suggests that bed

38 was Jacinta's own Gethsemani at the last, that she shared something of her Savior's awful agony.

It is, indeed, a bleak view from this side of the curtain, but on the other side, Our Lady of the Rosary must have come as she had promised to fetch her special child. And with Our Lady came Francisco, maybe, and vast armies of angels and the souls on whose behalf her sacrifices had pleaded God's mercy. All these to accompany her to the embrace of the no-longer-hidden Jesus.

Jacinta's ventures in the world of book-learning still hadn't progressed beyond the letter "H"; but, in fact, that was as far as she needed to go. On earth, it had often represented the Horror of Hell; now it could never mean anything but the Happiness of Heaven.

Portuguese law requires burial within twenty-four hours of death. Normally Jacinta's body would have been taken to the morgue and buried in a Lisbon cemetery the following morning. However, Dr. Eurico Lisboa, who had been responsible for bringing Jacinta to Lisbon in the first place, rightly reasoned that if there were to be an ecclesiastic inquiry into the Fatima apparitions, it would be wiser to have Jacinta's body in an accessible vault, rather than buried in the ground. In any event, the news of the death of the second Fatima seer was very quickly the talk of Lisbon.

As the children themselves had quoted the Lady predicting their early deaths, this was as creditable a proof of the authenticity of the apparitions to believers as the miracle of the sun had been two and a half years earlier. There were those who said that the Church had murdered Francisco and Jacinta to give Fatima credence, but variations on that sort of conspiracy argument have a familiar ring for Christians. The original one circulated around the sepulcher to divert attention from the resurrection of Christ.

Dr. Lisboa went to Father Reis at the Church of the Angels and asked if the body could remain there till a vault could be found to receive it. Given the possibility of the anti-religious authorities viewing the retention of the seer's body as a reactionary ruse and then using it as an excuse to close his church, the priest was understandably reticent. However, parishioners who were present when Dr. Lisboa made the request welcomed the idea, and the cleric relented.

Mother Godinho clothed Jacinta's body in a white first Communion dress with a new blue silk sash, provided by friends of the doctor, and placed it an open coffin. When the coffin arrived at the church, it was set out of sight, balanced between two stools, in a corner of the sacristy. Fortunately, Baron Alvaiázere welcomed the proposal that Jacinta's body be placed in his family vault in Ourem and insisted that he pay all the funeral expenses. The only difficulty this solution presented was that it involved a delay of several days. However, a quiet funeral was arranged for Tuesday, February 24, at the Angels church. Then the coffin was placed on a train to Chão de Maçãs.

The doctor figured that smooth, silent organization would prevent the authorities from being alerted to the circumvention of the burial law, but there's no stopping a happy bird from singing. Spontaneous queues of the Lisbon faithful formed at the church and filed through the sacristy to touch Jacinta's body with rosaries and other sacramentals, or simply to gaze at the hauntingly sweet expression on her face. The memory of the little girl in her coffin never dimmed for the undertaker, Antonio Almeida. Many years later he, who looked on dead bodies daily for most of his life, was able to write:

> I seem to see Jacinta still, looking like an angel. In her coffin she seemed to be alive; her lips and cheeks were a beautiful pink. I have seen many corpses, large and small, but I have never seen anything like that. The beautiful perfume which the body exhaled could not be explained

naturally and the hardest skeptic could not doubt it. One remembers the smell which so often makes it repugnant to remain near a corpse and yet this child had been dead three days and a half and the smell of her body was like a bouquet of flowers.

Father Reis, normally a quiet and well-mannered man, surprised everybody by becoming increasingly agitated about the whole business. On the civil front, the sanitary authorities could have fined, even imprisoned him. Or by alerting local government officials, they could have had his church closed. On the ecclesiastical front, the Church had made no judgments or offered any guidelines on the Fatima apparitions or on a cult of veneration for Jacinta. In desperation, he locked the coffin in an office, but that didn't prevent the people from coming. They sat in the church, waiting to see Jacinta.

Father Reis abrogated responsibility by having the undertaker move the coffin to a room above the sacristy used by the Confraternity of the Blessed Sacrament and giving him the key. Visitors gathered in the church and then, in small groups, were taken to the confraternity room nonstop until the funeral.

Happily heaven, too, kept a vigil over Jacinta's body. There was no interference from the authorities or from the cathedral to further provoke the consternation of the parish priest.

At eleven on the morning of February 24, Jacinta's body was placed in a lead coffin that was sealed, as the practice is. A number of witnesses testified to an extraordinary sweet odor emanating from the body. It was the odor of flowers, but flowers from fields no person had seen. The contrast with the odor that came from her wound just days before need not be labored.

Large crowds assembled at the Church of the Angels for the funeral, and they followed the hearse on foot through the streets of Lisbon to the station. Mother Godinho, as has been said, accompanied the coffin all the way to Chão de Maças.

Ti Marto went to the station to meet the train. A group of people stood around the little coffin. Ti Marto walked up to it, but the emotion of the moment was too much for him. He broke down and cried for his Jacinta. Relating the incident later, he said, "I cried like a child. I felt heartbroken and have never cried so much. I felt it had all been no good, all useless. She had been in the hospital here for two months and then gone to Lisbon and in the end she died all alone."

Ti Marto took the body to Ourem, where it was placed in the family vault of Baron Alvaiázere.

CHAPTER TWENTY-FOUR

When claims of heavenly sightings are made on earth, and they are legion, the Church, with the wisdom of centuries, maintains a cool reserve. As with a claim in a gold field, if the precious substance is there, it will reveal itself in time. The Church has come to recognize certain criteria, but they are very far from being aligned with the standards of this world. When these criteria have been met, the bishop of the diocese in which the apparition — or whatever is said to have occurred — launches an investigation. A committee is appointed, seers are interrogated and witnesses interviewed.

The Church does not hurry. If the investigations take a decade, well and good. If they take a century, so be it. In the case of Fatima, the ordinary, Dom José Alves Correira da Silva, appointed a Commission of Canonical Inquiry in May 1922. In October 1930 he officially declared that the apparitions at the Cova da Iria were worthy to be considered of supernatural origin, and he officially permitted devotion to Our Lady of Fatima. Note that the official pronouncement was not that it is indisputable that Our Lady appeared there at the times stated, and that we must believe it. The Church never says more than "worthy to be considered of supernatural origin." To a prospector this means there is reason to believe that gold is present, and with the map of Scripture and the tools of prayer, he can find the seam.

By September 1935, there was a popular feeling that the tombs of the two seers who had died so young should be in a place open to public veneration. Since their deaths, Fatima had — along with Guadalupe and Lourdes — grown into one of the major Marian shrines in the world. The bishop had a memorial constructed just inside a gate of the cemetery, opposite the parish church of St. Anthony in Fatima, at the head of the grave where Francisco had been buried. Bones thought to be Francisco's were exhumed, placed in an urn and reburied. The baron agreed to transfer Jacinta's coffin from the Alvaiázere vaults to this memorial, which also served as a mausoleum for her remains. As he did so, he paid tribute to the abundant graces he and his family received during her sojourn with them.

The transfer of Jacinta's coffin was set for September 12, 1935. Very few people were apprised of the operation: only her parents, some medics and clerics, the baron, and some "servitas"— the lay helpers attached to the Fatima Sanctuary. As soon as the coffin was removed from the vault it was opened, so that the body could be officially identified. As it happened, the full body wasn't even uncovered, because the face could be identified as soon as the top enshrouding material was unfolded. The normal process of corruption had not affected it.

Those present took the opportunity to touch the face with rosaries, medals, and handkerchiefs. Then the coffin was quickly resealed, covered with a silk pall and driven to the Cova. Bishop da Silva was waiting there, along with the archbishop of Evora who was to preside over the service. When the cortege of four cars arrived from Ourem, the inner coffin was lifted from the lead one and borne into the sanctuary.

The Cova da Iria in 1935 was no longer a wilderness of stones and furze. Though not quite as imposing as it is today, it featured large buildings on either side of the vast precinct, wide paths, paved areas around the Chapel of the Apparitions and, in the center, the "fontenario," giving access to the abundant water that sprang up in 1921. (If not miraculously, at least with the connivance of heaven.) On top of the high plinth in the center of the fontenario stood a life-sized statue of the Sacred Heart, emphasizing then, as it still does now, that Jesus is the center of the Christian life and the Fatima message.

At that time, the foundation stone of the Basilica of Our Lady of the Rosary hadn't yet been laid. The main church for pilgrims, called the Chapel of Penance, was on an incline, roughly half-way between where the basilica now stands and the Chapel of the Apparitions. This Chapel of Penance was demolished when the larger church was finally built and functioning. In spite of the absence of publicity surrounding the translation — the moving — of Jacinta's body, word of the Mass being celebrated by the archbishop of Evora in the presence of her coffin spread among the pilgrims. Crowds flocked to attend the Mass, pay their respects to the memory of the seer and, if they could, touch the

Dr. Fischer inspects the incorrupt face of Jacinta
September 12, 1935.

casket with anything they had to make a relic of it. After Mass, many hundreds followed the cortege, walking the mile or so along the Fatima road to the cemetery.

As Jacinta's body was being lowered into the grave, on top of what was thought to be Francisco's coffin, the archbishop leaned toward Ti Marto and said kindly, "Happy Father!" The response has since been quoted by popes and pilgrims alike. Ti Marto said, "The children are no longer mine; now they belong to the world." The inscription on the tomb reads:

Here lie the mortal remains
of
Francisco and Jacinta
to whom Our Lady appeared

Over the next fifteen years or so, this grave and the monument above it were in danger of being as denuded as the little holm oak of the apparitions had been. Pilgrims couldn't resist removing tiny fragments for their home altars or to keep with their rosaries, medals and other tangibles of devotion. The bishop planned to inter the seers in the basilica after it was consecrated — the consecration eventually took place on October 7, 1953 — but the mausoleum in the cemetery had been so vandalized, albeit with devout intentions, that rainwater was seeping through into the cavity housing Jacinta's coffin, and there was a danger of the remains interred there becoming polluted. Rather than erect a new mausoleum and headstones, which would be similarly desecrated, Bishop da Silva decided to bury them in the almost-completed basilica on May 1, 1951.

A grave that was to hold both Francisco and Jacinta was made ready in the north transept, on the "Gospel side" of the church. On the day before the transfer was to take place, again with a strict minimum of publicity, Jacinta's coffin and the urn beneath it thought to contain Francisco's remains were removed from the grave. They were taken to a nearby building belonging to the servitas to be formally identified and prepared for their tomb in the basilica.

When the doctors examined the bones thought be Francisco's, they found that they were the bones of an adult mixed with the bones of a baby. It was a custom in rural Portugal to bury a baby's body in the coffin of the next person to be interred. Francisco, shying off the limelight even after being dead for three times longer than he'd lived, couldn't be found. Ti Marto was adamant that they had the right grave. Further digging exposed more coffins, but for one reason or another none of them could have been Francisco's. At the end of the day, the grave was hastily filled in.

Meanwhile, the doctors had no trouble identifying Jacinta's body. It was still partially incorrupt. The face was light ocher and the skin dry, but it turned moist on exposure to the air. The lips were closed at first, but shortly after the body was moved they parted to show the tips of her white and even teeth. The eyes were sunk deep in the sockets. Some fair hair adhered to the top and the back of the crown. The cambric First Communion dress and veil she had been buried in had turned a light brown but had largely resisted the action of the lime that had covered the lower part of the body, a civil requirement for those dying of the flu epidemic. Most of this lower part had dried up and was in a semi-mummified state. The toes of her white kid shoes, also discolored but in fine condition, protruded from beneath the hem of the dress. The flesh on the upper part of the body was intact and proved soft to the touch. The incision made in her side during the operation to remove part of a rib was still seen under the surgical dressing, and a rubber drainage tube still inserted into it.

Ti Marto said sadly that it was like looking at a woman whom he had known when she was young now grown old.

There was no need to remove Jacinta's body. The old coffin was simply placed inside a new one, and the body was on view for selected people until the requiem Mass and burial service in the basilica on May 2. The funeral procession from the Fatima graveyard to the basilica was by foot. The coffin was covered with an elaborate pall and carried on a pallet surrounded by bouquets of lilies and roses. Residents from Fatima and the surrounding villages made up the procession, and they were joined by many pilgrims.

During the Mass the coffin stood before the altar, but after the service the congregation was permitted to file past and touch it with religious objects. Priests carried it to the vault sunken in the floor of the transept and lowered it in. A pink marble slab

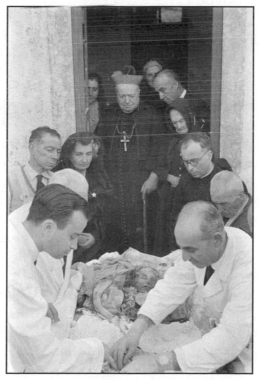

When Jacinta's coffin was opened for the second time in 1951, her body was found to be still largely incorrupt. Bishop Jose Correia da Silva and the Marto parents can be seen clearly here.

with metal handles at the corners was laid over the opening, and an upright was fixed at the head of the tomb with a picture of Jacinta. The memorial's inscription reads:

Here lies Jacinta Marto
to whom Our Lady appeared
Born 11.3.1910 Died 20.2.1920
Translated to this Basilica 2.5.1951

Jacinta remained alone in the basilica for more than nine months. Ti Marto, who was the very antithesis of a stubborn man, remained insistent that Francisco's original gravesite was the one he pointed out to Church officials. If they wanted to rebury his son's body in the basilica, it was pointless to go looking for it anywhere else. At length, Bishop da Silva ordered the plot to be re-excavated. On February 14, 1952, Ti Marto and his son José stood by while the workmen dug and unearthed coffin after coffin. But none of them was Francisco's. After more than six feet, they came across some skulls and a layer of cement. There was no accounting for the cement, but Ti Marto insisted that it be pierced. The workmen broke it, and there, immediately beneath, was the coffin that had been too short for Francisco's body, the yellow braid still tied around it.

The workmen gingerly brought the box to the surface but, because there were no doctors present, it was sealed and locked in the servitas house until February 17. When it was finally opened, it was clear that the skeleton, which almost immediately fell apart, was that of a body that had been buried sideways, with the knees bent up to fit it into the available space. The skull was pressed against the top end, and the feet against the lower. All this confirmed what Ti Marto had told about the measurements for the coffin being wrong and the body of Francisco being arranged to fit into it.

A part of a fifteen-decade bone rosary was still entwined between the boy's fingers. The rest — 148 beads — had fallen apart and was lying loose. These beads, made of bone, were flat, like buttons, not round. The cross, too, was bone. It had no figure attached to it. There were also real buttons among the skeletal bones, and bits of cloth, and coffin nails. The most striking object was a small red artificial flower attached to three metal ribbons, two white and the other blue. The cloth petals were unstained, despite the mud and damp inside the coffin, and shone like new.

Francisco's remains were placed in a new lead-lined ash coffin and kept in a sealed room while a new tomb was being prepared in the south transept of the basilica. The original plan to bury Francisco and Jacinta together had given way to the expediency of separate burial places so that the faithful could ask for either seer's intercession without being confused as to whose intercession they were soliciting. At the end of the twentieth century, another tomb was dug alongside Jacinta's. It lies there, covered but empty, waiting to receive the body of Lucia when God sees fit to call her from her Carmelite convent in Coimbra.

Francisco's new coffin was taken to the basilica on March 13, 1952. The procession took the same route as Jacinta's the year before and about the same number of people joined it. Ti Marto and Olympia walked with it all the way. A requiem Mass was said in the basilica, while the coffin stood on a catafalque surrounded by flowers. It remained there for a Mass for the sick, which followed. The statue of Our Lady of Fatima, brought from the Chapel of the Apparitions, stood a little to the left of the coffin, facing in its direction. After the Mass for the sick, four priests carried the coffin to the new tomb, lowered it in and placed a marble cover over it. The sign over Francisco's tomb reads:

Here lie the mortal remains of Francisco Marto
to whom Our Lady appeared

Born 11.6.1908 died 4.4.1919
Translated to this Basilica 13.3.1952

Olympia Marto died on April 3, 1956, and Ti Marto on February 3, 1957.

Maria da Purificação — "Mother" — Godinho passed away on June 24, 1960.

On May 13, 1989, Francisco and Jacinta Marto were declared "venerable" by a decree of the Congregation for the Causes of Saints.

On June 28, 1999, the decree announcing the beatification of Francisco and Jacinta Marto was promulgated. The beatification ceremony was formally carried out in the Cova da Iria by Pope John Paul II on May 13, 2000.

Epilogue

Basilica façade on the day of the beatification.

The Cova da Iria today is the center of a town with some ten thousand inhabitants. With the opening of the A1 freeway in the 1990s, access to the highland plateau was no longer restricted to donkey cart or vehicles with sturdy springs. Indeed, since now it's just more than an hour from Lisbon, its quiet streets and relative tranquility have made it attractive as a residential satellite for the capital. But the shrine is still the center, the heart, the justification for, and glory of, the town. It is, as has been said with poetic eloquence, the Altar of the World, and it is to this altar that between five and six million pilgrims make their way each year. They come to pay homage to the Lady of Light, to the Lady of Fatima, to the Lady of the Rosary, to the same Immaculate Heart that burns with love and mercy in all the aspects of herself that Mary presents to us.

The sanctuary has been built over the Cova da Iria until no feature of the original remains except one tree, the same holm oak that the children stood under during June and July of 1917 while waiting for the flash of celestial light to announce the approach of their visitor.

Pilgrims do not assemble here to admire the beauty and charm of the sanctuary, because it is not particularly beautiful or charming. They don't gather to be entertained, because no entertainment is provided. Perhaps some come for an indefinable religious experience, but if that means standing around waiting for sudden illuminations of the soul, then disappointment is certain. Miracles of spiritual regeneration do occur daily, but not on demand. They require a certain disposition of soul: not sinlessness, not guiltlessness, not even orthodox belief, but a desire for humility, a submission of the will, a disavowal of preconceptions, a frank connivance with the Divine.

If these attitudes are a problem, the pilgrim only has to shut himself away in his own mind for a short while with Francisco and Jacinta and to learn from them. And perhaps the greatest lesson they have to impart is the paradox that identifies their extreme youth as the basis of their spiritual maturity. It is not simply the state of childhood itself, otherwise we would all have been saints years ago; nor through any decision of their own, but because of their compliance with grace. Spiritual maturity must never be confused with physical adulthood. Physically we "grow up." Our spiritual growth requires a preposition that is not to be found in dictionaries.

There can be nothing adult about a soul's relationship with God. Jesus said it again and again. "Unless you become as little children…" "Whoever receives a child in my name receives me…" And, to the apostles at the Last Supper, "Little children, I shall not be with you much longer…" The Church presents Blessed Francisco and Blessed Jacinta Marto as role models for children, and rightly so, but the wise faithful, regardless of years, also take them as role models because "it is to such as these that the kingdom of heaven belongs."

Until the beatification of Francisco and Jacinta, the child — in religious thinking — had been relegated to the status of incipient adult. Since Lourdes and La Salette, those appearances of Our Lady's whose devotion has been approved by the Church have been made almost exclusively to children, which suggests that heaven wants us to reorder our thinking, to revert back to the mind of Christ. It might be said that the attitude that has been, "No one knows the Father except the Son and those over the age of twenty-one to whom the Son chooses to reveal Him" has now become "No one knows the Father except the Son and the children to whom the Son chooses to reveal Him." The children here being, of course, anyone big enough to be small.

The message of Fatima has many facets, but this one of spiritual childhood, exemplified in the Marto siblings, is the most overlooked. It's also one of the most important because it re-launches us, as it were, into the waters of baptism. With simplicity as the keel; trust as the radar; sacrifices as fuel; the rosary as rigging, lead-line and anchor; and all under the lee of Mary… safe passage is secured. The world has no access to that route. It would interpret innocence as shallows and peace as doldrums. It would see childlike love as rudderless navigation. People absorbed by the values of the world cannot grasp the terrible truth that they have no guiding star and no port.

Ships and sheep, sailors and shepherds, the fishermen of Genesareth, the shepherds of Bethlehem, what Jesus told his disciples by the lakeside, what Mary told the seers in the pastures of the Cova da Iria, was the same message. Both the first-century fishermen and the twentieth-century shepherds took it to heart

Pope John Paul II gives Holy Communion to Amelia Santos, a local woman who had been paralyzed from the waist down for twenty years. The Church accepted her healing, attributed to the intercession of Francisco and Jacinta, as heaven's sanction for the beatification of the seers.

and lived it until their lives became that message, just as a log on the fire becomes the fire.

Pope John Paul II beatified Francisco and Jacinta Marto at the altar of the Fatima Sanctuary on May 13, 2000, before an estimated one million people. Above the outdoor altar on the two faces of the basilica — on either side of the recess housing a fifteen-foot statue of the Immaculate Heart (a gift from the people of the United States) — two metal frames, each about thirty-by ten-feet, had been set in place before the ceremony. One was draped with an enormous Vatican flag, the other with the flag of Portugal. At the moment the Holy Father began to pronounce the beatification, the flags rolled down slowly to reveal what was beneath. On the north was a huge photo of Francisco with his stocking cap, shoulder bag and shepherd's staff. On the south was Jacinta with her left hand on her hip.

In his homily, the Holy Father made the poetic plea: "Parents, enroll your children in the School of Mary!"

After the pope had spoken, the Secretary of State for the Vatican, Cardinal Angelo Sodano, revealed the part of what the children had seen in "the light from the Lady's hands" during the July apparition that had never before been made public. It had been known as the "Third Secret" and seemed to refer to Pope John Paul II himself who, in fact, was not born until three months after Jacinta had died. The children's reverence for the Holy Father was being mirrored in the Holy Father's reverence for them.

Francisco and Jacinta had come a long way from being obscure peasant children, but that long way is for our sakes, that we might learn from them. They offer lessons very much at variance with the spirit of the world that surrounds us, lessons we and our children can only learn where Francisco and Jacinta themselves were taught, and where they are now teachers, in the School of Mary.

BIBLIOGRAPHY

Because I am not writing for academics I have eschewed footnotes. Anything of interest on the subject has been included in the body of this work. I have created nothing, unless commentaries and mild opinions can be categorized as creative. The facts of Fatima are too sensational to require fictionalization.

BOOKS CONSULTED:

Documentação Crítica de Fatima
I. Interrogatórios aos Videntes — 1917
II. Processo Canónico Diocesana — 1922–1930

Santuário de Fátima. 1992 and 1999

Fatima in Lucia's Own Words, Vols. I and II — 1976 and 1999
Secretariado dos Pastorinhos
Compiled Fr. Luis Kondor, S.V.D.
Translated by the Dominican Nuns of the Perpetual Rosary, Fatima

Fatima From the Beginning
Father John De Marchi, I.M.C.
Translated by I.M. Kingsbury
Missões Consolata, Fatima. 1950. Ninth edition. 1994

The Finger of God is Here
G.L. Barker
St. Paul Publications
Athlone, Co. Westmeath, Republic of Ireland. 1961

Fatima Revealed
Brother Michel de la Sainte Trinite
Translated by Tim Tindall-Robertson
Augustine Press
Devon, England. 1988

Our Lady of Fatima
Most Rev. Finbar Ryan, O.P.
Browne and Nolan
Dublin 1939. Fourth edition. 1948

Fatima, Russia & Pope John Paul II
Tim Tindall-Robertson
Augustine Press
Devon, England. 1992

Quando O Santuário Era Uma Azinheira
Manuel Pereira dos Reis
Fatima. 2000

A New History of Portugal
H.V. Livermore
Cambridge University Press
Cambridge, England. 1966

Marian Apparitions, The Bible and the Modern World
Donal Foley
Gracewing
Leominster, England. 2002

What Happened at Fatima
Leo Madigan
Catholic Truth Society
London. 2000

Princesses of the Kingdom
Leo Madigan
Kolbe Publications
9, North Main Street
Cork, Republic of Ireland. 2001

Fatima Handbook
Leo Madigan
Gracewing
Leominster, England. 2001

Vision of Fatima
Father Thomas McGlynn, O.P.
Skeffington & Sons Ltd.
London. 1951

Eye Witness at Fatima
Mabel Norton
C.J. Fallon Ltd.
Dublin, Republic of Ireland. 1950

RECOMMENDED BOOKS

Apelos da Mensagem de Fátima
Irmá Maria Lúcia de Jesus e do Coração Imaculado
Secretariado dos Pastorinhos
Fátima, Portugal. 2000

The Great Sign
Francis Johnson
Tan Books, Rockford, Illinois. 1975

About the Author

Leo Madigan lives as a hermit in Fatima, Portugal. He is the author of *What Happened at Fatima*, *The Fatima Handbook*, *The Princesses of the Kingdom: Jacinta Marto and Nellie Organ*, and *The Fatima Prayerbook*. His web site is www.theotokos.org.uk/leomadigan.

Our Sunday Visitor . . .
Your Source for Discovering the Riches of the Catholic Faith

Our Sunday Visitor has an extensive line of materials for young children, teens, and adults. Our books, Bibles, booklets, CD-ROMs, audios, and videos are available in bookstores worldwide.

To receive a FREE full-line catalog or for more information, call **Our Sunday Visitor** at **1-800-348-2440**. Or write, **Our Sunday Visitor** / 200 Noll Plaza / Huntington, IN 46750.

Please send me: __A catalog
Please send me materials on:
__Apologetics and catechetics   __Reference works
__Prayer books   __Heritage and the saints
__The family   __The parish
Name_____
Address_____Apt._____
City_____State_____Zip_____
Telephone (   ) _____
                                                     A33BBABP

Please send a friend: __A catalog
Please send a friend materials on:
__Apologetics and catechetics   __Reference works
__Prayer books   __Heritage and the saints
__The family   __The parish
Name_____
Address_____Apt._____
City_____State_____Zip_____
Telephone (   ) _____
                                                     A33BBABP

OurSundayVisitor

200 Noll Plaza
Huntington, IN 46750
Toll free: **1-800-348-2440**
E-mail: osvbooks@osv.com
Website: www.osv.com